The HABIT of a JUDGE

An etching entitled "The habit of a Judge", circa 1640, by Wenceslaus Hollar, which is based on his quarter-length oval engraving of Sir Richard Hutton (1560-1639), a Justice of the Court of Common Pleas, who (although in the minority) famously defied King Charles I and ruled against him in the Ship Money Case of R v Hampden (1637) 3 State Tr. 826. The keen observer would note the inaccuracies in this engraving in that it incorrectly portrays the robe with miniver lining down the entire front and bottom edges of the robe, and Hollar may have drawn this without having actually directly observed the full habit. The title of this etching provided inspiration for the title of this book.

The HABIT *of a* JUDGE

A History of Court Dress in England & Wales, and Australia

DANIEL YAZDANI

With a Foreword by the Honourable Wayne Stewart Martin AC, QC
Chief Justice of Western Australia 2006-2018

TALBOT
PUBLISHING
Clark, New Jersey

ISBN 978-1-61619-585-4

TALBOT PUBLISHING
AN IMPRINT OF
THE LAWBOOK EXCHANGE, LTD.
33 Terminal Avenue
Clark, New Jersey 07066-1321

Please see our website for a selection of our other publications and fine facsimile reprints of classic works of legal history: www.lawbookexchange.com.

Library of Congress Cataloging-in-Publication Data

Names: Yazdani, Daniel, author.
Title: The habit of a judge : a history of court dress in England & Wales, and Australia / by Daniel Yazdani ; foreword by Wayne Martin AC, Chief Justice Supreme Court of Western Australia.
Description: Clark, NJ : Talbot Publishing, an imprint of the Lawbook Exchange, Ltd. , [2019] | Includes bibliographical references and index.
Identifiers: LCCN 2018055532 | ISBN 9781616195854 (hardcover : alk. paper)
Subjects: LCSH: Judges--Clothing--England--History. | Judges--Clothing--Wales--History. | Judges--Clothing--Australia--History.
Classification: LCC K2146 .Y39 2019 | DDC 391/.0434742014--dc23
LC record available at https://lccn.loc.gov/2018055532

Front cover: Spectacular portrait of Sir Robert Chambers (1737-1803), Vinerian Professor of English Law (1766-1777), Chief Justice of the Supreme Court of Judicature at Fort William in Bengal (1789-1799), by Robert Home (1752-1834). A friend and contemporary of Dr Samuel Johnson, Chambers was appointed a Judge following the enactment of *East India Regulating Act 1773*, which established a Supreme Court of Judicature of Bengal, and departed for Bengal in May 1774. He was said to have been promised by Lord Apsley LC that if the office of Chief Justice ever became vacant, he would be offered that post, and he was eventually offered that position in 1789. He is wearing the full-bottomed wig, with its large lappets, and a scarlet robe and hood faced with miniver, a black cincture and laced cufflinks, and without a mantle (which was probably not worn due to the warm and humid Indian climate), which is the ceremonial dress of Judges of the Supreme Court of New South Wales. The letter pictured on his desk reads "The Rt Honourable Chief Justice Sir Robert Chambers Bengal".

Printed on acid-free paper

DEDICATION

I dedicate this book to my late grandparents, Dianatollah Yazdani (1923-2012) and Maliheh Yazdani (née Samimi) (1932-1997), who sacrificed so much for their children and grandchildren's future and well-being.

FOREWORD

The court attire worn by legal practitioners and judges has been a topic of occasional controversy during my time in the law. Contributions to that controversy have, in my experience, largely reflected the uninformed, idiosyncratic and subjective views of the contributor. Views expressed in the course of debate have seldom drawn upon a sound appreciation of the historical development of practices relating to court attire. That may well be the consequence of the shortage of available information on the topic readily available in a single convenient source.

This book fills that gap and provides, as far as I am aware, for the first time, a comprehensive history of the development of practices with respect to the attire of judges and lawyers in the courts of England and Wales, accompanied by a detailed analysis of the extent to which each Australian jurisdiction has varied those practices over the centuries since colonisation.

Mr Yazdani is to be congratulated upon the thoroughness of his research and the lucidity of his writing. The history which he traces commences in the reign of Henry II in the 12th century, although he notes that the first recorded occasion of distinctive judicial attire appears to be in 1292, during the reign of King Edward I. The development of judicial attire in England and Wales over the centuries which followed are traced in meticulous detail.

The breadth of the historical research reflected in the text is exceptional - drawing upon pictorial records as diverse as cathedral brasses, portraits, miniature illuminations, stained glass windows and judicial seals, and upon texts as diverse as wills and personal inventories. The book reveals a number of aspects of the development of court attire which are likely to be surprising to contemporary lawyers. For example, judicial attire has, over the centuries, involved a surprising range of colours, and has not been limited to the black and crimson gowns with which contemporary lawyers are familiar. To take another example, for many centuries, the traditional form of judicial headgear was the coif or skullcap. The judicial wig is a relatively recent phenomenon, emerging in the late 17th century when lawyers and judges endeavoured to keep up with the fashions of the day. However, the desire to remain à la mode appears to have dissipated, with the consequence that lawyers and judges retained wigs after they had been abandoned by the rest of society.

As lawyers and Supreme Court judges in Western Australia now only wear plain black gowns, it was of interest to me to note that such attire has a venerable history, being prominent in the court of Chancery in the 17th century and being later adopted by the common law courts for the purposes of civil trials on circuit.

Although the title of this book refers to "the habit of a judge", the historical development of the court attire worn by advocates is also covered in considerable detail, because of the connection between those developments and judicial attire.

Australian readers will be fascinated by the detailed analysis of the different practices which evolved in relation to court attire in each of the Australian jurisdictions. Although the colonists brought the traditions of England to Australia, different practices soon evolved in the different Australian jurisdictions, and there are now quite different practices amongst those jurisdictions. So, at one end of the spectrum, the judges of the Supreme Court of New South Wales wear three sets of robes and two types of wigs depending on the occasion, whereas at the other end of the spectrum, the judges of the Supreme Court of Western Australia wear only a single black robe, without wig, in all ceremonial sittings, appellate work, criminal work and civil trials. Other Australian jurisdictions have differing practices somewhere in between these two ends of the spectrum. Readers will find the details conveniently set out in this book.

The detailed analysis in this work underscores the significance of court attire. The uniforms worn by lawyers and judges are not superficial trappings of office, but reflect the dignity, solemnity and importance of court proceedings. The uniformity which they impose reduces the appearance of personal idiosyncracy and emphasises the fact that lawyers and judges perform their functions as officers of the court rather than as individuals.

I am very pleased to commend this book to all with an interest in the historical development of the courts of England and Wales, and the evolution of court practice in the different jurisdictions of Australia.

Wayne Martin AC
Chief Justice's Chambers
Supreme Court of Western Australia
May 2018

ACKNOWLEDGMENTS

This book would not have been written without the assistance and support of a number of individuals. First and foremost, I would like to sincerely thank the Hon. Wayne Martin AC, QC, former Chief Justice of Western Australia, for his foreword to this book. Having worn many of the various items of court attire the subject of this book, in particular the judicial "habit" of old, His Honour is able to personally relate to the subject-matter of this book, and his contributions in this particular area of court practice and procedure over the years are greatly acknowledged and appreciated. As His Honour retired from judicial office on 27 July 2018, I wish to also take this opportunity to pay tribute to his outstanding contribution and service to the law and the people of Western Australia as Chief Justice.

I would also like to particularly thank Professor Sir John Baker QC, leading English legal historian and Downing Professor Emeritus of the Laws of England at the University of Cambridge, for providing me with a hard-copy of his article on English Judges' robes back in 2010, and for permitting me to use a number of images from his personal collection in this book. It was one of Sir John's images (namely the etching of Sir Richard Hutton by Wenceslaus Hollar in circa 1640 entitled "the habit of a Judge" - see frontispiece) that inspired me to choose this title for my book. Sir John has over the decades written extensively on many aspects of English legal history, including the subject of court dress, leaving a wealth of knowledge for future practitioners and lovers of legal history to utilise and enjoy.

I wish to also thank Ms Val Buchanan of the Supreme Court of Western Australia for assisting me to take photographs of the various portraits of past Chief Justices of Western Australia at the Supreme Court building in Stirling Gardens.

I would like to also sincerely thank Mrs Valerie Horowitz and the entire team at Talbot Publishing/Lawbook Exchange for accepting my manuscript and working with me in preparing the manuscript for publication over the past year.

Lastly, I wish to thank my family, particularly my parents, Mr Nader Yazdani and Mrs Rawhia Yazdani, for their unfailing love and support, without which I would not be where I am today.

Daniel Yazdani
Perth, Western Australia
November 2018

CONTENTS

INTRODUCTION

Constancy and continuity in the law are valuable assets to any legal system, for people will have greater confidence in a legal system that has withstood the tests of time. The robes and gowns worn by the Bench and Bar are one such example of this continuity in the law, and are a marked expression of continuity in the practices and procedures of the courts and the administration of justice. In the words of the leading English legal historian, Sir John Baker QC:

> The robes worn by English judges ... were the robes of Coke, of Hale, of Holt and of Mansfield. They were worn through all the vicissitudes of our history, through the Wars of the Roses, the Civil War, and the Blitz, by the guardians of the common-law system of justice. They are well known everywhere and are still worn not only in many Commonwealth countries but even in some former Commonwealth countries. No other costume is more closely associated with freedom, judicial independence and fairness.[1]

However, this idea that there is a connection between the "habit" of a Judge and the proper administration of justice is not a new one. Indeed, the link between court attire and the administration of justice is clearly evident in the surviving speeches given at investiture ceremonies of newly appointed Serjeants-at-law, which date back to the fourteenth century. These speeches were given by the Chief Justice of the time and focused, *inter alia*, on the importance and symbolism of the distinctive attire worn by members of the Order of the Coif. One such speech was reported by Sir Richard Hutton, who has recorded that in 1627, Sir Thomas Richardson, Chief Justice of the Court of Common Pleas, gave an investiture speech at one of the creation ceremonies for new Serjeants-at-law. In his speech, Richardson CJ referred to the ancient dress worn by Serjeants-at-law and the symbolism it represented, saying:

> You have garments which are *vestimenta loquencia*. First your quoife, in fashion of an helmett, signifyeinge that you should be a man of courage and fortitude, not afrayd to speak the law, and to dow justice. This is a helmet of defence, the colour white and playne, pura immaculata. You must be without spott or blemish. Then your roabes, first black, signifyeing wisdome and gravity. ... You have scarlett, a rich and judiciall colour worne in ancient tyme onely by kings and princes and magistrates that exercised places of judicature. You have hoodes close, and all your garments are made close before, signifyeing that you are to be seacrett, a double seacrecie, to keepe councell, and to not reveale or discover seacretts that are commytted to you. You[r] sleeves are made wyde, signifyeing that you must be ready and easie of accesse, that suitors may have free accesse and be readily dispatched. ...[2]

---

1. Sir John Baker, *Collected Papers on English Legal History: Volume II* (Cambridge University Press, 2013), 812.

2. Sir Richard Hutton, *The Legal Diary of Sir Richard Hutton*, Cambridge University Library MS. Add. 6862, 6863 II, ff. 35v-

Although Richardson CJ was specifically referring to the vestments worn by Serjeants-at-law, it is equally relevant to robes worn by the judiciary and legal profession today, and even though Serjeants-at-law have long since disappeared,[3] elements of their dress still remain to this day and are now reflected in what is worn by modern-day Judges and lawyers. The numerous investiture speeches that have survived all highlighted the historical and symbolic nature of court dress and that each aspect of judicial attire was steeped in meaning and symbolism.

The ceremonial and criminal robes worn by Judges in the High Court of England and Wales, as well as the Supreme Courts of various Australian jurisdictions,[4] have essentially remained unaltered for centuries and are of great antiquity. It is, therefore, quite surprising that, to the writer's knowledge, no book has ever been written or published specifically on the question of English Judges' robes and/or the adoption of English court attire in Australian courts after British settlement in 1788.[5] This book redresses this anomaly and seeks to fill that large gap in English and Australian legal history.

The primary purpose of this book is to describe the "Habit" of a Judge - which at its core includes the full ensemble of robe, mantle and hood along with the girdle, casting-hood and black scarf. There are also additional items attached to or worn with, a Judge's habit, such as various forms of headdress and neckwear, among others. Although the focus of this book is on Judges' robes, this book will also look at the history of the gowns and other items of forensic attire worn by the legal profession, which, to some extent, has a completely different history to that of the robes worn by Bench but has, over time, become so interconnected (due primarily to the mutual use of many of the various items of dress by both the Bench and Bar), that to distinguish between the two is now almost impossible.

This book is also, quite deliberately, heavily illustrated, so as allow the reader to be as familiar as possible with the various elements of a Judge's Habit. All previous texts which have dealt with this topic in some way or another have, in large part, omitted illustrations (or at least colour illustrations) to assist the

---

38; quoted in Sir John Baker, *Serjeants-at-Law* (London: Seldon Society, 1984), 361-362. See also Wilfrid Prest, ed., *The Diary of Sir Richard Hutton 1614-1639*, (London: Selden Society, 1991).

3. The last Serjeant-at-law appointed was Lord Lindley who died in 1921. The decline of the Order of Serjeants-at-law was connected to the Judicature Acts for until 1875 only a Serjeant-at-law could be appointed to any of the Common Law Courts. The Order of Serjeant-at-law was never formally abolished but rather was dissolved when the Serjeants' Inn was sold in 1877. Apart from Judges' robes which can be traced back to the dress of Serjeants-at-law, the last vestiges of the Order of the Coif can be seen in the small circular depression on Judges' wigs and the practice of Judges referring to one another as "brothers", although even this practice has fallen into desuetude following the increased appointment of female judges since the 1980s.

4. The Supreme Courts of New South Wales and Queensland have, to varying degrees, retained the traditional scarlet robes. This is discussed in detail in chapter 5.

5. Although books have been published which have chapters devoted to this subject (e.g., Sir John Baker, *Collected Papers on English Legal History: Volume II, supra*; W. N. Hargreaves-Mawdsley, *A History of Legal Dress in Europe Until the End of the Eighteenth Century* (Oxford: Clarendon Press, 1963) 46-102), a detailed and authoritative book has never been published specifically on this subject, possibly due to the fact that many consider it to be such a superficial or ephemeral topic.

reader to understand what the writer is in fact talking about, and most of these texts leave the reader feeling more confused than enlightened on this rather ephemeral subject. It is hoped that the reader, after having read this book, will have a greater understanding of the history of Judges' robes and how these robes have evolved in Australia over the decades.

There is also another reason why this book has been written: change. Just as the common law does not remain in a state of stagnation and is constantly changing to meet the needs of society, so too is the dress worn by those who administer and interpret it. During the past four decades, in particular, there has been enormous change to the ceremonial and working-day dress of Judges, both in English and Australian courts, both to the despair and delight of many. Be that as it may, the purpose of this book is not to undertake an analysis of the advantages and disadvantages of retaining forensic garbs, for there are numerous texts and articles on this point. However, one point is noted: it is one thing to change a longstanding practice; it is entirely another thing to try and justify a change. In the words of former Justice of the High Court of Australia, Sir Victor Windeyer:

> The adoption of any new form of fancy dress is not easily justified. But the abandonment of a traditional costume is a very different matter, and the onus lies heavily upon those, who suggest this, to justify their proposal.[6]

Having researched the history and minute detail of English Judges' robes over many years, the writer has come to fully appreciate that the continued retention of robes and gowns by both the Bench and Bar is not due to some uninformed, dogmatic adherence to old customs and practices without reason; rather, it is clear that the continued use of these distinctive forms of dress, in numerous countries throughout the Commonwealth and beyond, is due to, *inter alia*, its effectiveness in promoting solemnity, uniformity and continuity in our legal system. On this point I again refer to the wise remarks of Windeyer J:

> The observance of old forms and customs is not simply a conservative adherence to usage. It is more; for it is a manifestation of the continuity of the law of the land. The present is visibly linked with the past, as a firm base from which the development and reform of the law can proceed in response to new social needs.[7]

---

6. Sir Victor Windeyer, "Of Robes and Gowns and Other Things," *The Australian Law Journal* 48 (1974) 394, 403.
7. *Ibid.* Similar views are made by de Jersey CJ who said that "[t]radition [of the Courts] is evident in the robes and wigs worn by Judges and barristers - a practice sometimes criticised, but I believe important in maintaining the dignity and serious nature of legal proceedings. You might find it amusing the traditional opening of the court - "Oyez, oyez, oyez. All persons having any business before this Honourable Court will draw nigh and give their attendance and they shall be heard. God save the Queen." But again, these words are of important legal effect - it is not meaningless tradition" (Speech by the Honourable Paul de Jersey CJ at the University of Queensland - TC Bierne School of Law "Welcome to Students", 9 February 2000).

On the importance of retaining court dress in some form or another,[8] the late Hon. David Kingsley Malcolm AC, QC,[9] former Chief Justice of Western Australia, had made the following important points:

> I'm not a person who upholds tradition purely for tradition's sake. It is necessary, I think, to identify some value to tradition apart from the sense of continuity and belonging.
>
> It is important to remember that practitioners and judges are all officers of the Court as it were, and when they are performing their official functions they assume responsibilities quite separate and apart from the individual person they are. The symbolism involved in robing, plays an important part in bringing home to people the sense of responsibility that must drive them in performing their function as officers of the Court.
>
> The conduct of public litigation is a State occasion. We have expectations of people who fulfil high public office and there is a symbolism which has an inherent value.
>
> The conduct of persons in Court ... [is] greatly affected and influenced by the atmosphere and sense of occasion which is created in the Courtroom. ... I think that people are much more conscious of their responsibilities and the public nature of the task they are called upon to perform it in surroundings and in a uniform. From that point of view it probably doesn't matter a great deal what the uniform is. The minutiae or the detail of the uniform is perhaps not as important as the sheer symbolism of having a uniform of some sort. Once you've got a uniform which is an identifiable uniform associated with the particular work that is being done, it's perhaps unwise to change too often because people then lose the sense of association between the uniform and the office.[10]

It is the writer's hope that this book shall keep, for posterity, an illustrative account of the rich and long-lasting legacy of court dress, in particular the Judges' habit, ensuring that it is more properly understood and appreciated by both the modern-day wearer and observer. There is a real risk that if such customs and traditions are not adequately recorded while still in use, their existence and usage will be eventually forgotten by future generations.

---

8. There are many Judges who support the wearing of some form of official regalia in order to symbolise the history and solemnity of Court proceedings, and yet at the same time support the modernisation of the current historical robes. This can be seen in the following speech of Wilson J of the Supreme Court of Queensland who said that "for many people the costumes of the Judges and barristers (the wigs and gowns) are an abiding impression of Court proceedings. To me, these costumes have always been simply uniforms - uniforms which symbolise the solemnity of Court proceedings and the continuity of the law. After all, individual Judges are merely ministers of the law, who will, in time, pass on their functions to others. That said, personally I think there is room for some modernisation of our uniforms!" (Speech by the Honourable Justice Margaret Wilson, "The Banco Court - Talk given to QUT 1st year architecture students", 23 September 2008 at [17]).

9. The Honourable David Kingsley Malcolm AC, QC was Chief Justice of Western Australia from 1988 to 2006, and passed away in 2014. His successor was the Honourable Wayne Stewart Martin AC, Chief Justice of Western Australia from 2006 to 2018. His Honour was succeeded by the Hon. Peter Quinlan on 13 August 2018.

10. "To Wig or be Damned", *Brief*, Volume 15, Number 7 (August, 1988) 8.

In 1955, James Derriman, a Barrister of Lincoln's Inn, wrote an extensive book on pomp and circumstance of the law of England and Wales entitled *Pageantry of the Law*. In it he made the following remarks:

> Of what use is the pageantry of the law? Is it perhaps time to do away with the wig, the robe and the black cap? These are questions on which no opinion is ventured in this book. It may be safely said, however, that pageantry without significance is mere superstition and rigmarole. If this book helps to make the significance and history of legal pageantry in this country more widely known, its existence will be justified.[12]

The writer would equally apply those aims and sentiments to the subject of this book too.

---

11. James Derriman, *Pageantry of the Law* (London: London, Eyre & Spottiswoode, 1955).
12. *Ibid*, 10.

The HABIT *of a* JUDGE

Westminster Hall, The First Day of Term. A Satirical Poem, coloured line engraving by Charles Mosley after original by Hubert-François Gravelot 1745. It shows the hammerbeam roof, looking towards the tripartite arched window at the far end of the Hall. On the left at the far end of the Hall is the Court of King's Bench. To the right of the Court of King's Bench is the Court of Chancery. Both courts are sitting on raised platforms against the far south end of the Hall, with a flight of stairs in between the two courts. On the right in the foreground is the Court of Common Pleas. Each court was only twenty-five feet square. Around the walls are the shops of booksellers, toymen, and haberdashers. In 1739, the Courts of King's Bench and Chancery were separated by ornate screens and in circa 1740-1741 a new Court of Common Pleas was built outside the west wall of the Hall.
WOA 952.

CHAPTER 1

Origins of English Judges' Robes

Although the High Court of Justice of England and Wales has been a creation of statute as a result of the enactment of *Judicature Acts* of 1873 and 1875,[1] the Queen's Bench Division of the High Court represents the former Court of Queen's Bench, the Court of Common Pleas and the Court of Exchequer, the three ancient Common Law Courts of England.[2] The Judges assigned to the Queen's Bench Division of the High Court had, until 2008, continued to wear the customary dress of the former Common Law Courts which until 1882 sat at Westminster Hall.[3] On ceremonial occasions, the same dress is also worn by puisne Judges of the Chancery and Family Divisions of the High Court, as they all hold the same office of Justice of the High Court of England and Wales. Although changes were made to the working-day dress of High Court Judges presiding over civil matters in 2008, the ceremonial court dress worn by High Court judges today is of great antiquity, and has essentially remained the same since the 15th century.

Note: illuminated letter from page 28.

1. *Supreme Court of Judicature Act 1873* (36 & 37 Vic. c. 66) and the *Supreme Court of Judicature Act 1875* (38 & 39 Vic. c. 77).

2. The Courts of Queen's Bench and Common Pleas were each presided by a Chief Justice and the Court of Exchequer was presided by a Lord Chief Baron. Originally, each of the three Common Law Courts exercised different jurisdictions. The Court of Common Pleas was concerned with actions between subjects particularly concerning land and debt issues. The Court of Queen's Bench was concerned with matters in which the Crown was interested and the Court of Exchequer was concerned initially with fiscal issues between the Crown and its subjects. However, by the end of the 17th century all these Courts had similar jurisdictions with broadly similar processes and procedures, and by the middle of the 19th century it was recognised that these arrangements could no longer be justified esulting in the passage of the Judicature Acts of 1873 and 1875 were passed. Its effect was to create a single post of Lord Chief Justice of England (which was filled by the then Chief Justice of the Court of Queen's Bench and one High Court of Justice with a number of Divisions (see *Lord Coleridge v Sotheby's* [2012] EWHC 370 (Ch) at [5]-[7] (Judge Pelling QC)).

3. Sittings at Westminster Hall took place for four terms, with each approximately three weeks long, the terms being Michaelmas (November/December), Hilary (January/February), Easter (April/May) and Trinity (June/July). The division of the year into these four terms is of great antiquity, possibly deriving from the reign of Edward the Elder (901-924): Derriman, *supra*, 191. The Courts of King's Bench, Common Pleas and Chancery were located in the open interior of Westminster Hall: James Oldham, *English Common Law in the Age of Mansfield* (Chapel Hill: University of North Carolina Press, 2004) 42-43. Westminster Hall was built for King William II (also known as William Rufus) in about 1099 and enlarged under King Richard II around 1395. With some physical changes and with the assistance of other courtrooms, Westminster Hall continued to be the home of the superior English courts until the opening of the Royal Courts of Justice in the Strand in 1882: Sir John Baker, *An Introduction to English Legal History* (London: Oxford University Press, 2002) (henceforth Baker, *Introduction*), 37.

Development of a Judge's Habit from the 12th Century to the Present Day

The present ceremonial dress of a Judge of the High Court of England and Wales—consisting of a long robe, a hood with a cowl worn around the shoulders, and a mantle over the hood,[4] all of which is made of the same cloth and facing—was essentially settled during the reign of King Edward III (who reigned from 1327 to 1377).[5] The Crown originally gave the material for these robes to the Judges as part of their livery.[6] The winter allowance included miniver (which is the white fur of ermine, without the tails) for the lining of the robes, and the summer allowance included a like quantity of taffeta (or silk) for the lining of the summer robes.[7] In the 15th century, the livery was commuted to an allowance of £8. 13s. 5d., which was added to the salary of each Judge.[8] It appears that the first form of illustrative evidence of a Judge's habit can be seen in an old seal affixed to an original grant of land by Sir Robert Grimbald—a justice during the reign of King Henry II (reigned 1154-1189)—to the canons of Osulveston, in the County of Leicester.[9] The seal depicts Sir Robert wearing a long tunic under a mantle, holding a naked sword in his right hand (representing the sword of Justice) and a broken sword in his left hand (representing the sword of Mercy) and a round cap over his head.[10] However, it is unclear whether the dress worn by Sir Robert as depicted in the seal would have been any different to the dress worn by laymen of distinction in the 12th century.[11]

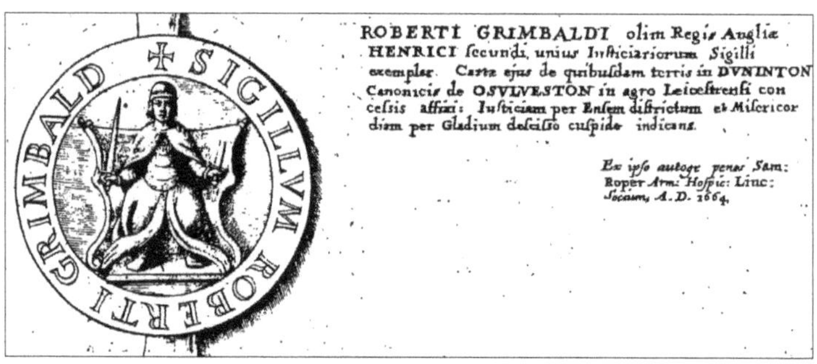

The seal affixed to an original grant of land by Sir Robert Grimbald from Dugdale's *Origines Juridiciales*.

4. The mantle has not been worn by Judges in Australia since the early twentieth century, and even at that point it was very uncommon, most likely due to the hot Australian summer.
5. Baker, *Collected Papers on English Legal History: Volume II,* (Cambridge: Cambridge University Press, 2013) (henceforth Baker, *Collected II*), *supra*, 813.
6. William Dugdale, *Origines Juridiciales* 3rd ed. (London: Printed for Christop. Wilkinson, Tho. Dring, and Charles Harper, 1680) 98. For example, William Westbury J of the Court of Common Pleas (died 1449) in his will bequeathed "one gown with sleeves and hood of the king's livery": Baker, *ibid*, 817.
7. Dugdale, *ibid.*
8. *Court Dress: a consultation paper issued on behalf of the Lord Chancellor and The Lord Chief Justice* (Lord Chancellor's Department, 1992) Appendix 1, 2.1.2.
9. Dugdale, *supra*; William Herbert, *Antiquities of the Inns of Court and Chancery* (London: Vernor & Hood, 1804) 95.
10. *Ibid.*
11. James Robinson Planche, *Cyclopedia of Costume* (London: Chatto and Windus, 1876-1879) 426.

The earliest known effigy of an identifiable Judge is the now destroyed brass of Ralph de Hengham which was in old St Paul's Cathedral, though he is depicted in an ecclesiastical appearance, with a round cap instead of a coif, which could be due to an unrealistic artistic reconstruction.[12]

The famous antiquary and scholar Sir William Dugdale (1605-1686) in his celebrated *Origines Juridiciales* has written that the first form of documentary evidence discerning the Judges' habit can be seen in the Close Roll of the 20th year of the reign of King Edward I (i.e., 1292), which commands the Keeper of the King's Great Wardrobe to deliver to the Chief Justices of the Courts of King's Bench, Common Pleas and Exchequer, and their respective fellow Justices, various materials of lighter weight for the Justice's summer robes and heavier materials for the Justice's winter robes:

> The King by his Praecept [sic] to the Keeper of his great Wardrobe, commandeth him to deliver unto William Scot and the rest of his fellow Justices of his Bench, there named; as also to John de Stonore and those with him, Justices of the Common Pleas, and likewise to Robert de Sadyngtone and the other Barons of his Exchequer; *viz* to each of them for their Summer Vestments (or Robes) for that present year, half a short cloth, and one piece of fine linen silk; And for the Winter season another half of a cloth colour Curt, with a hood, and three pieces of fur of white Budg. And for the Feast of the Nativity of our Lord, half a cloth colour Curt, with a hood of two and thirty bellyes [sic] of minever, and two furs of silk.[13]

Sir William Dugdale further recounts that the second form of documentary evidence of a Judge's habit can be seen in the Close Roll of the 21st reign of Edward III, where the Chief Justice of the King's Bench (Sir William de Thorpe) as well as his fellow Justices Sir William Basset and Sir Roger de Baukewell were permitted to have winter robes out of the King's Wardrobe:

> ... each of them a half cloth colour Curt; three furs of white Budg. And for their Liveries at Christmas, each of them half a likewise colour Curt, one hood containing xxxii [32] bellies of Minever, one Fur of Minever containing seven tires, and two Furs of silk, each of seven tires.[14]

Dugdale's drawing of the now destroyed brass of Ralph de Hengham which was located in the old St Paul's Cathedral, from Dugdale's *History of St Paul's Cathedral in London*, p. 102.

12. Baker, *Collected II, supra*, 813; Sir William Dugdale, *The History of St Pauls Cathedral in London from its Foundation untill these Times: Extracted out of Originall Charters. Records. Leiger Books, and other Manuscripts. Beautified with Sundry Prospects of the Church, Figures of Tombes, and Monuments* (London: Tho Warren, 1658) 100-101.

13. Dugdale, *supra*, 98. See also Herbert, *supra*, 92-93.

14. Dugdale, *ibid*; Herbert, *ibid*.

An etching of Sir William Dugdale by Wenceslaus Hollar dated circa 1656. Note the wide square collars which are the ancestors to the current bands worn by the Bench and Bar.

More pictorial evidence of Judges' robes is apparent from the 15th century. For example, there are a certain number of effigies and brasses of Judges in the first half of the 15th century, such as the brass of Sir John Cassy, one of the earliest of such brasses, as well as the four splendid 15th century illuminations of the Courts of Chancery, King's Bench, Common Pleas and Exchequer, now in the possession of the Inner Temple.[15]

During the 16th and 17th centuries, a less formal robing requirement began to come into operation when a judge was not sitting in banc in Westminster Hall, but rather was either sitting alone hearing civil cases on circuit, or was performing certain other functions and duties. Although the robe remained the same (according to the winter or summer season), the full hood and mantle were no longer worn on such occasions. In their place, the casting hood of a Serjeant-at-law would be worn on the right shoulder, with its liripipe hanging suspended on the front of the right shoulder, its modern day remnant being the scarlet "sash" incorrectly referred to by some as a "tippet" (which in the 1635 Rules refers to the stole worn over the shoulders by Judges).

15. These four illuminations are discussed in depth at pp. 44-51.

The Judges' Rules of 1635

On 4 June 1635, a solemn Decree and Rule was made by all of the Judges of the Courts of King's Bench, Common Pleas and Exchequer sitting at Westminster Hall,[16] which was to regulate the wearing of judicial dress by Judges sitting in the Common Law Courts at Westminster. The 1635 regulations by no means created new forms of dress; rather it formalised in writing what hitherto had been the norm, in the interests of uniformity of practice. The full text of the Rules is as follows:

> The Judges in Term Time are to sit at Westminster in the courts, in their black or violet gowns, whether they will;[17] and a hood of the same colour put over their heads, and their mantles above all, the end of the hood hanging over behind, wearing their velvet caps and coifs of lawn and cornered caps.
>
> The facing of their gowns, hoods and mantles, is with changeable taffeta,[18] which they must begin to wear upon Ascension-day,[19] being the last Thursday in Easter term,[20] and continue those robes until the feast of Simon and Jude;[21] and upon Simon and Jude's day the judges begin to wear their robes faced with white furs of minever, and so continue that facing till Ascension-day again.
>
> Upon all holidays which fall in the term, and are hall-days,[22] the judges sit in scarlet faced with taffeta, when taffeta facing is to be worn; and with furs of minever, when furs of minever are to be worn.
>
> Upon the day when the lord mayor of London comes to Westminster to take his oath, that day the judges come in scarlet; and upon the fifth day of November, being gunpowder day,[23] unless it be Sunday, the judges go to Westminster abbey in scarlet to hear sermon, and after go to sit in court; and the two lords chief justices and the lord chief baron have their collars of SS above their mantles for those two days.
>
> When the judges go to St. Paul's to the sermon, upon any Sunday in the time-term, or to any public church, they ought to go in scarlet gowns, the two lords chief justices and lord chief baron in their velvet and satin tippets,[24] and the other judges in taffeta tippets; and then the scarlet casting-hood is

16. These Rules were subscribed by Sir John Brampton CJ of the Court of King's Bench, Sir John Finch CJ of the Court of Common Pleas, Sir Humphrey Davenport CJ of the Court of Exchequer along with the rest of the Judges of the three respective Common Law courts "appointing what Robes they should thenceforth use, and at what times" (Dugdale, *ibid*, 101).

17. I.e., as they prefer.

18. The specific colour of the taffeta was not specified in these Rules. For more information on the various colours of taffeta used for the facings of the robes, see pp 56-59.

19. The Feast of the Ascension of Christ, also known as Holy Thursday, Ascension Day, or Ascension Thursday, commemorates the Christian belief of the bodily Ascension of Christ, and is one of the ecumencial feasts of Christianity. Ascension Day is traditionally celebrated on a Thursday, the fortieth day of Easter, although some Christian denominations have moved the observance to the following Sunday.

20. I.e., the third term of the legal year in England and Wales (from April to June).

21. The feasts of St Simon and St Jude falls on October 28 each year.

22. I.e., holidays.

23. I.e., the annual commemoration of the Gunpowder Plot of 5 November 1605.

24. The reference here to "tippet" is to the black stole or staff, rather than the casting-hood.

worn on the right side above the tippets, and the hood is to be pinned abroad towards the left shoulder;[25] and if it be upon any grand days, as upon Ascension-day, Midsummer-day,[26] All Hallow day,[27] or Candlemas-day,[28] the the two lords chief justices[29] and the lord chief baron[30] wear their collars of SS with long scarlet casting-hoods, and velvet with satin tippets.

At all times, when the judges go to the council-table, or to any assembly of the lords,[31] in the afternoons in term-time, they ought to go in their robes of violet, or black faced with taffeta, according as the time of wearing them doth require; and with tippets and scarlet casting-hoods pinned near the left shoulder, unless it be Sunday or holyday, and then in scarlet.

In the circuit the judges go to church upon Sundays in the forenoon in scarlet gowns, with hoods and mantles, and in afternoons to the church in scarlet gowns, tippet and scarlet hood, and sit in their cornered caps.

And the first morning at the reading of the commissions[32] they sit in scarlet gowns, with hoods and and mantles, and in their coifs and cornered caps; and he that gives the charge and delivers the gaol doth, or ought for the most part, to continue all that assizes the same robes, scarlet gown, hood, and mantle: but the other judge, who sits upon the nisi prius,[33] doth commonly (if he will) sit only in his scarlet robe, with tippet and casting-hood: or if it be cold, he may sit in gown, and hood, and mantle.

And where the judges in circuit go to dine with the shireeve, or to a public feast, then in scarlet gowns, tippets, and scarlet hoods; or, casting off their mantle, they keep on their hood.[34]

The scarlet casting-hood is to be put above the tippet on the right side; for justice Walmesley[35] and justice Warburton,[36] and all the judges before, did wear them in that manner; and did declare, that by wearing the hood on the right side, and above the tippet, was signified more temporal dignity; and by the tippet[37] on the left side only, the judges did resemble priests.

---

25. This refers to the pinning of the cowl part of the casting-hood across the back, so that it is squared on both shoulders of the Judge. This phrase has given difficulty to modern writers on court dress; it may refer to the old practice of wearing the hood scarflike or squared around the shoulder, with the cowl part of the hood pinned on the left shoulder, as can be seen in the 16th century coloured drawings of the Opening of Parliament in the House of Lords.
26. Also known as St John's Day, is the period of time commemorated by many Christian denominations and is centered around the summer solstice between 19 June and 25 June of each year.
27. Also known as All Saints' Day, is a Christian commemoration of all the saints, both known and unknown, and is celebrated between 31 October and 2 November each year.
28. Also known as the Feast of the Presentation of our Lord Jesus and the Feast of the Purification of the Blessed Virgin Mary, is a Christian Holy Day which commemorates the presentation of Christ at the Temple in Jerusalem, and falls on 2 February each year.
29. I.e., the Chief Justice of the Court of King's Bench and Chief Justice of the Court of Common Pleas.
30. I.e.., the Lord Chief Baron of the Court of Exchequer.
31. I.e., the House of Lords.
32. I.e., the Commissions provided to the Judges, upon which their jurisdiction depended. There were 5 such Commissions, namely, the Commissions of Assize, Nisi Prius (civil commissions), of the Peace, of oyer and terminer and gaol delivery (criminal commissions).
33. I.e., the Court of King's Bench.
34. I.e. the full hood lined with fur or taffeta which is worn underneath the mantle, with the cowl part of the hood hanging down behind.
35. A Justice of the Common Pleas 1589-1612.
36. A Justice of the Common Pleas 1600-1621.
37. I.e., the liripipe of the casting-hood.

Whensoever the judges or any of them are appointed to attend the king's majesty, they go in scarlet gowns, tippets, and scarlet casting-hoods, either to his own presence, or at the council-table.[38]

The judges and serjeants, when they ride circuits, are to wear a serjeant's coat of broad cloth with sleeves, and faced with velvet: they have used of late to lace the sleeves of the serjeant's coat thick with lace; and they are to have a sumpter, and ought to ride with six men at the least.

Also the first Sunday of every term, and when the judges and serjeants dine at my lord mayor's or the shireeves,[39] they are to wear their scarlets, and to sit at Paul's[40] with their caps at the sermon.

Drawing of the Court of Common Pleas in circa 1658, just over twenty years after the Judges Rules were issued by the Common Law Judges sitting at Westminster Hall. The two men seated beneath the Judges are wearing bonnets and are therefore the prothonotaries of the court. From G. Billinghurst's title page of *Arcana Clericalia* (1676). © Sir John Baker QC

38. This therefore implies that Judges do not need to wear their mantles and full-hoods when in the presence of the Sovereign, which therefore means that the current tradition of wearing full ceremonial dress in the presence of Her Majesty is technically incorrect.

39. I.e., sherrifs.

> When the judges go to any reader's feast, they go upon the Sunday or holyday in scarlet; upon other days in violet, with scarlet casting-hoods, upon other days with violet, with scarlet casting-hoods, and the serjeants go in violet, with scarlet hoods.
>
> When the judges sit upon nisi prius in Westminster or in London, they go in violet gowns and scarlet casting hoods and tippets, upon holydays in scarlet.[41]

Thus, the Judges Rules of 1635 Rules represent a clear picture as to the state of court dress by the early 17th century and is a significant piece of primary evidence from the Judges themselves as to their appropriate judicial attire.[42] It can also be seen from these Rules that a less formal dress was permitted for Judges undertaking civil trials on circuit, though any Judge could still wear the mantle if it was cold. However, it is not entirely clear what the practice was in fact for Judges when on circuit. There are portraits of Judges wearing black silk gowns and bag wigs, one of the earliest being the engraving of Lord Mansfield which appeared in the Gentleman's Magazine in the July volume of 1768. The use of the black silk gown was derived from the Court of Chancery, as the black silk gown was adopted for day-to-day use by the Lord Chancellors sitting in the Court of Chancery when it came into use as a Court gown at the end of the 17th century.[43]

An engraving of Lord Mansfield CJ which appeared in the *Gentleman's Magazine* in the July volume of 1768 (volume 38), wearing black silk gown with bands and a bag wig (which at this time began to replace the larger full-bottomed wig in ordinary court sittings).

On the other hand, there are portraits of Judges wearing violet robes without the full hood, such as the painting of Sir Soulden Lawrence by Hoppner. The fact that Lawrence J is without a full hood indicates that this could not have been *en banc* and must presumably have been worn on circuit.[44]

40. I.e., St Paul's Cathedral in London.

41. Dugdale, *supra*, 101-102; Herbert, *supra*, 96-98; E. Cave, "Ancient form prescribed for robing the Judges &c," *The Gentleman's Magazine, and Historical Chronicle* 38 (1768) 457-458; Sir Alexander Pulling, *The Order of the Coif* (London: W. Clowes & Son, 1897) 225-226.

42. Each of the elements of the Judges' habit as described in these rules shall be discussed with supporting illustrations in the following chapter.

43. Derriman, *supra*, 100. It has been suggested that the black silk gown was adopted by the Bench when they went into mourning following the death of Queen Mary II in 1694. See more at pp 106-107.

44. Baker, *Collected II*, *supra*, 826. This was the dress worn by

Portrait of Sir Soulden Lawrence by John Hoppner wearing violet robes faced with taffeta, wide bands, bar wig, black scarf, cincture and a scarlet casting hood over his right shoulder. Accession nos: 893-4.

In any event, it appears that by the 19th century, the practice had become to wear the black silk gown for civil trials on circuit. The use of the black silk gown by Judges on circuit, as opposed to the traditional *nisi prius* black and violet robes, can also be seen in this account by MacKinnon LJ:

> The judge trying civil causes wears his black gown, furred in the winter, silked in the summer. But formerly he used to wear a black silk gown, as a judge of the Chancery Division does now. … In Warren's *Ten Thousand a Year* in his

---

Judges sitting in the Queen's Bench Division of the High Court during the summer until October 2008. The violet robes currently worn by County Court and District Court Judges in England and Wales and Australia are partly derived from the violet robe worn by Lawrence J.

Coloured etching entitled "Court of Chancery, Lincoln's Inn Hall" published on 1 June 1808 in *Rudolph Ackermann's Microcosm of London illustrated* by Augustus C. Pugin and Thomas Rowlandson. Attributed to the British LIbrary

Coloured etching entitled "Court of Common Pleas" published on 1 June 1808 in *Rudolph Ackermann's Microcosm of London illustrated* by Augustus C. Pugin and Thomas Rowlandson. Attributed to the British Library

Coloured etching of the Court of King's Bench at Westminster Hall dated circa 1808 from the Microcosm of London illustrated by Rowlandson and Pugin, showing the presiding Judge wearing the Chancery black silk gown over court dress instead of the more traditional nisi prius violet or black robes.
Contributor: Lordprice Collection / Alamy Stock Photo

Coloured etching of the Court of Exchequer dated circa 1808 from the Microcosm of London illustrated by Rowlandson and Pugin.
Contributor: Lordprice Collection / Alamy Stock Photo

> account of the ejection action at the York Assizes he speaks of the Lord Chief Justice taking his seat wearing a 'short wig and a black silk gown', and in a footnote adds that this was the mode of the civil Court, while the judge of the Crown Court would wear his scarlet and ermine robe and a full bottomed wig. (New Edition, 1845, Vol. 1, p. 404.) Warren was a member of the Northern Circuit, and must have known the practice then current.[45]

It is also unclear what the position of dress was for Judges sitting *en banc* at Westminster Hall. There is a colour engraving by Robert Dighton of the Court of King's Bench at Westminster Hall where the Judges are sitting in the black robe and hood faced with miniver. However, there is also evidence indicating that Judges sitting *en banc* in the common law courts at Westminster Hall in the 18th and mid-19th centuries wore black silk gowns instead of the traditional black and violet robes as stipulated in the Judges' Rules of 1635, as can be seen in a number of engravings and etchings of the mid 18th and early 19th centuries.

This adoption of the black silk gown by common law Judges may have been due to the close interactions of the Common Law Courts with the Court of Chancery at Westminster Hall, which is plainly evident in the fact that the Courts of King's Bench and Chancery were not even fully partitioned prior to 1760.[46] This interaction between the superior courts at Westminster, along with the hustle and bustle of vendors selling all types of goods and services (until at least the reign of King George III), resulted in the atmosphere of the courts being quite informal and often undignified, as can be visualised by the following description of the courts at Westminster Hall[47] at that time:

> Various contemporary prints … depict the judges of the King's Bench and Chancery as sitting on raised platforms against the far (south) end of the Hall, with a flight of steps in between, while the Common Pleas bench was placed similarly against the west side.[48] The judges were distinguished by a backdrop of tapestries embroidered with the royal arms; clerks sat before them at a table covered by a green cloth, and the remaining space was occupied by the jurors one side, and counsel and attorneys in front. Seats and gothic screens were provided for the first time in the eighteenth century, but the barristers must have been almost on top of each other, for there were only four benches, and the working environment would have suffered considerably from the bustle

45. F. D. MacKinnon, "Judges' Robes - The Gun-Case," *The Law Quarterly Review* 61 (1945) 30, 32.
46. J. Trenchard, *A Collection of all the Humorous Letters in the London Journal* (London: J. Roberts, 1721), 48; H. Phillips, Mid-*Georgian London: A Topographical and Social Survey of Central and Western London about 1750* (London: Collins, 1964), 20; Oldham, *supra*, 121.
47. For a scale plan of Westminster Hall in 1807, see John Thomas Smith, *Antiquities of Westminster* (London: T. Bensley, Bolt Court, 1807), opp. 125.
48. In 1739, the Courts of King's Bench and Chancery were separated by ornate screens and in circa 1740-1741 a new Court of Common Pleas was built outside the west wall of the Hall: *The History of the King's Works: Volume V* 1660-1782, (London: H. Colvin; J.M. Crook, K. Downes & J. Newman, 1976) 389-390.

in the Hall, where (until George III's time) vendors sold all manner of goods and services, and passers-by strolled and conversed, sometimes with dogs at their heels. Before 1755 there was no ceiling to the courts, and in summer the participants complained of the heat, while in winter it was necessary to have braziers burning to counter the cold and damp, problems which were exacerbated by holes in the roof.[49]

Hand-coloured etching and aquatint entitled "Sittings at Westminster Hall in the Courts of Kings Bench Common Pleas Chancery Exchequer" dated circa 1814.
Museum number 1868,0808.8333.
© Trustees of the British Museum

49. David Lemmings, *Professors of the Law: Barristers and English Legal Culture in the Eighteenth Century* (Oxford: Oxford University Press, 2000), 47-48. See also the following description of the court environment at Westminster by Sir John Baker QC: "The interior of the hall is still best viewed from the great north door. On the far side is a flight of steps which used to divide the Court of King's Bench from the Court of Chancery. On the west side of the hall, near the door, was the Court of Common Pleas. The Exchequer was a large adjacent chamber which connected with the hall through a passage. Each court occupied a space marked out by a wooden bar at which counsel stood, and in the centre was a massive oak table covered with green cloth at which court officials sat and spread their records. Against the wall, on a raised platform or bench beneath tapestries with the royal arms, sat the judges. Until the eighteenth century there were no seats for counsel, nor any walls to divide the courts from the open thoroughfare; each court was scarcely out of earshot of the others, and speakers had to compete with the noise made by the throng of suitors, lawyers, shopkeepers, cutpurses and sightseers in the body of the hall. This arrangement seemingly impracticable to modern eyes, was a feature of English public life for six centuries. It survived two civil wars, and even in times of rebellion the judges and counsel kept up their attendance, sometimes with armour beneath their robes. Only in times of plague or flood did the courts leave Westminster Hall, and then only after a formal adjournment by proclamation" (Baker, *An Introduction to English Legal History*, *supra*, 37).

Developments in Judges' Robes Following the *Judicature Acts*

The 19th and 20th centuries brought about significant changes to the English judicial system, which also impacted on the ability of Judges to adhere to the Judges' Rules of 1635, and although the 1635 Regulations remained in force (and technically still remain in force as they have not been repealed), by the end of the 19th century only a few of the provisions of the 1635 Rules remained literally applicable and enforceable.

When the High Court of Justice was established on 1 November 1875 to replace the old Common Law Courts of Exchequer, Common Pleas and Queen's Bench,[50] it was decided by the Judges that the 1635 Judges' Rules would apply to all justices of the High Court, irrespective of whether or not they were Serjeants-at-law.

One of the immediate effects of the merger of the old Common Law Courts in 1875 following the *Judicature Acts* was the continuation of the practice by Judges of wearing the black silk gown at *nisi prius* and the winter or summer scarlet robe with a black scarf when on the Crown side.[51] It was also decided at the same time that the traditional *nisi prius* robes of black and violet worn by Judges when sitting *en banc* at Westminster Hall would now be adopted by Judges sitting in the Divisional Courts of the Common Pleas, Exchequer and Queen's Bench Divisions of the High Court,[52] meaning that the black robes and hood faced with miniver or the violet robes and hood faced with taffeta would now be worn by Judges sitting in those Divisional Courts.[53]

Following the great fire of 16 October 1834,[54] calls were growing for Parliament to move the courts from Westminster Hall to a new building of their

50. A Judicial Commission was appointed in 1867 to investigate into the division of work between the common law courts, the outcome of which was the enactment of the *Judicature Act 1873* which abolished the old common law courts and transferred their jurisdiction to the newly established High Court of Justice, though that Act came into force on the same date as the *Judicature Act 1875*, which provided for further reforms to the system of judicature in England and Wales: Baker, *ibid*, 50-51.

51. Baker, *Collected II*, *supra*, 828.

52. The Common Pleas and Exchequer Divisions of the High Court were abolished in 1880. The reason why were created as part of the reforms of 1875 in the first place was that at the time of the Judicature reforms of 1875, it was necessary to create three common law divisions because it was by then regarded as constitutionally unacceptable to force retirement or demotion on those Chief Justices of the respective Common Law Courts then in post who did not become Lord Chief Justice of England. Accordingly, Lord Coleridge CJ was the last Chief Justice of the Common Pleas Division and held office from 1873 until 1880. However, by chance, in 1880 Sir Alexander Cockburn CJ (formerly the Chief Justice of the Court of Queen's Bench and from 1875 the first Lord Chief Justice of England) and Sir Fitzroy Kelly (then the Chief Baron of the Exchequer Division) both died in office. Following these events, by an Order in Council made on 16 December 1880, the three common law divisions were merged into the one Queen's Bench Division, which thereafter assumed the work of all three former divisions. The Queen's Bench Division therefore became the sole representative of the old common law courts, and the then Chief Justice of the Common Pleas Division (Lord Coleridge CJ) was appointed Lord Chief Justice of England, and held that high office until his death in 1894: *Lord Coleridge v Sotheby's* [2012] EWHC 370 (Ch) at [6]-[7] (Judge Pelling QC); Baker, *ibid*, 51.

53. This can be seen in the painting of the famous Tichborne Claimant's Trial in circa 1873-1875 by Godefroy Durand.

54. Back in 1790, a Committee of the House of Commons made an adverse report about the worrying state of Westminster Hall, reporting, inter alia, that: "The court of exchequer, and exche-

Engraving of the Judges of the Court of Queen's Bench dated circa 1870, showing them wearing the nisi prius winter robes and hoods.
Contributor: Chronicle / Alamy Stock Photo

own.[55] In 1882 the courts physically moved from Westminster Hall to the newly built Royal Courts of Justice at the Strand, and it was at this point that the trial Judges of the now Queen's Bench Division reverted to wearing the traditional black and violet robes with matching hood for civil trials, along with the stole and casting hood, instead of the black silk gown which had been adopted by Judges by the early nineteenth century.[56]

Upon the establishment of the Court of Criminal Appeal in 1907, the Judges of that Court adopted the traditional dress worn by Judges in the former Court for Crown Cases Reserved, namely the summer and winter scarlet robes and the corresponding hoods according to the season.[57] However, once the Court of Criminal Appeal was abolished and its jurisdiction transferred to the Criminal Division of the Court of Appeal, the Lords Justices of Appeal adopted the black silk gowns worn by Judges of the Civil Division of the Court of Appeal.

---

quer chamber, contiguous to and connected with, Westminster-hall, are very old, but not in a state of actual ruin. On the ground-floor, under the court of exchequer, is the custos brevium of the court of common pleas, and treasurer's office belonging; the ceiling and walls of them are lined with deal, and insecure from fire, and very damp. … The public-houses and coffee-houses on the south side of New Palace-yard, immediately adjoining the custos brevium of the court of common pleas, are particularly dangerous, as they have several chimneys and coppers; the roofs are under, and close to, the windows of the custos brevium, and some of them covered with sail-cloth pitched; the smoke of one of the chimnies is conveyed by a slight tin funnel … near the windows of Westminster-hall" (The Annual Register: World Events 1790 (ProQuestrel, 1793), 249-250). Unfortunately, nothing came about from this report, and the great fire of 1834 may have been avoided had Parliament heeded to the concerns in this report: Baker, *Collected II*, *supra*, 809.

55. The problems arising from the courts sitting at Westminster Hall during the 18th and 19th centuries were numerous. Although the Hall itself was quite large, the three common law courts which sat within the open interior of Westminster were each only approximately 25 square feet in size and were not even fully partitioned off from each other prior to 1760 (Lemmings, *supra*, p 46; H. Phillips, *Mid-Georgian London: A Topographical and Social Survey of Central and Western London about 1750* (London: Collins, 1964), 20).

56. Baker, *Collected II*, *supra*, 829. The black silk gown was retained by Judges sitting in the Chancery Division and the Probate, Divorce and Admiralty Division of the High Court, as they had no historical links with the old common law courts at Westminster Hall.

57. *Ibid.*

Painting of the Opening of the Royal Courts of Justice at the Strand by Queen Victoria, 1882, by Henry Tanworth Wells (1828-1903), GAC Number RCJO/124 © Image; Crown Copyright: UK Government Art Collection

Prior to 1971, Judges of the Queen's Bench Divisional Court wore black robes faced with miniver and matching hood in winter and violet robes faced with taffeta with matching hood during the summer, and scarlet robes on Red Letter days. However, after 1971 this practice was abolished due to the inconvenience of having to change robes in the course of sitting when Judges of the Queen's Bench Divisional Court were transmuted into a panel of the Criminal Division of the Court of Appeal (which required them to wear scarlet robes rather than black or violet robes).[58] It has therefore been the case that the violet and black hoods (which were last worn by Judges sitting in the Queen's Bench Divisional Court), has since 1971 gone into desuetude.[59]

Thus, a single Judge of the Queen's Bench Division would wear winter or summer scarlet robes with the black stole and casting hood when sitting in a criminal trial.[60] However, a single Judge of the Queen's Bench Division sitting in a civil trial would wear black robes or violet robes depending on the season with a black stole and casting hood (without the matching hoods which had been discontinued by single Judges by this time), and all Judges of the Queen's Bench Division would wear scarlet robes for the appropriate season on Red Letter Days (which include the Queen's Birthday and certain Saints' Days), as prescribed in the Judges' Rules of 1635.[61]

58. *Court Dress, supra*, Appendix, 2.3.2; Baker, *Collected II, supra*, 829.
59. *Ibid.*
60. *Ibid.*
61. *Ibid.*

Painting of Judges sitting in the Court of Criminal Appeal in 1916 entitled "High Treason, Court of Criminal Appeal: the Trial of Sir Roger Casement 1916" by Sir John Lavery (1856-1941). GAC Number 0/128. The Judges are all wearing the summer scarlet robes and hoods faced with taffeta, bands and bench wigs. This exact dress is worn by Judges in the Court of Criminal Appeal in New South Wales. © Image; Crown Copyright: UK Government Art Collection

The working day Court dress worn by all other Judges of the Senior Courts of England and Wales (namely, the Chancery and Family Divisions of the High Court and Judges of the Court of Appeal) comprised of a court coat and waist-coat worn with bands and a skirt or trousers underneath a black silk gown, and a bench wig.[62] This form of dress was already the traditional dress of Judges sitting in the Court of Chancery, and was no doubt adopted when the Probate, Divorce and Admiralty Division (now the Family Division) was formed after the *Judicature Acts* due to the fact that no more distinctive dress was available or academic gowns worn by ecclesiastical judges were no longer appropriate to be worn.[63] The black silk gown over a court coat with bands and a bench wig is the current dress of Judges sitting in the criminal division of the Court of Appeal as well as Judges sitting in the Old Bailey in London.

62. Court dress is generally not worn in Chambers.
63. Derriman, *supra*, 100.

Development of County Court and Circuit Judges' Robes

The dress of Judges sitting in the County Court (which was created pursuant to the *County Courts Act 1846*)[64] originally comprised of black silk gowns over court dress,[65] though a few Serjeants-at-law who were appointed as County Court Judges are said to have worn their scarlet and violet robes.[66] However, in 1915 Judge Woodfall suggested to the Lord Chancellor that a new robe—similar to those worn by High Court judges—be introduced.[67] It has been suggested that more than half the County Court Judges were in favour of their own distinctive robe, although some argued that a black silk gown would be easier to transport to the various courts in the country.[68] Lord Buckmaster LC approved of the new robes, which consisted of a violet robe faced in lilac or mauve taffeta—to distinguish it from the violet robe worn by High Court Judges—along with a lilac casting hood and black girdle, but no black stole.[69] However, Lord Buckmaster did not make the new robes compulsory and due to wartime conditions the new robes did not come into use by County Court Judges until 1919.[70] However, even at this point the new robes were not permitted to be worn at court functions.[71]

Upon the enactment of the *Courts Act 1971* (UK) all County Court Judges and Chairmen of the Quarter Sessions became Circuit Judges and as such Judges of the Crown Court, which was established in 1971.[72] The question that then arose was that of the appropriate form of dress for Circuit Judges sitting in the newly created Crown Court. Lord Hailsham of St Marylebone issued a direction that a Circuit Judge sitting in the Crown Court would be able to choose between wearing either the violet robe faced with lilac and a scarlet casting hood (instead of the lilac casting hood) or the black silk gown.[73] It was reported in the *New Law Journal* that:

> [a]t a dinner at Lincoln's Inn at which he addressed county court judges … the Lord Chancellor said, on the subject of robes for the new circuit court bench, that he had never been personally very attracted by the county court

---

64. 9 & 10 Vic c 95.
65. See e.g., *County Courts Chronicle* 5 (1852) 59, 77-78.
66. *Court Dress*, *supra*, Appendix, 2.2.2.
67. *Ibid*. The County Court robes are very similar to the traditional nisi prius violet robes faced with taffeta, with some writers presuming that the violet robes are "vestiges of the violet gowns of the 17th century serjeants and justices" and "a happy recalling of tradition" (Derriman, *supra*, 179).
68. *Court Dress*, *supra*, Appendix, 2.2.1.
69. Derriman, *ibid*. Consideration was also given to the adoption of a scarlet robe, but Lord Buckmaster decided upon the violet robe: *Court Dress*, *supra*. Some writers incorrectly refer to it as a black robe faced with violet: *see e.g.*, Derriman, *ibid*.
70. Law Journal, *County Court Reporter* 5 (1916), p 50; Derriman, *ibid*.
71. Public Record Office, Lord Chancellor's Office, 12/43.
72. *Court Dress*, *supra*, Appendix, 2.2.3.
73. Speech of Lord Hailsham of St Marylebone at a dinner in Lincoln's Inn on 30 October 1971, reported in 121 New Law Journal at 985. Sir John Baker has rightly pointed out that Lord Hailsham referred to the casting hood as a "tippet", even though the Judges' Rules of 1635 use the word "tippet" for the black stole: Baker, *Collected*, *supra*, 830.

> judge's purple robe and had hoped that the changes in the court system which would take place ... under the Courts Act [1971] "might provide a convenient opportunity for getting rid of it", His own view was, Lord Hailsham said, that when a circuit court judge sat in the Crown Court, "his robe should include a dash of red [as] customary colour for ... judges when exercising criminal jurisdiction". But the great majority of those Lord Hailsham had consulted were in favour of keeping the purple robe, substituting a red for a purple tippet when sitting in the Crown Court.
>
> He had been assured also that judges preferred a robe to a court coat and silk gown in the summer. The Lord Chancellor's office had "managed to persuade the Civil Service Department to meet from public funds the cost of purchasing a robe for every judge, such as a full-time chairman of quarter session or an additional judge of the Old Bailey, who does not already possess one". But, the Lord Chancellor added, he had no intention of requiring a judge to wear a purple robe if he preferred to sit in a black silk gown.[74]

Therefore, a Circuit Judge sitting in the County Court would wear a violet robe faced with lilac with a black girdle and lilac casting hood, whereas a Circuit Judge sitting in the Crown Court would wear the same violet robe faced with lilac and girdle but with a red casting hood, which was introduced in 1971 upon the establishment of the Crown Court.[75] However, unlike Judges of the High Court, Circuit Judges of both the County Court and Crown Court wear their casting hood on the left (meaning that the liripipe of the hood falls on the left side) and without the black stole. The working day dress of Circuit Judges also comprises of bands worn over a violet robe with lilac facings and a bench wig. Ordinary day dress is worn beneath the robe. In 1937, Viscount Hailsham LC authorised the use by County Court Judges of a matching violet hood faced with lilac on ceremonial occasions.[76]

On some occasions and in certain courts Circuit Judges do not wear the violet robe described above but the short wig and black silk gown over a court coat and/or waistcoat. This was worn by Circuit Judges sitting to deal with certain types of High Court business, by Official Referees and by Circuit Judges sitting at the Central Criminal Court (formerly known as the Old Bailey)[77] in London. Prior to October 2008, a District Judge sitting in open court also wore a black gown and bar wig over ordinary business attire and on ceremonial occasions, District judges wore a short black coat, waistcoat and striped trousers.[78]

74. *Ibid.*

75. Thomas Woodcock, *Legal Habits: A Brief Sartorial History of Wig, Robe and Gown* (London: Ede & Ravenscroft, 2014), 69.

76. *Ibid.*; *Court Dress*, *supra*, Appendix, 2.2.3.

77. The Old Bailey was renamed the Central Criminal Court in 1834: Derriman, *supra*, 144.

78. For further information on the ceremonial dress of English Judges and reforms to working day dress for Judges in England and Wales, see chapter 4.

Portrait of Sir Edward Montagu (1485-1557), Lord Chief Justice of both the Court of King's Bench (1539-1545) and the Court of Common Pleas (1545-1553), during the reign of King Henry VIII. This is said to be the oldest extant portrait of a Lord Chief Justice in his ceremonial scarlet robes, although the extended miniver lining down the robe below the waist is incorrect and the artist may have drawn this without having actually directly observed the full habit. It is also the first illustrative example of the change in the fastening of the mantle directly under the chin rather than on the right shoulder. This habit is almost identical to that worn by the present Lord Chief Justice of England and Wales, albeit the mantle is now much shorter and pulled back so that the lining is only visible, the girdle is now much wider and a full-bottomed wig has replaced the black cornered cap and skull cap.

CHAPTER 2

Elements of a Judge's Habit

As is the case with the common law, the development and evolution of English legal and judicial dress has occurred largely without written rules and regulations.[1] The "Habit" of a Judge refers to the full ensemble of a robe, hood and mantle and is of great antiquity,[2] so much so that the common law Judges sought to codify the ancient conventions for the wearing of the different types of robes, for the sake of uniformity, by way of the *Judges' Rules* of 1635.[3] Indeed, the antiquity of an English Judge's habit can be clearly seen in the following humorous account by a Victorian observer of a masquerade ball held at Buckingham Palace:

> The official dress of the judges of England has, with some slight exceptions, remained unchanged for many centuries. When Her Majesty the Queen, some twenty years since, gave a grand masquerade ball at Buckingham Palace, at which all the guests were directed to be arrayed in the costume of the reign of Charles II, two learned judges who attended, the late Lord Chief Justice Campbell and Baron Parke, congratulated themselves upon the trifling cost of their costumes. They had merely to purchase two black silk skull-caps, edged with white satin, to be worn instead of their ponderous "full-bottom" George I wigs, polished boots with high heels, and then donning their usual scarlet and ermine robes, they were in the dress of the judges of the period. Indeed, except in colour, the state and criminal robes of the judges have remained almost unaltered since the time of Henry III.[4]

Each of the elements of a Judge's habit (namely, the robe, mantle and hood) and its accessories (namely the casting-hood, cincture and black scarf (or stole)) shall each be discussed in turn.[5] Other additional items of legal dress, such as the black silk and stuff gowns and the various types of neckwear and headwear worn by the Bench and Bar over the centuries - none of which are derived from the original Judges' habit and each have a different history altogether - shall also be discussed as they now form part of the history and tradition of court dress and legal attire.

Note: illuminated letter from page 66.

1. *Court Dress, supra*, 1.1.

2. Pulling, *supra*, 218. It seems that the essentials of a Judge's "habit" were settled by the time of King Edward III (1327-1377): *Court Dress, ibid*, Appendix, 2.1.2.

3. There are many references to "habits" in Judges' wills which evidently refer to the robe, mantle and hood. For example, William Calow J of the Court of Common Pleas left in his will "habits and gownes" (Probate Records of the Prerogative Court of Canterbury, PCC 7 Milles (1485)); Sir Thomas Lyttleton J of the Court of Common Pleas left 3 habits, "that is to saie gowne, cloke and hode" (Will of Thomas Lytilton or Lyttleton, 8 November 1481, Probate Records of the Prerogative Court of Canterbury, PROB 11/7/74); Thomas Tremayle J of the Court of King's Bench left "*unam togam et unam clamidem de vestimentis et habitibus meis existentibus apud London*" (Will of Thomas Tremayll, of East Meon, Hampshire, 19 September 1508, Probate Records of the Prerogative Court of Canterbury, PROB 11/16/104).

4. "Judicial Costume," *Leisure Hour* 26 (1877) 707.

5. The 1635 Judges' Rules refer to the robes as "gowns" as do a number of early Judges' wills (see above at n3).

JUDGES' ROBES

It is difficult to trace with exact precision the origins of English Judges' robes, given that very little illustrative evidence exists.[6] However, it is apparent that during the 14th century, the Judges wore the habit of the order of Serjeants-at-law, as it was from their ranks that Judges were exclusively appointed by the Crown.[7]

It has been suggested that the term "robe" in this instance is derived from the Latin *roba*.[8] However, Sir Victor Windeyer - a former Justice of the High Court of Australia - has clearly outlined the origin of "robe" as deriving, rather, from the Old French word "*rob*":

> The word "robe" is of the same stem as "rob". It came into English from Old French. "Robe" meant originally plunder, spoil. This linguistic relationship later led to Coke to propound an inverted etymology. He said that robbery, a felony, got its name from the conduct of the offenders: "Either because they bereaved the true man of his robes or garments or because his money or goods were taken out of some part of his garment or robe about his person [3. Inst. c.16]." To say that robbers "bereaved" a man of his goods is today an unusual, although perfectly correct, use of the word "reave". Coke's explanation of the derivation of the word "robbery" is remarkable, yet less so than his derivation of the word "robberdsmen" in two old statutes (5 Ed. III c.14 and 7 Rich. II c.5) which he said came from Robin Hood's name, he being a great exponent of their methods [3 Inst., 197]. However, the word "robe" had come to mean a garment longe before Chaucer wrote. The Man of Law's robes were, along with his fees, lawful takings of his office - not plunder, whatever some of his patrons and clients may have thought. In mediaeval legal Latin a robe, in the sense of a garment, was "roba" [e.g., Bracton, 147]. Incidentally, "roba" was later, and by an Italian route, to come into English with quite another meaning. In Shakespeare's time a "bona-roba" was a wench, particularly an attractive and and immodest wench, as Doctor Johnson said "a showy wanton". Shallow, boasting to his fellow justice of the peace, Silence, of youthful roistering when he was a student at Clement's Inn with his companions - "not four such swinge bucklers in all the Inns of the Court again" - said that "we knew where the bona-robas were": and Falstaff remembered that Jane Nightwork had been a bona-roba [Henry IV, Pt II, Act 3, Sc. 2, 26, 220].[9]

The "robe" in this instance refers to the garment of cloth - similar to a cassock in shape - which is closed down the front with a straight front fastening and a high neck without any lapels.[10] The cuffs of this judicial robe

6. Baker, *Collected II*, *supra*, 822.
7. *Ibid.*
8. Indeed, it is referred to as "*roba*" by Sir John Fortescue CJ: "...*Nam Serviens ad Legum ipse existens, Roba longa, ad instar Sacerdotis*..."(*De Laudibus* 128).
9. Windeyer, *supra*, 396.

were trimmed with either miniver or silk and the front edges of the robe were trimmed with the same material for most of the robe's length. The "robe" is therefore distinguishable from a "gown" which is historically known in the Latin as a *toga*[11] and, in contrast to the robe, refers to a garment which is open in front (such a barrister's gown), though these terms have, both in the past and at present, been used by Judges and academic writers interchangeably.[12] In any event, in order to understand the origins and development of Judges' robes, it is critical that one reviews the development of the robes worn by those of the Order of the Coif.[13]

The Habit of a Serjeant-at-law

The habit of Serjeants-at-law consisted of a long robe or cassock, a hood, a tabard (also known as a *collobium*[14]) with two tongue-shaped labels[15] at the neck and a white coif. As is the case with the current official dress of the Bar, it appears that this dress was retained by Serjeants-at-law as their official costume from the lay fashions of the time.[16] Initially, the habit of a Serjeant-at-law was worn by laymen of all classes in the 13th century, with people of all ranks (from monarchs to peasants) all wearing tabards and coifs.[17] However, it is clear that the version worn by Serjeants-at-law was distinguished from the garments in lay use by both the length (the robe and hood of a Serjeant-at-law required five and a half yards, along with three yards for the tabard) and the quality of the material (that is, a white coif and ray or parti-coloured robes).[18]

10. Derriman, *supra*, 85.
11. It has been suggested by some writers that the English Judges' robes and barristers' gowns derive from the Roman *toga*, given that Roman jurists wore such robes which were subsequently emulated by European jurists: Wayne Martin, "Forensic Fashions," *Brief* (June, 1986), 8.
12. Baker, *Collected II*, *supra*, 812. Sir Viktor Windeyer J has stated that the words "gown" and "robe" "are today generally interchangeable, although one properly denotes a form of the other. Doctor Johnson defined a robe as a "gown of state, a dress of dignity". That description is apt for either the scarlet or black garb of a judge, although sometimes a judge's robes are spoken of as his ceremonial apparel, his working dress as a gown." (Windeyer, *supra*, 395). Planche has described "robe" as deriving from the French which originally was a general term for a gown, but that the English word is limited to state and official garments, such as the coronation and parliamentary robes of the sovereign, and the robes worn by peers and judges (Planche, *supra*, 420).
13. Although this text does briefly refer to the history of the robes worn by Serjeants-at-law, a more fuller and detailed analysis of their habit can be obtained from Baker, *Serjeants-at-Law*, *supra*, 67-83.
14. The term "*collobium*" refers to a sleeveless or short-sleeved tunic used traditionally as an ecclesiastical vestment, but which was ampler than the Greek chiton worn during the Archaic period (circa 750-500 B.C.).
15. The term "label" refers to two tongues of white fur or silk and were rounded at at bottom to give it a tongue shaped appearance, and were turned outwards in a gourd-shape which made them appear to be either part of the hood or an extension of the collar of the Serjeants' robe: Hargreaves-Mawdsley, *supra*, 83. Although they look similar in appearance to the bands worn presently by the Bench and Bar, bands were not derived from labels and were simply a development of the falling collar which was part of the lay fashion during the mid seventeenth century: *ibid*, p 84.
16. Baker, *Serjeants-at-Law*, *supra*, 68.
17. *Ibid*, 69.
18. Serjeant Ayloffe has recorded that for the 1577 call of Ser-

An example of the contrasting nature of the dress of laymen and persons of higher status is a miniature in a manuscript known as Bracton, in which King Edward I (1239-1307) is presenting a sword to a group of six knights and a sealed charter to a group of six seated Judges. Of the six Judges, three of them are wearing *capae manicatae* and *pilei* (which presumably indicates that they were also of the clergy), while three others wear white coifs which were forbidden to be worn by the English clergy. [19]

Up until the turn of the 15th century (if not earlier), Judges and Serjeants-at-law wore almost identical robes of no great distinction. Illustrative evidence from the 14th century shows that judges and Serjeants-at-law had acquired a distinctive habit by the middle of the 14th century.[20] There are a number of 14th century miniatures which depict Serjeants-at-law in long robes of either plain or rayed colour, along with hoods and coifs, with the *collobium* being more associated with Judges of the time.[21] One illustrative example is in James le Palmer's historiated initial of "A" in "*Advocatus*" in his encyclopedia *Omne Bonum*.[22]

In addition to the various fourteenth century miniatures, there are a number of existing effigies which show this distinctive costume, such as the worn effigy of John de Stonore (died 1354) in the the abbey church at Dorchester, Oxfordshire, and the oaken effigy of Sir John de Stouford (died 1359) at West Down, Devon, among others.[23]

The Serjeants-at-law maintained their distinctive dress for centuries until their gradual abolition in the late nineteenth century,[24] and there are numerous interesting accounts in which Judges have described the traditional dress of Serjeants-at-law during creation ceremonies.[25]

---

jeants he required: "v yeardes and a halfe of fine scarlet at xxvi s. viii d. the yeard, for your gown and hood, vii li. vi s. viii d. for v yeardes and a halfe of fine vilett in graine at xiii x.iiid. the yeard, for your gown and hood, iii li. xiii s. iiii d. For viii yeardes [and a] halfe of fine morraye in graine and London rosset at xii s. the yeard, for your gown and hood [and] taybott (and abbe), v li. ii s. For v yeardes of morraye and rosset at ix s. The yeard for your men's liverayes for x cootes, vi li. xv s." (British Library MS Add. 35329, folios 33-39; Baker, *ibid*, 310).

19. The Archbishop of Canterbury, John Peckham (1230-1292), forbade the wearing of coifs in 1281 by English clergymen: William Lyndwood, *Provinciale* (Oxford, 1679), 120.

20. Baker, *Serjeants-at-Law*, *supra*, 70.

21. *Ibid.*

22. Royal MS 6 Edward VII, folio 52 (two advocates and two judges in *collobia*). This can be seen on page 29.

23. Baker, *Serjeants-at-Law*, *supra*, 70.

24. The last Serjeant-at-law appointed was Lord Lindley in 1875. Following the *Judicature Acts* of 1873 & 1875, the requirement for a common law Judge to have formerly been a Serjeant-at-law ceased, leading to the demise of the Order of the Coif. The Serjeants' Inn was sold for in 1877 and demolished in 1910: *ibid*, 127-129.

25. Baker, *Ibid*, 291-292, 287.

Miniature in Bracton of the King presenting a sword to a group of six knights and a sealed charter to a group of six seated Judges. Of the six Judges, three of them are wearing capae manicatae and pilei (which presumably indicates that they were also of the clergy), while three others wear white coifs which were forbidden to be worn by the English clergy.
The British Library (MS Add 11353, folio 9)

Fourteenth century miniature of a Judge facing Serjeants-at-law who are wearing plain robes. The Judge is wearing a blue collobium or tabard with white lining and a brown (or red) hood pulled over his head with two tounged-shaped labels extending from the hood which appear to be an extension of the collar of the blue robe. This image is probably one of the earliest images showing a Judge wearing a collobium.
© The British Library Board (MS Harley 947, folio 107)

Another fourteenth century miniature of a Judge facing Serjeants-at-law, with one wearing light red rayed with white, with the hood lined in green, and another wearing blue-grey rayed with white with a scarlet hood. The Judge is wearing what appears to be a green tabard and a white coif. © The British Library Board (MS Egerton 656, folio 122).

Royal MS 6 Edward VII, folio 52, Detail of a historiated initial 'A'(dvocati) of two advocates and two judges showing two Judges and two Serjeants standing and facing each other. The two Judges are wearing collobia and have two tongue shaped labels on their necks. The British Library (Royal MS 6 Edward VII, folio 52).

The Change from a Serjeant's Habit to a Judge's Habit

It can be seen that by the fifteenth century (if not earlier), the habit of a Serjeant-at-law consisted of a sleeveless or short sleeved tabard, a full length robe with either small bell sleeves or narrow sleeves and a corresponding hood which as with the robe was lined with lambswool or budge with the cowl part of the hood hanging from behind, and a white coif.[26] By the end of the 14th century, however, newly appointed Judges had replaced the tabard[27] and *collobium* for a mantle or cloak (also known as a "*chlamys*"[28]), which was fastened on the Judge's right shoulder.[29] Indeed, there are no monuments or brasses which depict the *collobium* or tabard being worn by judges after 1400.[30] The habit of a Judge therefore became by 1400, if not earlier, a robe, hood and mantle and this habit has, to a large extent, remained unaltered to the present day.

The result of this development was that the *collobium* formed part of the exclusive habit of Serjeants-at-law.[31] This change from the *collobium* to the mantle by Judges and its retention by Serjeants-at-law is particularly evident in the writings of Sir John Fortescue CJ (himself becoming a Serjeant-at-law in 1438 and then a Judge in 1442) who wrote in circa 1470, while in exile in France, that on becoming a Judge the Serjeant-at-law would give up the *collobium* and would wear a mantle in its place:

> From thenceforth, he changes his habit in some few particulars, but not in all: for when only a Serjeant at Law, he is clothed in a long robe, not unlike a sacerdotal habit, with a furred cape about his shoulders, and a hood over it, with two labels or tippets ... with a coif ... But after he is made a Judge, instead of the hood he shall be habited with a cloak, fastened upon his right shoulder; he still retains the other ornaments of a Serjeant, with this exception, that a Judge shall not use a party-coloured habit, as the Serjeants do, and his cape is furred with minever, whereas the Serjeant's cape is always furred with white lamb.[32]

---

26. *Ibid*; Hargreaves-Mawdsley, p 74; Pulling, *supra*, 228-229.
27. The tabard may not have been worn from the fifteenth century onwards in court, as it is not shown being worn by the Serjeants-at-law in either the Inner Temple illustrations or window paintings at Long Melford. However, they are shown in the sixteenth century brasses of Thomas Pygot (died 1520) at Whaddon, Buckinghamshire, John Brooke (died 1522) in St Mary Redcliffe, Bristol and John Newsegate (died 1528) at Harefield in Middlesex, which is the last brass depicting the tabard: Baker, *Serjeants-at-Law*, *supra*, 74. What is clear, though, is that the tabard was in fact still worn over the hood during creation ceremonies, resulting in the tail of the hood being pulled out from behind ("apon theire hoodes were put theire tabbertes, and the said hoodes a little pulled owte both behinde and before above theire tabertes": Baker, *ibid*, 273; Dugdale, *Origines Juridiciales*, *supra*, 122). The tabard was worn during the last general call of Serjeants in 1736 ("party-coloured robes and the tabord over them": Edward Wynne ed., *Observations touching the Antiquity and Dignity of the Degree of Serjeant at Law* (1765) 111) and thereafter in private calls up until the late eighteenth century, for the last mention of the tabard's use was in the drawing by Robert Dighton of the coifing of Serjeants Kirby and Rooke in 1781 which shows a mantle being worn underneath the liripipe of the hood as well as two angular appendages on the upper arm which are ledged with plain lace which probably derive from the original lapels on the medieval version of the tabard and may be the explanation for the reference in 1675 to "parti-coloured robes with scallops" being worn by Serjeants (Baker, *ibid*, 75, 410).
28. The *chlamys* of *chlamis* is now referred to as a mantle, although in early Judges' wills it is referred to as a cloak: Baker, *Collected II*, 813.
29. Baker, *Serjeants-at-Law*, *supra*, 72.
30. Baker, *Collected II*, 813. The *collobium* continued to be worn by Serjeants-at-law at their creation ceremonies until at least 1781 and was part-coloured (Baker, *Serjeants-at-Law*, *supra*, 72).
31. *Ibid*.
32. A. Amos, *Fortescue De Laudibus Legum Angliae: The Trans*

The earliest known effigy of an English Judge was the monumental brass of Ralph de Hengham CJ of the King's Bench (1274-1290) by Wenceslaus Hollar in Sir William Dugdale's *The History of St Paul's Cathedral* which was depicted on his tomb at the Old St Paul's Cathedral in London,[33] before it was most likely destroyed by the Great Fire of London in 1666, although he is portrayed with a round ecclesiastical cap rather than a white coif which was probably due to the misinterpretation of the artist.[34] By the third quarter of the 15th century it seems that the front of the Judges' robes began to be slit edged with fur, with this partial opening down the front of the robe continuing to this day.[35] This can be seen in the brass of Sir Richard Bingham, a Justice of the Court of King's Bench (circa 1476) at Middleton Church, Warwickshire, which depicts a partial opening down the front of his robe up to the point where his cincture is fitted, over which he wears the mantle.[36] The bottom of his robe also appears to be faced with some form of fur.

Brass of Bingham J of the Court of King's Bench (circa 1476) with his wife Lady Bingham at Middleton Church, Warwickshire, which depicts a partial opening down the front of his robe up to the point where his cincture is fitted, over which he wears the mantle. The bottom of his robe also appears to be faced with some form of fur.

The finest piece of evidence depicting 15th century Judges' robes can be seen in the four illuminations on four surviving folios of a law treatise executed during the final years of the reign of King Henry VI, which in 1894 came into the possession of the Inner Temple from Whaddon Hall, Buckinghamshire, now commonly known as the Inner Temple illuminations or miniatures.[37]

By the 16th century, the robes became looser at the wrists and the practice became to turn back the sleeve-lining by about 3 to 6 inches,[38] while the opening of the robe at the front was extended down to the waist, with the edge of the lining also shown, but unlike the wrists, the edge of the lining here was not folded back but rather was faced with miniver or taffeta.[39]

Between the 18th and 19th centuries, the lining of the sleeves which were turned up were now converted into facings with deep cuffs which were carried up until almost the elbow (as if the sleeves are turned back to display the miniver or taffeta 'lining') and this practice has continued to the present day.[40]

---

lation into English (London: J. Smith, 1825) 195. See Latin: "*iusticiarius factus, loco collobii clamide induetur, firmata super humerum eius dexterum, ceteris ornamentis servientis ad huc permanentibus*" (*De Laudibus*, 128). However, there is evidence that this change in judicial dress occurred many decades before Sir John Fortescue, as the effigies indicate that the change from the *collobium* to the mantle occurred at the end of the 13th century at the latest.

33. Dugdale, *The History of St Pauls Cathedral*, *supra*, 100-101.

34. John Schofield, *St Paul's Cathedral before Wren*, (Historic England Publishing, 2011), 281-284.

35. Hargreaves-Mawdsley, *supra*, 54.

36. Sir William Dugdale, *The Antiquities of Warwickshire illustrated* (London, 1656), 758.

37. Discussed below at p. 44-51.

38. It has been suggested that this change in the sleeves being turned back to display the miniver lining was as a result of changes to court fashion during the reign of Henry VIII: Hargreaves-Mawdsley, *supra*, 60.

39. Baker, *Collected II*, 815. F. N. Newark, "Judicial Robes," *Northern Ireland Legal Quarterly* 6 (1944-1946) 206, 212.

40. Derriman, *supra*, 86.

The Colour of Judges' Robes

The colours of the robes worn by Judges between the thirteenth to sixteenth centuries was of great variation.[41] This was due to the fact that, historically, the colour of a Judge's robe varied with the taste of the reigning monarch, out of whose Wardrobe the robes were furnished to Judges as a royal livery.[42] What had become established since early times, however, was the practice of Judges having both winter and summer robes, the former being lined with miniver (as opposed to ermine)[43] and the latter lined with taffeta or sarsent.[44]

There are a number of early records of the accounts of the King's Wardrobe which show allowances by the Crown to Judges of violet, miniver and green cloth. For example, Dugdale discovered records showing that Judges had summer robes of green cloth lined with green taffeta in 1387, during the 10th year of the reign of King Richard II:

> In R. 2 Sir Walter de Clopton Knight then Chief Justice of the King's Bench, and John Hull his fellow Justice in that Court; Sir Robert Charleton Chief Justice of the Common Pleas, and William Thyrning, William Rykill, John Wadham, and Richard Sydenham Justices also of the same Court had for their summer robes these following liveries; viz, each of the Chief Justices ten ells[45] of green cloth long, and xxiiii [23] ells of green taffata; and each of the rest ten ells of green cloth long. The like (viz ten ells of green cloth long) at the same time had John Cassy Chief Baron of the Exchequer.[46]

Dugdale has further recorded that in 1442, during the 22nd year of the reign of King Henry VI, the Judges had winter robes of violet cloth lined with miniver and summer robes of green cloth lined with tartarin:[47]

---

41. Dugdale, *Origines Juridiciales*, *supra*, 99.
42. *Ibid*; "Judicial Costume", *supra*, 707. Dugdale himself has noted that from the accounts t his disposal that "the colour of their robes was not constantly the same, there being so much variation in those times abovementioned; though for the fashion of them (I presume) they did not much differ": *ibid*, 99. An example of a Judge referring to his robes as a royal livery can be seen in the Will of William Westbury J of the Court of Common Pleas (died 1449), who bequeathed "one gown with sleeves and hood of the king's livery": Lambeth Palace, Reg. Stratford, 180b.
43. Miniver is the unspotted white fur of ermine but without the distinctive black tails, although many writers incorrectly state that the robes are lined with ermine. The term "ermine" itself is the name of the stoat (*Mustela erminea*) and is also used to refer to the stoat's pure white winter coat. Although writers "are fond of the romantic sound of 'ermine'" (Hargreaves-Mawdsley, *supra*, 46), Judges have never worn ermine as it was very costly and used only for the robes of peers and the sovereign, as described by the English historian and poet Edmund Bolton (1575-1633): "They are commonly called *polwdred Ermin,* and both the *white,* and *black* in them are skin with the haires on, for I haue seene a royall satten mantle, the furre wherof was the whole cases of *Ermin,* their tail-tips (all that was black in them) not stitcht in, but Pendent, and Dangling, and ... I must tell you also ... that there is a counterfet sort, which notwithstanding is very rich, made of the soft white bellies of Squirrel, Mineuer, and the like, drawn-in, and powldred with little specks of black Italian budge" (Edmund Bolton, *The Elements of Armories* (London: George Eld, 1610), 171-172) As to the use of miniver, however, in practice many Judges also use rabbit (coney) or fake fur for their scarlet robes instead of pure miniver which is much more expensive.
44. Baker, *Collected II*, *supra*, 817. See also below at pp 56-59 for an analysis of the taffeta facings of Judges' robes.
45. An "ell" is a unit of measurement, originally a cubit, i.e., approximating the length of a person's arm from the elbow to the tip of the middle finger.
46. Dugdale, *Origines Juridiciales*, *supra*, 99.
47. Tartarin was an expensive form of silk or taffeta from Tartary, which in the Middle Ages was a term designated for the great tract of northern and central Asia.

> And in 22 H. 6. John Fray then Chief Baron of the Exchequer, had for his winter robe against Christmas allowed unto him x [10] ells of violet in grain,[48] fur of xxxii [32] bellies of minever pur[e], for his hood. Another fur of cxx [120] bellies of minever gross and two furs each of seven tyres [i.e., tires][49] of silk. As also for his summer robe, against Whitsuntide,[50] ten ells of green cloth long, and half a piece of green tartarin.
>
> And at the same time Roger Hunt, Robert Frampton, and William Fallan (the other Barons of the Exchequer) had for the like summer robes, each of them ten ells of violet in grayn [i.e., violet dyed in grain]; with one fur of cxx [120] bellies of minever gross; and another fur of xxxii [32] bellies of minever pur[e], for the hood, as also two furs of silk, each of seven tyres [i.e., tires].[51]

Thus, it seems that it was customary for Judges to wear green robes during the summer, violet for winter and scarlet for special occasions. It is not entirely clear why violet robes were adopted by Judges from the 13th century onwards,[52] though one 19th century observer has suggested that the wearing of violet robes was in recognition of the Seamless robe of Christ which, according to the Bible, was also purple in colour.[53] However, this scheme of green for summer, violet for winter and scarlet for special occasions was not universally observed by all Judges. For example, Sir Peter Arderne CB (d. 1467) referred to the following judicial robes in his will, although he does not state for which season or on what occasion they were worn by him:

> Two of my best clokes furred, my best cloke lyned with tarteryn ... a murrey[54] cloke furred with Calaber[55]... my side [i.e., long] Scarlett gowne furred the Coler and Sleves with the hoode of Scarlett furred ... my green gowne and my grene cloke of the same lyned with Reede Tarteryn ... my best new side Skarlett gowne, hoode and cloke lyned with Tarteryn ... my side Crymesyn gowne engreyned [i.e., dyed in grain] with the hode lyned of the same ... my murrey

48. The word "grain" was the Medieval word for the red dye derived from the dried bodies of the female scale insects of the genus *Kermes* (the word "kermes" itself is derived from the Perso-Arabic word *qirmiz*, which means "red" in Persian and "crimson" in Arabic). The phrase "*dyed in the grain*" refers to dyed with kermes, or kermes in combination with another dye, producing various colours such as *crimson in grain* or *violet in grain*: John H. Munro, "Medieval Woollens: Textiles, Technology, and Organisation" in David Jenkins ed., *The Cambridge History of Western Textiles* (Cambridge University Press, 2003) 214–215.

49. The word "tire" or "tyre" is an archaic Middle English word referring to attire or dress. The word in this context is no longer in use, though it was commonly used in this meaning during the 14th century.

50. I.e., the week following Whitsun (or Whitsunday), which was the Christian festival of Pentecost, the eighth Sunday after Easter, which commemorates the Holy Spirit's descent upon the disciples of Christ.

51. Dugdale, *Origines Juridiciales*, *supra*, 99.

52. The violet robe is said to date from the reign of King Edward I (1272-1307): Derriman, *supra*, 86.

53. Matthew says that the soldiers "put a scarlet robe" on Jesus (27:27-28), Mark says that "they clothed Him with purple " (15:16-17), and John states that the soldiers put "a purple robe" on Him (19:1-2).

54. Murrey is a deep purple red cloth. This colour may well have been worn by Ardene CB given that murrey was one of the two livery colours of the House of York (the other being azure), during which period Ardene CB was a Judge. Murrey is also depicted on the shields of the Falcon of the Plantagenets and the White Lion of Mortimer, two of the ten heraldic statutes representing the genealogy of Her Majesty the Queen, known as the Queen's Beasts: H. Stanford London. *The Queen's Beasts* (London: Newman Neame Ltd, 1953) 25–33.

55. Referring to Calabrian squirrel fur, which was brown in colour: Baker, *Collected II*, *supra*. 818.

Photograph taken of an extant stained glass windows painted in circa 1486 at Long Melford, Suffolk which depicts Sir William Howard CJ of the Court of Common Pleas (1297-1308) in scarlet with miniver linings. The hood is unconventionally worn over the mantle, and there are only a few such representations of hoods over the mantle, and it is unclear whether such depictions are simply artistic errors or permissible variations to the conventional dress.

gowne side engrayned with the hoode furred of the same … my blewe side gowne cloke and hode of the same lyned with grene Tarteryn … my skarlett gowne furred with martyrns ….[56]

Another example of the variation in the colour of judicial robes can be seen in the will of John Holgrave, a Baron of the Court of Exchequer (d. 1487):

> A gowne of scarlet furryd with martrons with the hoode … a gowne of scarlet purfyllyd with menyver with the hoode … a scarlet gown lynyd with wollyn with the hoode … a cremesyn gowne lyned with wollyn with the hoode … a grene gowne sengyll with hode … a blew goune lynyd with wollyn with the hoode … a scarlet cloke sengyll … a blew cloke sengyll … ij rounde hoodes, oone of cremesyn and that other of vyolet with ij rollys.[57]

Scarlet Robes

Although those records noted by Dugdale do not make any reference to scarlet robes, it is clear that by at least the 15th century scarlet was worn by Judges. This can be clearly seen in the miniature illuminations of the Inner Temple Library which depict the Judges sitting in scarlet robes faced with miniver, as well as stained-glass windows which depict Judges wearing scarlet robes. For example, the extant stained glass windows painted in circa 1486 at Long Melford, Suffolk which depicts Sir William Howard (d. 1308), Chief Justice of the Court of Common Pleas (1297-1308) in scarlet with miniver linings.

BL MS Harley 1498, folio 76, depicting a historiated initial of "T" for "This", which is one of 4 historiated initials in colours and gold of Henry VII currently located at the British Library. The British Library (MS Harley 1498, folio 76)

Another early pictorial example of Judges in scarlet robes is the miniature of 1503, depicting a historiated initial of "T" for "This", which is one of 4 historiated initials in colours and gold of Henry VII currently located at the British Library.[58] The

56. Will of Peter Arderne of Latton, Essex, 10 July 1466, Probate Records of the Prerogative Court of Canterbury, PROB 11/5/245.

57. Will of John Holgrave, one of the Barons of the King's Exchequer, 22 September 1487, Probate Records of the Prerogative Court of Canterbury, PROB 8/11/63.

58. British Library MS Harley 1498, folio 76.

historiated initial depicts a Judge wearing scarlet robes with a hood and mantle faced with miniver and is wearing a coif.

Scarlet was the most solemn of the colours worn by Judges, partly due to its cost as well as the fact that laymen were forbidden by law to even wear it.[59] Indeed this connection between the upper ranks of society and scarlet can be clearly seen in the initial etters of the foundation charters of Eton College (1440) and King's College (1446) with both depicting two judges in scarlet wearing coifs and kneeling behind the peers who are also wearing scarlet mantles. The peers' robes are similar to those worn by Judges but have additional bars of miniver on their mantles which indicate the rank of the peerage (i.e., a Duke, Marquess, Earl or Baron), which are still worn by peers at the State Opening of Parliament in the House of Lords and which have to a large extent retained their medieval form.

Illumination from the Founder's Charter of King's College, dated 1446. The Lords and Commons petition King Henry VI, who prays for his College (Henry founded King's College in 1441). © King's College

59. The statute of 3 Edward IV, c. 5 forbade inferior persons from wearing scarlet, and by the mid sixteenth century scarlet cost 33s 4d. a yard (Dugdale, *Origines Juridiciales*, *supra*, 129). Similarly, the *Act of Apparel 1532* (24 Hen. VIII, c. 13) banned the use of scarlet and violet by anyone earning less than 5 pounds in income a year.

Green Robes

It is apparent that green was the most favoured colour (or, at least, the colour of Judges' robes during the summer) until scarlet became the Judges preferred colour, from the mid 16th century onwards, beginning during the second half of the reign of King Henry VI.[60] The last reference to green robes being worn by Judges was during the trial of Lord Dacre in 1534 where Sir John Spelman noted that "the justices were in their green robes, not scarlet."[61] The change in preferences from green to scarlet may have been due to the fact that the colour of the House of Lancaster was red,[62] which is in conformity with the historical custom that the colours of a Judge's robes were based on the preference of the reigning sovereign of the day.

The Man of Law from Geoffrey Chaucer's *Canterbury Tales* written in circa 1387. EL 26 C 9, folio 50v The Huntington Library, San Marino, California

Parti-Coloured and Rayed Robes

Sir John Fortescue has described the habit of a Serjeant-at-law as being either rayed or parti-coloured.[63] By the 14th century it had become fashionable for the Bench and Bar (more particularly so the Bar) to wear parti-coloured garments, which were either striped in different colours or half one colour and half another.[64] The parti-coloured robes arose from the lay fashion of the fourteenth century and were worn by Judges and Serjeants as a livery.[65] For example, Geoffrey Chaucer in his *Man of Law's Tale* described his fictitious Serjeant as appearing in parti-coloured robes:

> He rood but hoomly in a medlee cote
> Girt with a ceint of silk, with barres small
> Of his array telle I no longer tale.[66]

---

60. Hargreaves-Mawdsley, *supra*, 51. Green robes have been referred to in the inventory of the goods and chattels of William Rastell, a Justice of the Court of Queen's Bench (1558-1562).
61. Sir John Hamilton Baker, ed., *The Reports of Sir John Spelman* (London: Seldon Society, 1977) 55. Sir John Baker has also noted that a green robe is referred to in the Will of a Judge who died in 1553 which indicates that green robes may have been worn by Judges even after the trial of Lord Dacre in 1534 (Baker, *Collected II*, *supra*, 819). In any event, there is no reference to green robes being worn by Judges after 1553: Spelman, *ibid.*
62. Hargreaves-Mawdsley, *supra*, 51.
63. Amos, *supra*, 125; *De Laudibus* 128. The terms "ray" or "rayed" cloth indicates cloth which was "made of one dominant colour woven with rays or stripes of a lighter colour or of several colours" (Baker, *Serjeants-at-Law*, *supra*, 73).
64. Windeyer, *supra*, 397.
65. Pulling, *supra*, 221. It seems that not only the King, but also nobles, presented Serjeants-at-law with parti-coloured livery dress along with their retaining fees, for the Act of 1469 of Edward VI provides that no person of any condition was to give any livery to any person other than his menial servant, officer or man learned in the one law or the other: G. R. Corner, "Observations on Four Illuminations," *Archaeologia* 39 (1863) 357-366. In general, between the reigns of Edward III and Henry VIII numerous statutes were passed which restricted the wearing of parti-coloured robes, but the Serjeants-at-law were exempted from any such legislative restriction: F. A. Inderwick, *The King's Peace: A Historical Sketch of the English Law Courts* (London: Swan Sonnenschein & Co, 1895) 122.
66. *Canterbury Tales*, Prol. 1462.

The "medlee cote" of Chaucer's Serjeant-at-law was a long robe of two different colours which were divided vertically in the middle of the robe, known as a "parti-coloured" robe. When Judges during the fifteenth century began to exclusively wear one coloured robes the parti-coloured robes came to be entirely identified with Serjeants-at-law.[67]

In addition to being parti-coloured, the robes of Serjeants-at-law were also "rayed" vertically with parallel lines of cloth of a contrasting colour, as outlined by Sir John Baker:

> Parti-coloured garments were made of two different cloths, one for the right side and another of contrasting hue for the left side. Often one side was plain and the other side was rayed. Robes of that pattern were worn not only by serjeants and apprentices but also by legal and civil officials and by liverymen.[68]

One early example of parti-coloured and rayed robes can be seen in the window paintings of Serjeants Pygot and Haugh in the glass windows of Long Melford Church in Suffolk. These beautiful paintings show the Serjeants dressed in robes of murrey parted with blue ray cloth, with vertical rays of yellow and white (similar to Howard CJ's painting, they are depicted wearing the hoods over the mantle). Another clear example of the parti-coloured robes are those depicted in the Inner Temple miniature illuminations dated circa 1460, which show various parti-coloured robes being worn by the Serjeants-at-law standing at the bar in court, as well as by apprentices and barristers and other court officials, with the predominant colours being blue and green although occasionally a neutral buff or grey colour can also be seen.

Although the colours of Serjeants' robes were not fixed during medieval times, by the Tudor period the Serjeants had adopted standardised colours of murrey and blue,[69] which have been described by Sir Edward Montagu CJ in 1540 as "very sumptuousse and precyusse [i.e., precious] colours".[70] It appears that rayed robes went out of use in Tudor times, and it has been recorded in 1525 the city officers in London had permission to cease wearing ray cloth

---

67. Hargreaves-Mawdsley, *supra*, 75; Amos, *supra*, 125; *De Laudibus* 128. In later times parti-coloured robes became exclusively used by the Serjeants-at-law and for centuries were used in the course of ceremonies and festivities which would mark the creation of a new Serjeant-at-law, such ceremonies lasting several days: Windeyer, *supra*, 397.

68. Baker, *Serjeants-at-Law*, *supra*, 73-74.

69. This can be seen in the Long Melford glass window paintings of the Serjeants-at-law which date to circa 1485. Although murrey and blue were the livery colours of the House of York (1385-1485), it is not clear whether the robes of Serjeants were initially derived from a royal livery, for the Inner Temple illustrations (which were undertaken in circa 1460, during the Lancastrian period) do not show any of the Serjeants wearing the Lancastrian colours of white and blue and there was no change to the Tudor livery colours of green and white after 1485. However, on the other hand, the court officials in the Court of King's Bench may have worn the royal livery colours, for some of the court officials in the Inner Temple miniature are depicted wearing the Lancastrian colours of blue ray and white, and in the coronation of King Henry VIII in 1509 the tipstaves and court officials in the Court of King's Bench wore the Tudor livery colours of green and white: *ibid.*

70. British Library MS Harley 361 ff. 75-80; Baker, *Serjeants-at-Law*, *supra*, 298. Lord Chief Justice Montague links the two colours of murrey and blue to "two high qualyties inheretens every of you. To one is the highe talante of learninge, the other of auctoritye and power": *ibid.* In an earlier speech to newly ap-

Photograph taken of an extant stained glass windows painted in circa 1486 at Long Melford, Suffolk which depicts Serjeant Pygot.
© Long Melford Church, Suffolk, UK / Bridgeman Images

Photograph taken of an extant stained glass windows painted in circa 1486 at Long Melford, Suffolk which depicts Serjeant Haugh.
© Long Melford Church, Suffolk, UK / Bridgeman Images

pointed Serjeants-at-law in circa 1521, the Chief Justice noted the colour of the hood and tabard as being "blew and murrye, rather then of any collors, I shall tell you mine opinion. The blew dothe represent unto us the the elyment, in token that we shuld lift up our yees to hevine and remembre that we suffer not our selfes so to be drowned in worldlye matters that we forgett heaven and heavenlye cogitations. The murrye signifiethe unto us the blode that Christ sched for us all when he suffered his passion, which thinge we that be Christians owgth alwayes to have in memorye": Baker, *Serjeants-at-Law*, *supra*, 287.

because of it being badly wrought.[71] It appears that Serjeants-at-law also abandoned ray cloth at the same time, as it is no longer mentioned after this period.[72] However, for some unknown reason, parti-coloured robes were retained by Serjeants-at-law for much longer and lasted well into the late eighteenth century (although earlier accounts state that they went into disuse much earlier),[73] with Serjeants wearing them for their creation ceremonies and certain appearances in court.[74]

By the 1550s, following the disuse of rayed robes, the traditional murrey and blue cloth gave way to a murrey and "mustard" or "russet", which was of a darker colour closer to black than blue.[75] Following the Restoration, the parti-colours of robes began to be varyingly described as "purple and murry",[76] brown and blue,[77] brown and violet[78] and by 1736 it was described as "Gowns and Jacquets of blew and purple".[79] Sir John Baker has described the discrepancies in the parti-colours, noting that the colours were not changed at random:

> Law reporters who described creations in some detail never mentioned the colours, which suggests that they were fixed and well known. Indeed, making due allowance for the difficulty of describing colours, it is probable that the pre-1649 russet or black had simply been replaced by violet or bluish purple: in which case, consciously or otherwise, there was a reversion to the older colours.[80]

In any event, the coifing of Serjeants Kirby and Rooke in 1781 (as illustrated by Dighton), which showed the robes on the right hand side of the Serjeant as violet which are laced and edged with murrey, was most likely the last occasion when parti-coloured robes were worn by Serjeants-at-law (even for creation ceremonies).[81]

---

71. J. Stow, *Survay of London* (London, 1598) 539.
72. Baker, *Serjeants-at-Law*, *supra*, 74.
73. Mr Serjeant Pulling had stated that parti-coloured robes eventually came into disuse during the reign of King Henry VIII (Pulling, *supra*, 228), although it was suggested by Mr Serjeant Atkinson that parti-coloured robes continued to be worn by Serjeants-at-law until the time of the Commonwealth Protectorate, when a great change took place in all forms of dress in England (Corner, *supra*, 63).
74. Baker, *Serjeants-at-Law*, *supra*, 74.
75. The colour of "russet" has been described as "somewhat lighter than black" (G. Leigh, Accedens of Armorie (1562), p 116, and "mustard" has been described by Dugdale as "mouse": Dugdale, *Origines Juridiciales*, *supra*, 136. Chief Justice Sir Edward Coke in a call to Serjeants in 1614 described the Serjeants' robes as "murrey and black, [signifying] wisdome and gravitie" (Baker, *Serjeants-at-Law*, *supra*, 324) and the *Judges' Rules* of 1635 refers to the Serjeants' parti-coloured robe as being "of black and murrey". Following the Restoration up until the early eighteenth century, the parti-colours of robes began to be described as murrey and purple, brown and blue, brown and violet and by 1736 it was described as purple and blue.
76. Sir Henry Chauncy, *The Historical Antiquities of Hertfordshire, Vol 1*, (London, JM Mullinger), 156: "The first Year after their Creation, every Serjeant shall wear his party-colour'd Robe of purple and Murry, with a Hood of the same close over his Neck, the Tip hanging back and down behind, every Day at Westminster, and in their Circuits."
77. E. Chamberlayne, *Angliae Notitia or the Present State of England* (1671 ed.), II, 245.
78. J. Strype, ed., *Stow's Survey of London* (London, 1720), I, 122.
79. Arthur Robert Ingpen ed., *Master Worsley's Book on the History and Constitution of the Honourable Society of the Middle Temple* (London: Chiswick Press, 1910), 301.
80. Baker, *supra*, 76-77.
81. Parti-coloured robes had most certainly fallen into desuetude by 1809: E.W. Brabrook, *Transactions of the London & Middlesex Archaeological Society* 7 (1877) 249.

Unlined Robes of Serjeants and Barons of the Exchequer

The earlier quoted passage from the will of Baron Holgrave referred to "single" (i.e., unlined) robes and a robe "lyned with wollyn" (i.e., a robe with woollen lining) which were worn by Judges who were not Serjeants-at-law and were accordingly Judges of lower rank.[82] These Judges were mostly appointed to the Court of Exchequer and until the 19th century wore unlined robes highlighting their inferior position to that of Judges who were formerly from the Order of the Coif.[83]

Pictorial evidence of Barons of the Exchequer wearing unlined robes can be seen the brasses of Ursewyk CB (died 1479) at Dagenham, Essex, Brian Roucliff B (died 1495) at Cowthorpe, Yorkshire and Nicholas Luke B (died 1563) at Cople, Bedfordshire. The Barons of the Exchequer in the 15th century Inner Temple miniature are shown wearing mustard-coloured robes, hoods and mantle. The painting of Baron Sotherton, cursitor Baron of the Exchequer 1579-1605, also clearly depicts the unlined scarlet robe traditionally worn by Barons of the Court of Exchequer.

Painting of John Sotherton B, cursitor Baron of the Exchequer (1579-1605), who is wearing an unlined scarlet robe, hood and mantle with a black cincture, the traditional dress of Barons of the Exchequer during the 15th to 18th centuries. © Southampton Museum

As for Serjeants-at-law, by the end of the fifteenth century they had also (along with their parti-coloured robes) adopted single coloured robes, which by this time were almost identical to those worn by Judges (that is, the scarlet, black and violet robes), the only difference being that the Serjeants' robes no longer had any lining whereas the Judges' habits had miniver linings for winter and silk linings in the summer.[84] A clear example of the unlined scarlet robes can be seen in the portrait of William Bendlowes, which depicts the robes in the same form as a monastic habit with the hood and large cowl being worn over the loose robe which has wide sleeves and is closed at the front.[85]

82. Druitt, *supra*, 226.
83. *Ibid.*
84. The use of unlined robes for Serjeants is mentioned by the Chief Justice in 1521, who remarked that the Serjeants' robe "must be single and nott lyned, for that you should remembre to beware of dublenes and dissimulation, *Quia ve duplici cordi* (for owt upon him which have a duble hart)": Baker, *Serjeants-at-Law*, *supra*, 287.
85. By the middle of the eighteenth century, the folded part of the sleeves began to be caught up with tapes or cords and by the nineteenth century the sleeves were caught up by three tapes and buttons as was the case with the barrister's stuff gown: Baker, *ibid*, 78.

Portrait of William Bendlowes (dated 1564), clearly showing the unlined scarlet habit. He is wearing a cowled hood over a loose robe which is closed at the front and has wide sleeves. He is also wearing small ruffs as neckwear and a close fitted white coif along with gloves in his right hand.
By permission of the Master and Fellows of St John's College, Cambridge

Portrait of Sir John Maynard (Serjeant-at-law 1654), wearing almost the exact same dress as worn a century earlier by William Bendlowes, except that the hood had grown larger in size and the sleeves had now begun to be turned back at the wrist. It was the exact same dress of Judges when wearing scarlet, save that the Judges had miniver or silk facings on their robes and hoods. Note also the wide rectangular collar replacing the large ruffs of the late Elizabethan and early Stuart periods.

Illuminations of the Inner Temple

The use by Serjeants-at-law, Judges and Masters of their parti-coloured, scarlet and mustard robes respectively, as well the colourful robes of other court officials, meant that court trials in the 15th century would have been highly colourful affairs. No where else can this spectacular array of robes and colours be more clearly seen than in the miniature illuminations which date back to circa 1460, now in the hands of the Inner Temple.[86] Four such illuminations have remained largely intact, each depicting a specific court, which shall each be discussed below. Above the heads of the Judges in each of the four illuminations are three shields, the one on the left bearing the arms of King Edward the Confessor, which consist of five doves or martins surrounding a patonce cross; the middle shield bears the arms of the reigning monarch, the arms of France and England having been equally borne by Henry VI and Edward IV, and the shield on the right hand side bears the arms of England which consist of three identical gold lions with blue tongues and claws, walking past but facing the observer, arranged in a column on a red background.[87]

Illumination of the Court of Chancery

This illumination depicts two Judges sitting in scarlet robes with hood and mantle lined with miniver, one of them (the Master of the Rolls) without a coif and tonsured, the other (the Lord Chancellor[88]) wearing a black skull cap. On each side of the two scarlet Judges are two persons (most likely ecclesiastical Masters in Chancery, some of whom used to sit with the Lord Chancellor in the Court of Chancery until the time of Lord Brougham and Vaux LC),[89] wearing mustard-coloured robes, three of whom are evidently tonsured. The Master of the Rolls is holding a deed with a large seal attached to it from which he appears to be delivering his judgment.[90] Below the Judges are registrars and other officers with various rolls before them.

The table is covered with green cloth, on which stands one of the six clerks or a clerk in court reading a record which he holds in his hands. To his left is a court usher or tipstaff in a parti-coloured robe of green and blue, rayed diagonally. On the right of the table can be seen a sealer pressing down the matrix of

86. The illuminated manuscript now in the library of the Inner Temple, originally belonged to William Fleetwood, Recorder of London in the time of Queen Elizabeth I, which then eventually passed on to a Mr Selby Lowndes who then passed it onto the Inner Temple, and was produced for the first time by the Society of Antiquaries in 1860 (Inderwick, *supra*, 121).
87. Inderwick, *ibid*.
88. The Lord Chancellor is most likely Richard Neville, Earl of Salisbury (1400-1460), one of the very few laymen who held the office of Lord Chancellor during the early period: Inderwick, *ibid*, 122. He also appears to have been one of the last Lord Chancellors to have worn scarlet robes.
89. Corner, *supra*, 359.
90. Inderwick, *supra*, 122.

Illumination of the Court of Chancery.
Contributor: ART Collection / Alamy Stock Photo

Illumination of the Court of King's Bench.
Contributor: ART Collection / Alamy Stock Photo

the court seal with a roller on the wax attached to a court document of some sort (possibly a patent), and before the sealer lie a number of sealed writs folded up with pendant labels, as subpoenas and Chancery writs were prepared in this manner until the 19th century.[91]

Three Serjeants-at-law stand at the bar wearing coifs and parti-coloured robes of blue and green and blue and brown, along with two apprentices of the law or barristers wearing parti-coloured robes of blue and light brown and green and light blue. All of these parti-coloured robes worn by the Serjeants-at-law and barristers are striped or rayed either vertically or diagonally, and the divisions of the respective colours are separated straight down from the front and back of the robes.

Behind the row of Serjeants and barristers sit two other apprentices of the law or barristers, one of whom is reading a document, and three solicitors or clerks in court, one of whom is examining the point of a pen after having possibly mended it, another is delivering a paper to his colleague and the third individual is writing.

Illumination of the Court of King's Bench

The illumination of the Court of King's Bench portrays five Judges all of whom are wearing coifs and scarlet robes lined with miniver. Below them are sitting the King's Coroner and Attorney, and the Masters of the Court, as was the case in the mid 19th century prior to the Judicature reforms of 1875, all of whom wear parti-coloured robes of blue rayed and white,[92] or murrey and green.

On the table covered in green cloth are rolls and writing materials, and on which two ushers stand each holding a staff, the one on the left wearing a parti-coloured robe of mustard and blue rayed who is administering an oath on the Bible to one of the members of the jury, and the one on the right wearing a parti-coloured robe of murrey and green who appears to be speaking.

At the bar stands a prisoner in chains by the legs holding out his right hand as if he is addressing the Judges, who appears to be in custody of the court marshall or tipstaff. A Serjeant-at-law appears on each side of the prisoner, both of whom are wearing a coif and parti-coloured robes of green and blue rayed.

Behind the Serjeants stand six prisoners, all of whom are chained together by the legs and who appear to be in the custody of two tipstaff or gaolers, the one on the left wearing a blue robe holding a staff, and the one on the left is wearing a high cap and a mustard coloured robe.

---

91. Corner, *supra*, 358.

92. Blue and white were the colours of the House of Lancaster, which indicates that the parti-coloured coloured robes worn by the court clerks are royal liveries, then the date of the illumination must be before 4 March 1461, which is the date of the end of the first reign of King Henry VI: Baker, *Serjeants-at-Law*, *supra* 74-75.

Illumination of the Court of Common Pleas

This illumination of the Court of Common Pleas is smaller than the others and has the commencement of an alphabetical table of contents on the lower part of the manuscript. It depicts seven Judges, all of whom are wearing coifs, scarlet robes and scarlet hoods underneath scarlet mantles, which are lined with white budge.[93] The fact that there are seven presiding Judges indicates that the illumination dates between 1450 and 1466, during the reign of King Henry VI, as it was during his reign that the number of Judges appointed to the Court of Common Pleas was seven.[94]

Below the Judges sit the registrars and other officers of the court wearing parti-coloured robes of blue and light brown, rayed with blue stripes, and green and similarly rayed light brown with blue stripes. Similar to the other illuminations, the table is covered with a green cloth, on which are the rolls, a closed book and writing materials, and two ushers bearing staffs stand on the table both wearing parti-coloured robes, the one on the left wearing light brown and green rayed with white stripes and the other blue and green rayed with white stripes.

At the bar is a defendant in the custody of a tipstaff or marshall, in his shirt only with bare legs, and on his right is a Serjeant-at-law in a parti-coloured blue and green robe with white stripes and wearing a white coif. There are two other Serjeants-at-law similarly dressed at the far right, while on the left is another Serjeant similarly attired talking to an old man with a bald head, dressed in a parti-coloured robe of mustard blue rayed with white stripes, with a penner hanging from his cincture.

Illumination of the Court of Exchequer

This illumination (dated *circa* 1460) depicts five presiding Judges, the one in the centre dressed in scarlet robes, hood and mantle lined with miniver and wearing a turban-like hat of the same colour. Sitting with him are four Barons of the Exchequer,[95] two on each side, all wearing mustard-coloured robes, with two of them wearing their hats of the same colour, while two others hold their hats in their hands. At the table are clerks and officers of the court, two of whom sitting on the left are counting a large quantity of gold before them. There is also an usher standing on the table bearing a staff and apparently speaking. Interestingly, the table is not chequered but green like the tables in the oth-

93. Pulling, *supra*, 229-230.

94. Corner, *supra*, 360.

95. Planche has suggested that the four accompanying persons sitting on the Bench wearing robes of mustard colour were not in fact Barons, as the robes issued to all of the Barons of the Exchequer were always the same colour as that issued to the Chief Baron (Planche, *supra*, 427).

Illumination of the Court of Common Pleas.
© The Masters of the Bench of the Inner Temple

Illumination of the Court of Exchequer.

er illuminations, thus raising some doubt in the mind of the observer as to whether in fact this illumination in fact depicts the Court of Exchequer, which derives its name from the table covered with a chequered cloth.[96] However, the following statement from Corner explains why there should be no doubt that this illumination is that of the Court of Exchequer:

> There does not appear to be any sufficient reason for doubting whether the present illumination does represent the Court of Exchequer simply because the table covering is of a single colour. It must be remembered that, in keeping with the great accounts of the court, there were two distinct operations, one relating to the *summing-up* of the amounts due from the King's debtors, and the other to the receipt of them. The duty, therefore, of the most skilful of the Exchequer officers was to make those calculations and reduce them to writing; and for this purpose the chequered board or cloth was used, with the proper counters. But it is the receipt of the Exchequer which is represented in this painting, the mere payment of the several sums due, as is indicated by the gold coin lying on the table to be counted, and the small white sheepskin bags in which the money was kept. In the many entries on the great roll relating to the cloth for the Exchequer table, it is simply called *Pannus Laneus*, without any mention of its being chequered. It must be observed, also, that there were two chambers belonging to the court, each of which had a table covered with a cloth.[97]

At the bar are three Serjeants-at-law in parti-coloured and rayed robes of blue and green rayed with blue stripes and blue and green robes which are not rayed, all of whom are wearing white coifs. Standing alongside the Serjeants-at-law are barristers who are identifiable by them not wearing coifs, also in parti-coloured robes of blue and light brown rayed with blue stripes, and the barrister on the far right has his hat cast over his left shoulder, resembling the casting-hood which remnant can be seen on the back of left side of a barrister's stuff gown. Both barristers are also wearing black girdles around their waists.

In the foreground behind the Serjeants and barristers is a square cage which is barred and grated made out of strong wooden bars with a door of solid planks which is nailed and having a large lock. The cage seems capable of holding up to five prisoners, and appears to be erected on the lower floor of the court, against some solid part of the chamber in which the court is sitting. It also seems that the cage was a form of temporary confinement for the common defaulters until the court hearing was concluded.

96. Corner, *supra*, 362.
97. Corner, *ibid.*

Black Robes and Violet Robes

Although there are many early references to violet robes,[98] it is only until the mid 15th century that we see violet robes becoming an alternative to black robes. One of the earliest reference to the alternative black and violet robes worn by Judges appears to be in the inventory taken in 1479 of the goods and chattels of Sir Thomas Ursewyk (or Urswick) CB of the Court of Exchequer which lists robes of scarlet, violet, black, green and "Kentyshe kendal", though it is not clear if all of these items were judicial dress.[99]

Another early reference to black and violet robes being worn by Judges is in the Will of Edmund Mervyn J of the Court of Common Pleas dated 1550 who bequeathed robes of scarlet, green, violet and a "browne blew abbet".[100] A further early example of references to black and violet robes is in the inventory of the goods and chattels of William Rastell J of the Court of Queen's Bench (1558-1562), which was taken pursuant to a special commission issued by the Court of Exchequer in 1562 immediately after he had retired and fled from England to Leuven for religious reasons, without the permission of Queen Elizabeth I. The inventory included the following items pertaining to Rastell J's judicial robes:

> a violet gowne and cloke and hood fased with furre and lyned
> a skarlet gowne, cloke and hood fased with furr and lined with cotten
> a skarlet gowne, cloke and iii hoods fased with grene sarsenet unlined
> a violet gowne, cloke and hood lined with blake say and fased with sarsenet
> a gowne, cloke and hood fased with whit pure and lyned with cotten.[101]

In 1635, the Common Law Judges sitting in Westminster Hall issued regulations relating to judicial dress which, inter alia, formalised the wearing of black and violet robes:

> The Judges in Term Time are to sit at Westminster in the courts, in their black or violet gowns, whether they will; and a hood of the same colour put over their heads, and their mantles above all, the end of the hood hanging over behind, wearing their velvet caps and coifs of lawn and cornered caps.
>
> The facing of their gowns, hoods and mantles, is with changeable taffeta, which they must begin to wear upon Ascension-day, being the last Thursday in Easter term, and continue those robes until the feast of Simon and Jude; and upon Simon and Jude's day the judges begin to wear their robes faced with white furs of minever, and so continue that facing till Ascension-day again.[102]

---

98. *See e.g.*, Dugdale, *Origines Juridiciales, supra*, 99.
99. Public Record Office, Exchequer: King's Remembrancer and Treasury of the Receipt: Inventories of Goods and Chattels, Inventory of the goods of Thomas Ursewyk paper, E 154/2/2. See also: F. W. Steer "A Medieval Household: The Urswick inventory," *Essex Review* 63 (1956) 4-20.
100. Will of Sir Edmund Mervyn, 16 November 1553, Probate Records of the Prerogative Court of Canterbury, PROB 11/36/285. It is most likely that this reference to "browne blew" was an alias for a black coloured robe (see Cro. Car. 67).
101. "Legal Retrospections," *The Law Magazine or Quarterly Review of Jurisprudence* 31 (1844) 54, 58-59.
102. Dugdale, *Origines*, p 101. The full text of the Judges Rules of 1635 can be see at p. 7-10.

Thus, by 1635, the black robe had become an alternative to the violet robe, although it is not entirely clear when the modern practice of wearing the black robes faced with miniver in winter and violet robes faced with shot taffeta during the summer began. However, the Judges' Rules of 1635 in fact allowed Judges to alternate between the black and violet robes throughout the year, thereby providing them with additional flexibility. This can also be seen in the account-book of Stephen Frewen, who was a London skinner, which states that between 1637 and 1642 it was customary for some Judges to have the same fur facings of "minifur and armenes" added to their summer robes every winter, which the records state would have cost a Chief Justice 8 pounds and a Puisne Judge 5 pounds.[103] The Will of Sir Anthony Fitzherbert, a Justice of the Court of Common Pleas (d. 1538), also indicates this practice of Judges removing one form of lining and replacing it with another:

Colour engraving of Sir Edward Coke (1552-1634), by Pierre Duflos (1742-1816), in circa 1780. Coke is wearing the black robe, hood and mantle lined with miniver, which was the dress traditionally worn at Westminster Hall by common law Judges. © Private Collection / The Stapleton Collection / Bridgean Images

> And I will that … to my Cosyn Alice his wyfe oon of my best habites with the Cloke and Hood and the Lynyng and the furr of the same.[104]

One of the earliest portraits of Judges wearing the black robe faced with miniver is a colour engraving of Edward Coke by Pierre Duflos (1742-1816), though it is not contemporary and may be based on an original which is no longer in existence. Another early portrait is that of the coifing of Serjeants Cranley Thomas Kirby and Sir Giles Rooke by the Earl of Mansfield and the Earl of Rosslyn entitled "A Peep into Westminster Hall on a Call of Serjeants" by Robert Dighton dated 1 March 1781. Later portraits and pictures depicting the winter black robe include a number of later Victorian watercolours, some of which were reproduced in the Vanity Fair series (such as the watercolour of Sir Alexander Cockburn CJ dated 11 December 1869) as well as two portraits of Lord Justice Darling - one is an oil painting by George Henry dated 1898, at the time of his appointment to the Queen's Bench Division of the High Court, in which he is wearing the black robes faced with miniver, cincture and scarlet casting-hood over the black scarf, and the other by Reginald Grenville Eves dated 1916 in which he is wearing the same dress with the addition of the accompanying black hood faced with miniver.[105]

It is therefore clear that until the English Civil War, Judges wore both violet and black robes during the winter, as was permitted by the 1635 Judges' Rules which stated that the Judges may sit "in their Black or Violet Gowns, whether they will". However, by the 19th century, the rule of violet faced with change-

103. East Sussex Record Office (Lewes), MS FRE 521, 34, 43.

104. Walter W. Skeat, *The Book of Husbandry by Master Fitzherbert* (London: Trubner & Co, 1882) xix.

105. This portrait of Lord Darling was sold for £1,800 in November 2009 at Bonhams's, Knightsbridge. Its current owner and location is unknown.

able taffeta for summer and black faced with miniver for winter had become the norm, as clearly stated by the following 19th century contemporary writer:

> Sitting in banc in Hilary and Michaelmas Terms the judges wear black cloth robes trimmed with ermine. In Easter and Trinity Terms purple robes trimmed with "sad-coloured silk", in commemoration of the purple robe worn by our Saviour, are assumed.[106]

By the late nineteenth century it had also become settled that the violet and black coloured robes would be worn in the following terms:

- At *Nisi Prius* (i.e., when trying civil cases) during winter (Michaelmas and Hilary) terms: black robe faced with miniver, with black scarf, girdle, casting-hood, bands and bench wig;
- At *Nisi Prius* during summer (Easter and Trinity) terms: violet robes faced with changeable taffeta with black scarf, girdle, casting-hood, bands and bench wig.[107]

Portrait by Robert Dighton of the coifing of Serjeants Cranley Thomas Kirby and Sir Giles Rooke by the Earl of Mansfield and the Earl of Rosslyn, dated 1 March 1781, showing the Judges in their *nisi prius* black robes, hood and mantle faced with miniver. Mansfield is placing the coif over the wig of one of the newly appointed Serjeants, both of whom are wearing parti-coloured robes of violet which are laced and edged with murrey. The mantle is worn underneath the liripipe of the hood, and the two angular appendages on the upper arm which are ledged with plain lace are probably derived from the original lapels on the medieval version of the tabard and may be the explanation for the reference in 1675 to "parti-coloured robes with scallops" being worn by Serjeants. The coifing ceremony is conducted in private rather than in open court and was the last known occasion when part-coloured robes were worn by Serjeants-at-law. WA1924.9.420 Robert Dighton I, 'A Peep into Westminster Hall on a Call of Serjeants' Image © Ashmolean Museum, University of Oxford

106. "Judicial Costume", *supra*, 707.
107. Derriman, *supra*, 95-96.

The alternative violet and black robes continued to be worn by Judges of the High Court of England and Wales until the adoption of the new robes in October 2008.[108] However, they are still worn in Northern Ireland.

Photograph of Mrs Justice Hallett (now Lady Justice Hallett) on 20 April 2004, as a Judge of the Queen's Bench Division, wearing the winter nisi prius robes of black with miniver facings, with a scarlet casting-hood, black cincture, bands and a bench wig, which was the working day dress of Judges sitting in the Queen's Bench Division of the High Court during winter until they were discontinued on 1 October 2008.

Watercolour of Sir Alexander Cockburn, Lord Chief Justice of the Court of King's Bench and later Queen's Bench Division, reproduced in the Vanity Fair series, dated 11 December 1869. Cockburn LCJ is wearing the nisi prius robes and hood of black faced with miniver, along with bands and a bench wig.

108. See more at pp 173-175.

Colour of Taffeta Facings for Scarlet and Violet Robes

The colours of the silk or taffeta[109] facings of Judges' robes have varied over the centuries, and have never been authoritatively defined. For example, Chief Baron Sir Peter Arderne of the Court of Exchequer had red facings on his green robes (circa 1448-1467),[110] and Rastell J of the Court of Queen's Bench had green facings on his scarlet robes. Unfortunately, there is scant literary evidence on this subject, and most portraits of Judges portray them in their winter scarlet robes lined with miniver. Even the 1635 Judges' Rules are unclear as to the proper colour of the taffeta facings, stating that the facings of the gowns, hoods and mantles are to be with "changeable [i.e., shot] taffeta".[111]

Painting of Chief Justice Martin Howard of North Carolina by Copely, dated 1767. Martin CJ is wearing a scarlet robe with a black cincture, though without a hood, mantle, black stole or casting-hood, and the the front of the robe as well as its pulled back sleeve lining is with shot pink-grey taffeta with a bronze appearance which becomes slightly grey in the shadows - a clear example of the 'changeable' nature of the taffeta facings. © Fundación Colección Thyssen-Bornemisza, Madrid

The taffeta facings have been also referred to as "changeable taffeta", "shot silk", "sad-coloured silk", and "variable taffety".[112]

The earliest extant portrait of a taffeta facing is an unidentified portrait of a Chief Justice (possibly Bankes CJ) showing him in a scarlet robe, black cincture, ruff neck-

109. Taffeta (also historically referred to as "taffety") is a crisp, smooth, plain woven fabric made from silk or cuprammonium rayons. The word is Persian in origin and means "twisted woven".

110. In his will he states "my green gowne and my grene cloke of the same lyned with Reede Tarteryn": Will of Peter Arderne of Latton, Essex, 10 July 1466, Probate Records of the Prerogative Court of Canterbury, PROB 11/5/245.

111. Dugdale *Origines Juridiciales*, *supra*, 99.

112. "Judicial Costume", *supra*, 707. The term "shot silk" (also referred to as "changeable silk" and "changeable taffeta") is a fabric which is made up of silk woven from warp and weft yarns (which are the two basic components used in weaving to turn either thread or yarn into fabric) of two or more colours producing an iridescent appearance. The "shot" here is a single throw of the bobbin (i.e., the spindle or cylinder, on which the yarn or thread is wound) which carries the weft thread through the warp, and shot silk colours can be described as "[warp colour] *shot with* [weft colour]." This weaving technique can also be applied to other fibres such as cotton, linen, and synthetics. It has been suggested that "shot silk" was also described as *purpura* at around the 7th century, the Latin word mainly applied to purple although there are multiple references to *purpura* being red, green and black-and-red, as well as "varied": C. R. Dodwell, *Anglo Saxon Art, A New Perspective* (Manchester: University Press, 1982), 145-150.

wear and a black cap and hood (it is not clear whether the hood or the front of the robe was lined with taffeta) and the mantle fastened in the middle at the chin.

A similar but clearer form of this type of taffeta facing can be seen in Copely's portrait of Chief Justice Martin Howard of North Carolina dated 1767. The portrait depicts Howard CJ in scarlet robe with a black cincture, though without a hood, mantle or black stole, and the the front of the robe as well as its pulled back sleeve lining is with shot pink-grey taffeta with a bronze appearance which becomes slightly grey in the shadows - a clear example of the 'changeable' nature of the taffeta facings.

There are clear variations in the types of changeable taffeta used by Judges for their facings. For example, a small coloured engraving of Bayley J dated 1820 shows him in scarlet faced with shot pink taffeta.[113] However, by 1844, the taffeta facings for the summer scarlet robes had become plain dove-grey or slate grey,[114] although some Judges continue to this day to wear scarlet robes with shot pink taffeta facings.[115]

A small coloured engraving of Bayley J wearing the scarlet robes faced with pink taffeta dated 1820 from *Portraits of the Worthies of Westminster Hall*. The fact that Bayley J is wearing the black cap indicates that he is most likely delivering a death sentence. © Sir John Baker QC

A lawyer interrogating a witness in front of jury and judges at Westminster Hall. The judges include Chief Justice Sir Charles Abbot, and barristers Raine, Pollock, Ashworth, Courtney. The Maiden Brief, Dick Gradus' first appearance among the Worthies of Westminster Hall. Hand-coloured copperplate drawn and engraved by Robert Cruikshank from *The English Spy*, London, 1825. The Judges can be seen wearing the scarlet robes and hoods faced with shot pink taffeta. Contributor: Florilegius / Alamy Stock Photo

113. As can be seen in *Portraits of the Worthies of Westminster Hall, with their Autographs* (London, 1823), plate [2].
114. Baker, *Collected II*, *supra*, 821. An early extant example of which is the summer scarlet robes of Sir Frederick Pollock CB (1844-1866), on loan from the London Museum to the permanent exhibition of legal costume in the Royal Courts of Justice (particularly no. 2 in the catalogue).
115. See e.g., the photograph of the late David Malcolm AC, QC, former Chief Justice of Western Australia 1988-2006 wearing his scarlet robes and hood with shot pink taffeta facings, he being the only Judge with such facings, and the other Judges of the Supreme Court are shown wearing robes with the more common plain slate-grey facings.

Coloured engraving of the Judges sitting in the Court of Crown Cases Reserved, Illustration for *The Illustrated London News* dated 12 June 1847. It appears that the Judges are wearing scarlet faced with slate-grey taffeta, though it is not wholly reliable because the cowl part of the hood is in one colour and the facing of the actual hood is in another, which is clearly incorrect and may have arisen out of the artist's misconception of the robes' facings.
© Daniel Yazdani

The violet summer robes[116] were originally faced with exactly the same taffeta used for the scarlet summer robes, namely, a rich salmon pink shot with blue or grey as to give a bronze appearance in the light and grey in the shadow.[117] This is clearly evident from a number of oil paintings, such as the paintings of Sir Soulden Lawrence, Justice of the Court of King's Bench (1794-1808) (showing the scarf and casting hood, but without the full hood), Sir Edward Hall Alderson, Baron of the Court of Exchequer (1834-1857), by Eden Upton Eddis, Sir John Taylor Coleridge, Justice of the Court of King's Bench (1835-1858), by Margaret Sarah Carpenter, as well as a number of later Victorian watercolours, some of which were reproduced in the Vanity Fair series.

It appears that the colour of the taffeta facings on the violet robes slightly changed in the 20th century, due to the older material being unavailable, though it was still within the range of the original colour of the facing.[118]

116. The earliest extant violet robe is that of Sir Thomas Molony CJ of Ireland (1918-1924) in the permanent exhibition of legal costume in the Royal Courts of Justice (particularly no. 5 in the catalogue). The robes are faced with shot silk: Baker, *ibid*, 821.
117. *Ibid*.
118. *Ibid*, 822.

The taffeta facings on Judges' robes have always been a problem, partly because they were never defined, but mainly because the finer material kept going out of production which resulted in variations of the colour of the changeable taffeta facings. One 19th century writer, however, stated the modern rule (i.e., as applied by the judges of the High Court prior to October 2008) as to the colour of Judges' robes and the colour of the requisite facings clearly as follows:

> The colours have now been fixed at black, purple [i.e., violet], and scarlet: the black always trimmed with ermine, the purple always with "shot silk," or variable taffety, as it is called in the old books, and the scarlet with ermine in winter and spring, and with shot silk in the summer.[119]

Photograph of (left to right) the Hon. Justice Murray, the former Chief Justice of Western Australia the late David Malcolm AC, QC and the Hon. Justice Owen at the farewell ceremony of Chief Justice Malcolm in the Supreme Court building in Stirling Gardens, Perth on 7 February 2006. Note that the facings on the robe and hood of the Chief Justice is shot pink taffeta, whereas the facings of the other two Justices' robes and hoods are slate grey taffeta, which is now more commonly worn. © West Australian Newspapers Limited

Although the violet robes faced with taffeta are no longer worn by High Court Judges sitting in the Queen's Bench Division (although they are still worn in Northern Ireland), the same cannot be said with the equivalent scarlet robes faced with taffeta, for although the new robing directions of Lord Phillips CJ, introduced in October 2008, no longer refer to the summer scarlet robes, Judges are still permitted to wear them pursuant to Part A.2 of Division XII of the *Criminal Practice Directions 2015* [2015] EWCA Crim 1567. Indeed, Lord Thomas of Cwmgiedd CJ (2013-2017) wore these robes during the swearing-in ceremony of the then Lord Chancellor Lidington in 2017.[120]

119. "Judicial Costume", *supra*, 707.

120. In correspondence with the Lord Chief Justice, his Lordship advised the writer that he would tend to wear the summer robes on hot days, as those robes were in his possession having been handed down to him from previous Lord Chief Justices: personal correspondence from the Rt. Hon. The Lord Thomas of Cwmgiedd to the writer dated 11 September 2017.

Portrait by Peter Tillemans (circa 1684-1734) of Queen Anne (1665-1714) in the old House of Lords, most likely during the opening of a new session of Parliament. This is one of a pair of paintings showing the two houses of Parliament, which must have been painted between Tillemans's arrival in England in 1708 and the death of Queen Anne in 1714. The chamber appears with its distinctive coffering pattern in the vault and walls hung with the 'Armada Tapestries'. A long-case clock shows the time to be approaching 1:00 pm. The Queen is shown attended by her Ladies-in-waiting, Officers of the State, Heralds and Pages. The peers (Lords Temporal) appear on the right and in the centre in their scarlet robes (which are still worn by peers in the House of Lords); the bishops (Lords Spiritual) appear on the left (with the two Archbishops beside the clock). The Lord Chief Justice and lesser Judges and legal dignitaries sit immediately in front of the woolsack; next to them a row of clerks sit at their desks. In the foreground are members of the House of Commons crowded at the bar, some holding the white staffs indicating their position within the Royal Household. Although not entirely clear, it appears that the Judges by the woolsack are wearing their violet (or black) robes with taffeta facings. The Judge sitting on the left of the portrait can be seen also wearing a black cap over his wig. Royal Collection Trust / © Her Majesty Queen Elizabeth II 2018

Oil painting of Sir Soulden Lawrence by Hoppner wearing violet robes faced with taffeta, bands, bar wig, black scarf and a scarlet casting hood over his right shoulder.

Oil painting of Sir Edward Hall Alderson, Baron of the Exchequer (1834-1857) by Eden Upton Eddis (1812-1901). Baron Alderson is wearing the summer violet robe faced with changeable taffeta, and a scarlet casting-hood over his right shoulder underneath the black scarf along with white bands.

Watercolour of a Judge wearing the summer *nisi prius* violet robes and hood faced with taffeta, though the taffeta facing is quite thick due most likely to the drawer's misinterpretation of the facing. © Sir John Baker QC

Watercolour of a Judge of the High Court wearing the summer *nisi prius* robes, without the hood, reproduced in the Vanity Fair series dated 14 January 1898. © Daniel Yazdani

JUDGES' MANTLE

The mantle was a loose gown which was, originally, fastened on the right shoulder, from which it opened and closed on the left shoulder.[121] The origins of the mantle (also referred to by some as a cloak (*chlamys*) or *armelausa*),[122] can be traced to the late Roman and early Byzantine periods.[123] A mantle of a similar shape (known as a lorum) was worn by the late Roman and early Byzantine emperors, as well as by Roman Consuls in their diptychs.[124] It

Portrait of Sir James Dyer CJ, by an unknown artist, based on a work dated 1575 wearing the mantle in the traditional form which totally conceals both arms. Dyer CJ is also wearing the SS collar of the Common Pleas. NPG 1294. © National Portrait Gallery, London

---

121. Hargreaves-Mawdsley, *supra*, 49; D. Yarwood, *English Costume: From the Second Century B.C. to the Present Day, with Introductory Chapters on the Ancient Civilisations* (B.T. Batsford, 1967) 67.

122. Hargreaves-Mawdsley, *ibid*; Baker, *Collected II*, *supra*, 813.

123. Hargreaves-Mawdsley, *ibid*.

124. Charles du Fresne Du Cange, in his *Glossarium mediæ et infimæ latinitatis* (originally composed in 1678), defines the "*lorum*" as follows: "*Vestis Imperatoriæ et Consularis species....*

had, in turn replaced the *toga* worn during earlier Roman times.[125] The *lorum* was made of gold or silk cloth and was fastened on the right shoulder with an ornate jewelled clasp known as a fibula and, depending on the wearer's status, was heavily jewelled.[126]

The mantle was viewed as a symbol of magisterial and regal authority, and was worn by both the royalty and nobility.[127] An early illustration of the regal mantle can be seen in the effigies of King Henry II, Queen Eleanor of Aquitaine and their son King Richard the Lionheart, illustrations of which were carefully drawn and coloured by Charles Alfred Stothard from the original effigies located at Fontevraud Abbey in Normandy.[128] It is believed that the mantle was presented to Judges by the Crown as a Royal livery, for Judges were regarded as being not only part of the nobility by virtue of their office but were also seen to be allies of the Crown.[129]

Originally, the mantle was a lined semi-circular cloak which was fastened with buttons onto the Judge's right shoulder down to within 6 inches of the bottom of the robe.[130] From the point where the mantle was fastened on the shoulder, one edge of the mantle would hang straight down the back, while the other edge went over the Judge's left arm with the lining folded back, or alternatively if both hands were not needed the mantle would be so hung so as to completely cover the left arm.[131]

As discussed earlier, the mantle replaced the *collobium* as an integral part of a Judge's habit by 1400, if not earlier.[132] It appears that the earliest illustrative example of a mantle being worn by an English Judge is the brass of Sir Robert Thorpe (d. 1372), Chief Justice of the Court of Common Pleas (1365-1371), which was located in the Peterborough Cathedral until its destruction during

---

Deinde diadema, videlicet coronam capitis nominis nostri, simulque Phrygium, necnon et superhumerale, videlicet Lorum, quod Imperiale circundare assolet collum.

Leo Grammaticus in Basilio pag. 472 :Ἐνθρονίζεται καὶ ἐγκαινίζεται ἡ ἐκκλησία ἣν ἔκτισεν ὁ βασιλεύς, καὶ ἐκαλλώπισε κοσμῷ πολλῷ, παρὰ Φωτίου Πατριάρχου, τοῦ Βασιλέως ἐν τῷ αὐτῆς καινισμῷ λῶρον φορέσαντος, καὶ χρήματα πολλὰ δόντος, *etc.*
Quid sit Lorum, seu λῶρον, *quivis deprehendet ex Diptychis Consularibus Compendiensi, Bituricensi, et Leodiensi, apud Sirmond. et Wilthemium, et ex numismatibus posteriorum Imperatorum, maxime Mauricii, in quibus effinguntur Imperatores et Consules cum toga Imperatoria vel Consulari, et fascia desuper, cujus pars a dextro humero, circa pectus ad pedes usque descendit, eumdemque circumvolvens, sinistrum humerum amplectitur, ac circa dorsum delabens, rursum a dextro latere pectus circumfundit, et infimam sinistri brachii partem, qua manus conjungitur, involvit, reliqua fasciæ parte retro pendula. Hæc fuit* lori *forma, cujus mentio est in Instrumento donationis Constantini perantiquo, licet fictitio : ex quo tandem percipitur ejusmodi ornatus nomenclatura, eumdemque esse cum summorum Pontificum pallio ; quod ii ab Imperatoribus accepere, ut et CPolitani, et cæteri fortean Patriarchæ et Archiepiscopi, maxime Græci, quibus id genus ornatus* ὠμοφόριον *dicitur. Plura de hac veste annotamus in Dissertatione de Imperatorum Constantinopolitanorum nummis.*": Charles du Fresne Du Cange, *Glossarium mediæ et infimæ latinitatis*, (La Favre, 1883) t. 5, col. 143A.

125. Tom Tierney, *Byzantine Fashions* (Mineola: Dover Publications, 2002) 3.

126. *Ibid*; Hargreaves-Mawdsley, *ibid.*

127. Baker, *Collected II*, *supra*, 814.

128. Planche, *supra*, 356.

129. Hargreaves-Mawdsley, *supra*, 49; Baker, *Collected II*, *supra*, 814.

130. *Ibid.*

131. *Ibid.*

132. There is an early but unidentified example of an early mantle being worn by a Judge from a sketch by Elias Ashmole from a monument in St Alkmund's, Shrewsbury (Bodleian Library MS Ashmole 854, 208). Another possible early example of the mantle is the weeper at Clifton Reynes, Buckinghamshire which may represent Sir Henry Green CJ of the Court of King's Bench (1361-1365), which shows the mantle hanging straight down and concealing both of the Judge's arms (Baker, *ibid*, 814).

the Civil War but was drawn by Sir William Dugdale in the 17th century in his *Book of Monuments*[133] before its destruction.[134] Dugdale records this as being in the nave of the old cathedral which shows a marble slab upon which lies the effigy of Thorpe CJ who is wearing a coif, robe, hood and mantle and whose hands are pressed together as if he is in a state of prayer, with his head reclined on a lozenge-shaped cushion and his feet resting on a lion.[135] The mantle is fastened to his right shoulder, in the style that was traditionally worn by Judges of the time.[136]

Another early example is that of an miniature illustration to the historiated initial "I" in "*Iudicium*" (i.e., '*Judicium*') in James le Palmer's encyclopedia *Omne Bonum*[137] (*circa* 1360-1375), depicting a court of five Judges sitting *in banc* in scarlet with mantles pulled around them and wearing their hoods over their heads,[138] which is thought to represent the Court of Common Pleas during the time of Thorpe CJ.[139] This can be also seen in the historiated initial "I" in "Iudex" (i.e., 'Judex') which shows a bare-headed Judge who is seated wearing a pink-violet mantle over his robes with the liripipe of his scarlet hood hanging down behind with the actual hood lined with miniver around his neck.[140] Another illustration from the *Omne Bonum* detail of an historiated initial "A" (i.e., 'Assessor') of a prisoner with two court officers before a Judge accompanied by two assessors (i.e., advisers to a Judge) which depicts what appears to be an amalgam of both the *collobium* and mantle.[141]

Brass of Sir Robert Thorpe (d.1372), 1372), Chief Justice of the Court of Common Pleas 1365-1371, which was located in the Peterborough Cathedral until its destruction during the Civil War but was drawn by William Dugdale in the seventeenth century before its destruction.

133. British Library, Add. MS 71474, f. 121.
134. Baker, *Collected II*, *supra*, 814. It is also illustrated in ed. William Lack, H. Martin Stuchfield & Philip Whittemore eds., *The Monumental Brasses of Huntingdonshire* (Stratford St. Mary, 2012), 125. Thorpe CJ was of the Thorpe family of Northamptonshire, which was one of the most successful legal dynasties in England in the 14th century, for the family produced two Chief Justices, one of the first lay English Chancellors and a peerage: Robert Kinsey, "Each according to their Degree: the Lost Brasses of the Thorpes of Northamptonshire", *Transactions of the Monumental Brass Society* 18 (2012) 311.
135. Kinsey, *ibid*, 314. There is a slightly mutilated Latin marginal inscription in Dugdale's brass which reads: "Hic ia[cet] [dom]inus Robertus de Thorpe miles quondam cancellarius d[omi]ni regis anglie qui obiit vicessimo nono die Junnii anno [Domini] millessimo trescentissimo septuagessimo secundo cuius anime propitietur deus amen amen" (which translates as: "Here lies buried Robert de Thorpe, knight, formerly chancellor of our Lord the King of England, who died 29 June 1372. On whose soul may God have mercy Amen Amen"): *ibid*, 316.
136. *Ibid*, 318.
137. Meaning "all good things" in Latin. The encyclopedia extends to 1100 folia and includes more than 650 illustrations. James le Palmer described his work with: 'Virtually all good things [are] contained herein', hence the title "Omne Bonum". There are 1350 entries arranged under the 23 letters of the medieval Latin alphabet, with each letter comprising a book, and over 750 of these entries are accompanied by historiated initials. The 1094 pages are divided into two volumes, held at the British Library and each surviving in two parts: Royal MS 6 Edward VI/1, Royal 6 E VI/2, Royal 6 E VII/1, and Royal 6 E VII/2.
138. Royal MS 6 Edward VII, folio 356v. Cf., folio 52 (Detail of a historiated initial 'A'(dvocati) of two advocates and two judges) which depicts Judges wearing the collobium.
138. Royal MS 6 Edward VII, folio 356v. Cf., folio 52 (Detail of a historiated initial 'A'(dvocati) of two advocates and two judges) which depicts Judges wearing the collobium.
139. Baker, *Collected II*, *supra*, 814. James le Palmer was a clerk at the Court of Exchequer and so would have seen at first hand the dress of Judges of his time.
140. Royal MS. 6 Edward VII, folio 345.
141. Royal MS. 6 Edward VII, folio 150v.

Above, left. Royal MS 6 Edward VII, folio 365v, showing the Judges (most likely sitting in the Court of Common Pleas) wearing scarlet with their mantles wrapped around them and their hoods over their heads. Note the three figures at the bar wearing short coats, presumably they are plaintiffs rather than advocates. © British Library

Above, right. Royal MS 6 Edward VII, folio 150v, showing three Judges wearing what seems to be an amalgam of both the mantle and collobium. © British Library

Royal MS 6 Edward VII, folio 345, showing a Judge wearing a pink-violet mantle lined with miniver over his tight-sleeved robe. The liripipe of the hood hangs down behind the Judge and the hood itself is lined with miniver around the neck. Detail of an historiated initial 'I '(udex) of a Judge. © British Library

Another early example of the change from the *collobium* to the mantle can be seen in the brass of Sir John Cassy CB of the Court of Exchequer (died 1400) at Deerhurst, Gloucestershire, who is depicted with his wife on dexter side, wearing coif, robe and mantle lined with vair, with the sleeves of his undertunic ending with buttoned mittens.[142] Other examples include the alabaster effigy of Sir William Gascoigne (died 1419) at Harewood, Yorkshire, the brasses of Sir Hugh de Huls (died 1415) at Watford, Hertfordshire,[143] Sir John Juyn CJ of the Court of King's Bench at St Mary Redcliffe in Bristol (1439),[144] Cottesmore J in Brightwell Baldwyn, Oxon,[145] and Sir Thomas Urswyk (or Ursewyk), a Baron of the Court of Exchequer, in Degenham, Essex (1479).[146] There are numerous examples of such brasses after this date.

Above. Brass of Sir John Cassy (died 1400) at Deerhurst, Gloucestershire, who is depicted with his wife Lady Cassy on dexter side, wearing a mantle lined with vair, with the sleeves of his undertunic ending with buttoned mittens. © National Portrait Gallery, London

Below. Brass of Sir John Cottesmore in Brightwell Baldwyn, Oxon. (1439). From Edward T. Beaumont's *Ancient Memorial Brasses* (1913), 68

Left. Brass of Sir Thomas Urswyk (or Ursewyk), Baron of the Court of Exchequer, in Degenham, Essex (1479). One of the earliest references to the alternative black and violet robes worn by Judges appears to be in an inventory taken in 1479 of Ursewyk's goods and chattels, which lists robes of scarlet, violet, black, green and "Kentyshe kendal", though it is not entirely clear if all of these items were judicial dress.
Brass from Edward T. Beaumont's *Ancient Memorial Brasses* (1913), 122

142. Baker, *Serjeants-at-Law*, *supra*, 72; Druitt, *supra*, 226; Kinsey, *supra*, 318.
143. Baker, *ibid.*
144. Mary G. Houston, *Medieval Costume in England and France: The 13th, 14th and 15th Centuries* (Dover Publications, 1996) 157.
145. Edward T. Beaumont, *Ancient Memorial Brasses* (London: Oxford University Press, 1913) 122.
146. *Ibid*, 68.

Above. Portrait of Sir John Glanville, the elder (1542-1600), showing the mantle fastened on the right shoulder and opening showing the miniver facing on the left. Glanville J was the first Judge to have been an attorney prior to his appointment. He was killed while riding on circuit when he fell off his horse and broke his neck on 27 July 1600. Reproduced courtesy of The Benchers of The Honourable Society of Lincoln's Inn (the Licensor). Copyright; the Licensor

On some rare occasions, the hood would be placed over the mantle, with the tail of the hood pulled out so that it hung down behind, and the opening of the hood which showed the lining would be displayed over the mantle in front. This can be clearly seen in the extant portrait of Sir William Howard CJ on a stained glassed window in the church of Long Melford, Suffolk which was painted circa 1486. Th Chief Justice and two Serjeants-at-law are depicted on this stained glass window, from left to right: Howard CJ, Richard Pigot and John Haugh J. Although all three Judges are wearing coifs and are kneeling on green cushions, along with hoods trimmed with miniver, the Chief Justice is distinguishable of the three by wearing a scarlet mantle underneath the hood and cowl, which are trimmed with miniver. The shoulder piece and robes of the two Serjeants-at-law are faced with blue down the front, although their 'shoulder pieces' are trimmed with miniver. However, only a few such representations of hoods over the mantle are available depicting the hood and cowl over the mantle, and it is unclear whether such depictions are simply artistic errors or permissible variations to the conventional dress.

Below. Portrait of Sir Christopher Wray CJ, dated 1582, wearing the mantle in the traditional form concealing the arms. Wray CJ is also wearing the SS collar of the Queen's Bench. NPG 1484. © National Portrait Gallery, London

Right. Portrait of Sir Edmund Anderson CJ by an unknown artist dated circa 1592, showing the mantle fastened on the right shoulder but the mantle has been pushed back showing the miniver lining. The robe opens only down to the waist and the black girdle is narrow, with ruffs forming the neckwear and a black cornered cap worn over the white coif. NPG 2148. © National Portrait Gallery, London

Up until the end of the 16th century (and at least until 1592), the mantle continued to be fastened on the right shoulder and closed on the left shoulder. This can be clearly seen in the anonymous portrait of Sir Edmund Anderson CJ of the Court of Common Pleas (1582-1605) dated circa 1592.[147] There can also be seen portraits of the mantle falling straight from the shoulder and concealing both arms, as can be seen in the portraits of Sir James Dyer CJ of the Court of Common Pleas (1559-1582), Sir Christopher Wray CJ of the Court of Queen's Bench (1574-1592), and Thomas Owen J of the Court of Common Pleas (1594-1598).

By 1600, however, the practice of having the mantle fall straight from the shoulder concealing the arms was discontinued, and it now became customary for the mantle to be turned sharply back from the right towards the left shoulder so as to avoid any encumbrance of movement,[148] as can be seen in the portrait of Sir John Glanville J of the Court of Common Pleas dated 1600, which is located in Lincoln's Inn.[149]

A later engraving of Sir Edmund Anderson CJ showing the mantle fastened directly under the chin. © National Portrait Gallery, London

It also appears that another change began to occur from the mid 16th century when the mantle began to be now fastened under the chin rather than on the right shoulder. The first illustrative evidence of this change in the fastening of the mantle can be seen in the portrait of Sir Edward Montagu LCJ who was Lord Chief Justice of both the Court of King's Bench

Portrait of Sir Thomas Fleming LCJ dated 1609 by Marcus Gheeraerts, similar to that of the earlier portrait of Glanville J, showing the traditional fastening of the mantle on the right shoulder. It also shows the robe opening only down to the lower chest with a narrow black girdle, and the SS collar is also worn. © Abingdon-on-Thames Town Council

147. MacKinnon, *supra*, 30.

148. *Ibid.*

149. Glanville J was appointed as a Justice of the Court of Common Pleas in 1598, but died suddenly on 27 June 1600 as he was riding on circuit he fell off his horse causing him to break his neck.

Line engraving of Sir Henry Hobart LCJ by Simon de Passe dated 1671, presumably based on an earlier portrait, depicting him with his mantle incorrectly fastened on the left shoulder rather the right shoulder. © National Portrait Gallery, London

(1539-1545) and the Court of Common Pleas (1545-1553). A second portrait of Sir James Dyer CJ (most likely dating prior to his death in 1582), also shows a centre fastening of the mantle with the mantle turned back showing the miniver lining, in stark contrast to his earlier portrait showing the mantle falling straight from the shoulder and concealing both his arms. The change becomes more prevalent after 1600, for in a later print of Sir Edmund Anderson CJ by William Faithmore dated 1605, the mantle is now opened in front under the chin, rather than from the right shoulder.

The traditional fastening of the mantle on the right shoulder can still be seen in the portraits of Fleming CJ (dated 1609), Sir Thomas Foster J of the Court of Common Pleas (1607-1612) and Sir Thomas Walmsley J of the Court of Common Pleas (1589-1612). Sir Henry Hobart CJ of the Court of Common Pleas (1613-1625) wears the mantle in the old fashion in one engraving but in the new style in another portrait. This can also be seen in the portraits of Sir John Popman CJ, who in an earlier portrait has the mantle fastened to his right shoulder but in a subsequent portrait shows the mantle fastened in the modern way under the chin with both sides of the mantle folded back showing the miniver lining - the same style worn by English Judges today.

Portrait of Sir Henry Hobart LCJ by an unknown artist dated 1624, showing him fastening the mantle in the new style under the chin. © National Trust Images

Between 1613 and 1625, it becomes clear that the ancient practice of fastening the mantle on the right shoulder was abandoned altogether,[150] and instead the mantle was folded back symmetrically from a fastening under the chin, resulting in most of the mantle being worn at the back with only the lining being visible from the front, and leaving the hood as the Judges' principal upper garment.[151] It is unclear as to why such a change in the fastening of the mantle occurred; however, it has been argued that the centre fastening of the mantle is in accord with the mantle's origins as a cloak, which is disputable.[152]

In the first half of the 18th century, it can be seen that the mantle still reached to well below the waist, as can be seen in the portraits of Lord Chief Justice Willes (1685-1761) by J. B. van Loo and Sir Charles Pratt (1714-1794), Lord Chief Justice of the Court of Common Pleas, by Thomas Hudson. However, as the hood grew larger, the mantle became shortened to such an extent that, by the end of the nineteenth century, the mantle looked more like a cape than a cloak, and it has remained as such to the present day.

Left. Portrait of Sir John Bramston the elder (1577-1654), Lord Chief Justice of the Court of King's Bench (1635-1642). Most of the mantle is worn at the back with only the lining now being visible from the front, leaving the hood as the Judges' principal upper garment. Reproduced with the kind permission of the Corporate Custodian of Art, Essex County Council

Right. Portrait of Sir Wadham Wyndham (1609-1668), a Justice of the Court of King's Bench (1660-1668). The diminution of the mantle can be clearly seen. The sleeves can also be clearly seen pushed back to show the miniver lining and he is holding a black cornered cap in his left hand. Reproduced courtesy of The Benchers of The Honourable Society of Lincoln's Inn (the Licensor). Copyright; the Licensor

150. It has been suggested that Sir Edward Coke LCJ was responsible for this innovation soon after becoming Lord Chief Justice of the Court of King's Bench in 1613: Baker, *Collected Papers on English Legal History: Volume II, supra*, 815.

151. Baker, *Collected Papers on English Legal History: Volume II, supra*, 816.

152. Derriman, *supra*, 89. This view was also supported by MacKinnon LJ who stated that he "cannot understand how the earlier mode came to be used. For the top corners of the mantle to meet beneath the chin and its sides to be turned back over the shoulders is in accord with its origin as a cloak": MacKinnon, *supra*, 30. This is questionable, however, given that the origin of the mantle may not in fact be a cope, but rather the original mantle was always worn on the right shoulder in the form of a *lorum*.

Right. Portrait of Sir Charles Pratt (1714-1794), Lord Chief Justice of the Court of Common Pleas by Thomas Hudson (1701-1779). The black girdle is now much wider, and the miniver cuffs are much deeper, coming almost to the elbow © Exeter Guildhall

Above. Portrait of Lord Gorell (1848-1913), a judge of the Probate, Divorce and Admiralty Division of the High Court of Justice, from 1892 to 1905, by William Llewellyn in 1896. © Image; Crown Copyright: UK Government Art Collection

Left. The Rt Hon. Kenneth Clarke QC MP (left) and the Rt. Hon. the Lord Judge, former Lord Chief Justice of England and Wales (2008-2013), standing outside the Royal Courts of Justice before being sworn in as Lord Chancellor on 14 May 2010. The scarlet robe, hood and mantle, with some modifications, has largely remained the same to that worn by Sir Edmund Montagu LCJ in circa 1539. © Crown Copyright

At the swearing-in ceremony of the Lord Chancellor, the Rt. Hon. David Lidington MP on 19 June 2017 at the Royal Courts of Justice. The scarlet robe, hood and mantle faced with taffeta mantle was worn by Lord Thomas CJ at the swearing-in ceremony of Lord Chancellor Liddington. The taffeta lining of the mantle is folded back so that the mantle appears to be reversed, i.e., with the taffeta outside. © Josh John

The Judges' Rules of 1635 only provided for the wearing of the scarlet mantle, meaning that the mantle was technically not worn when black or violet robes were worn,[153] and is now worn at the opening of the legal year, in the House of Lords for State Openings of Parliament and in the presence of the Sovereign (see a recent example of this when Her Majesty visited the new Rolls Building in 2011). According to the 1635 Judges' Rules, the mantle could also be worn at Westminster Hall by Judges when trying criminal cases "if it be cold".[154]

---

153. Newark, "Judicial Robes," *supra*, 209.
154. Dugdale, *Origines Juridiciales*, *supra*, 101.

Above. High Court Judges wearing the full habit of scarlet robe, hood and mantle with bands and a full-bottomed wig during opening of the Rolls Building in 2011 by Her Majesty the Queen. © Crown Copyright

The hood and mantle of High Court Judges from behind as they enter Westminster Parliament through the St Stephen's entrance arriving from Westminster Abbey on 1 October 2009. Although the mantle is made out of scarlet cloth, that is hardly visible due to the fact that the lining of miniver is folded back so that the mantle appears to be reversed, i.e., with the miniver outside. The cowl part of the hood is worn over the mantle hanging down from behind. Contributor: David Levenson / Alamy Stock Photo

Judges wearing their full habit, including mantle, sitting on the woolsack in the House of Lords during the most recent State Opening of Parliament on 21 June 2017. The Prince of Wales accompanied Her Majesty during the ceremony due to the Duke of Edinburgh's ill health. © House of Lords 2018 / Photography by Roger Harris

At present, the mantle is worn over the cowl or 'shoulder piece' portion of the hood, with the headpiece or cowl of the hood thrown back over it.[155] The mantle is the form of a short cloak of scarlet cloth, lined with miniver, although there is a corresponding mantle lined with silk taffeta that is worn in the summer (see the recent photograph of the Lord Chief Justice pictured in June 2017 at the swearing-in-ceremony of the former Lord Chancellor, the Rt. Hon. David Lidington MP, wearing the taffeta-faced mantle). Although the mantle is made out of scarlet cloth, that is hardly visible due to the fact that the lining of miniver is folded back so that to the lay observer the mantle appears to be reversed, that is, with the miniver outside.[156]

155. Derriman, *supra*, 89.
156. *Ibid*.

JUDGES' HOOD

The hood is the most complicated of the items worn by Judges, for it is a term that refers to different elements of a Judge's habit. The hood in fact consists of two parts: the "shoulder piece" which is worn over the shoulders covering most of the chest, underneath the mantle, and the actual hood itself or the "cowl part" of the hood which falls behind looking like a big bag of miniver.[157] The hood is very similar to an academic hood, and from the front view appears as if it is a short shoulder-cape, but this was not always the case.

The term "hood" is derived from the Saxon "*hod*" and were initially worn by wayfarers and rustics after the Norman invasion.[158] It first appears in the 13th century and was known by its Norman French name of chaperon.[159] The chaperon worn by men during the reign of King Edward II looked similar to a pointed bag with an oval opening for the face, while the tail (known as a liripipe), which was sometimes of great length, hung down from behind or was twisted around the head.[160] By the end of the 15th century, as caps and bonnets became more fashionable, the hood was slung over the shoulder, and it ceased to be worn over the head at all, but continued to form part of the ceremonial dress of various institutions (such as the Order of the Garter, Judges and Serjeants etc), by whom it was worn over the shoulder only.[161] This custom of Judges wearing such a hood with a liripipe hanging down the back continues to this day.

One of the earliest images of this early type of hood can be seen in the brass of Sir John Cassy (died 1400) and the tomb effigy of Sir William Gascoigne in which he is seen wearing the miniver hood and its liripipe hanging forward over his left shoulder.[162] Another early illustration of the "shoulder piece" of the hood can be seen in the illustration by Wenceslaus Hollar of the monumental brass of Ralph de Hengham CJ of the King's Bench (1274-1290) in Sir William Dugdale's *The History of St Paul's Cathedral* which was depicted on his tomb at the Old St Paul's Cathedral in London,[163] before it was most likely destroyed by the Great Fire of London in 1666.

By the 16th century, the hood itself had developed to a great size, with the cowl still joined to the scarlet cloth 'shoulder piece' of the hood.[164] The cowl part of the hood now depended behind the robe like a large bag of miniver, with the scarlet liripipe (which had also increased in breadth and length), hung down from the hood.[165] For example, a brass dated circa 1563 depicts a hood being held by a ribbon in position at the front of the robe.[166]

157. "Judicial Costume," *supra*, 708.
158. Planche, *supra*, 291.
159. *Ibid*, 292.
160. *Ibid.*
161. *Ibid*, 295-296.
162. Hargreaves-Mawdsley, *supra.*
163. Dugdale, *The History of St Pauls Cathedral, supra*, 100-101.
164. Hargreaves-Mawdsley, *supra*, 54.
165. *Ibid.*, 55.
166. L. Edwards, "The Professional Costume of Lawyers illustrated principally by Monumental Brasses," *Transactions of the Monumental Brass Society* 8 (1936-1938) 155, 157.

Oil painting on canvas of Sir John Bankes (1589-1644) as Lord Chief Justice, aged 54 by Gilbert Jackson in 1643. He is wearing a black skull cap over a white coif, a "cartwheel" ruff, black girdle, a scarlet robe, hood and mantle trimmed with miniver and the SS collar. Note the front of the hood which has now developed into a V-shape.
© National Trust Images

During the 17th century, the hood became even more fuller. This can be clearly seen in an engraving of Judges sitting by the woolsack (as indicated by the letter "E") in the House of Lords before Queen Elizabeth I who is seated on the throne, in frontispiece of a work entitled 'Journals of All the Parliaments during the Reign of Queen Elizabeth' by Simonds D'Ewes in 1682. By the mid 17th century the hood became more similar to an academic hood than to a cowl of a monk, due to the fact that the opening of the hood had been lengthened so that the hood's lining could be displayed at the back, while the front of the hood developed into a V-shape, as can be seen in the portraits of Sir Henry Hobart LCJ and Sir John Bankes LCJ by Gilbert Jackson.

Engraving of Queen Elizabeth I seated in the House of Lords, in the frontispiece of a work entitled *Journals of All the Parliaments during the Reign of Queen Elizabeth* by Simonds D'Ewes in 1682. The Judges can be identified as they are sitting by the woolsack in the centre and are indicated as such by the letter "E". The Judges are shown wearing the hood, but without the mantle.

By 1635, the cowl part of the hood had so increased in size that it came over the shoulder piece of the hood in front and descended onto the chest in a V-shape, being held in position by a ribbon.[167] It has been argued by some writers that some time after this period (probably by 1674), it appears that the cowl and hood became separate, as can be seen in the oil painting of Sir Richard Rainsford LCJ (1676-1678) at Lincoln's Inn, London.[168] However, such views appear to be incorrect, for the cowl part of the hood never in fact separated from the hood itself and it was only because the cowl had enlarged in size and was worn over the mantle that some artists and writers may have misinter-

Above. Portrait by George Frederic Watts (1817-1904) of Sir Alexander Cockburn (1802-1880), Lord Chief Justice of the Court of Queen's Bench, and later Lord Chief Justice of the Queen's Bench Division of the newly created High Court of Justice. The hood is quite large, coming down to the forearms and almost reaching the miniver facings of the robe, and the mantle is less visible. He is also wearing the black girdle and white bands and a full-bottomed wig with sets of uneven curls on each side.
By permission of the Master and Fellows of Trinity Hall

Portrait by Herbert James Gunn (1893-1964) of Lord Roche (1871-1956), as a Judge of the King's Bench Division of the High Court, showing the enlarged hood which seems almost as large as the diminished mantle. The black scarf is also now invariably worn beneath the hood and the robe is now a fully open garment. His full-bottomed wig now clearly has the the "doormat effect" of having equal number of curls on each side.
By permission of the Warden & Fellows of Wadham College. Photographer: Studio Edmark, Oxford

167. Hargreaves-Mawdsley, *supra*, 63.
168. *Ibid.*, 63-64.

preted the hood as being separate from its cowl. Between the 18th and 19th centuries, the cowl part of the hood became quite large coming down over the forearms, as can be clearly seen in the portraits of Sir Alexander Cockburn LCJ and Sir Alexander Roche LJ (later Lord Roche). The current hood worn by Judges has remained largely the same to that worn by Judges since the eighteenth century, with the cowl part of the hood connected to the hood with the cowl hanging behind over the mantle.

Thus, by 1635 there were 5 types of hoods worn by Judges at various occasions. These were as follows:

1. black *nisi prius* hood faced with miniver;
2. violet *nisi prius* hood faced with taffeta;
3. winter scarlet hood faced with miniver;
4. summer scarlet hood faced with taffeta; and
5. scarlet casting hood (discussed below).

Putting aside the question of the casting hood (which is discussed below), the ordinary hoods were traditionally worn in the Divisional Courts, at Westminster on weekdays, at church on circuit on Sunday mornings, at assizes at the opening of the Commission and when trying criminal cases.[169] A further development to the role of the hood arose in 1919 when the County Court Judges adopted a violet hood to correspond with their newly created violet robes, which is worn on ceremonial occasions, but without a mantle.

The hood worn by County Court (and some Australian District Court) Judges on ceremonial occasions. Note also the distinctive rosette, which represents from the "wig bag" which was worn by the Bench and Bar to protect the powder from the wig soiling their silk velvet coat, for the powder would fall from the queue of the wig and damage the delicate fabric of the velvet coat. The rosette is worn by County Court Judges as well as Queen's Counsel in England and Wales and some jurisdictions in Australia. Photograph taken during the annual procession of Judges at the Opening of the Law Term © Crown Copyright

169. Newark, *supra*, 208.

Casting-hood

It is not entirely clear what is the precise origin of the casting-hood. It is probable that the casting-hood was derived from the 15th century fashion of wearing a *chaperon a bourlet* (which was a hat fastened to a scarf), which itself was derived from a hood. The chaperon would be 'cast' off the head to rest over the right shoulder, with the liripipe hanging down in front, or being tucked into the cincture, or brought across the breast towards the left shoulder.[170]

The original practice of wearing the casting-hood may have been to wrap the entire hood around the neck, similar to the wearing of a modern-day scarf, with the liripipe on one shoulder and the cowl part of the hood on the other shoulder.[171] This is clearly evidenced in the 15th century illumination of the Court of Chancery, in which the Masters of the Court are depicted wrapping their hoods around their necks like a scarf, with the liripipe falling on the left side,[172] and can also be seen in the drawing of the State Opening of Parliament in 1523 during the reign of King Henry VIII, in which the Common Law Judges sitting on the woolsacks are wearing scarlet robes have their hoods wrapped around their necks in the same fashion.[173]

It is also clear that, originally, the casting-hood was in fact the same hood that Judges would wear over their heads. This is proven by the first hand account of Sir John Spelman, who was one of the Judges present at the coronation of Queen Anne Boleyn in 1533. Sir John recounts as follows:

> And when the queen had ascended into the high place, they and all the lords went down to the door of the Hall, and there took off their coifs, cloaks and hoods, and put on their tippets, collars, and hoods upon their shoulders as before.[174]

In a later account it is stated that the Judges "put off their robes, mantles and cloaks and tooke their hoods from their necks and cast them about their shoulders."[175] This style of wearing the hood suggests that the Judges wore the hood in the fashion of a scarf over their shoulders, which is the style as can be seen being worn by Judges in the 16th century illustration of King Henry VIII's Parliament in 1523 in the Garter Book of Thomas Wriothesley. However, the former account of Spelman seems to indicate that the hood was first worn over the shoulders beneath the mantle, and that when the mantle was removed

170. Hargreaves-Mawdsley, *supra*, 56.
171. Baker, *Collected II*, *supra*, 822.
172. It is not entirely clear why the liripipe was worn over the left side in this instance rather than the right, though Walmsley J has suggested that that the wearing of the liripipe over the left side resembled the clerical style and spiritual dignity: see Dugdale, *Origines Juridicales*, *supra*, 101.
173. Senior Judges continue to sit on the woolsack during State Openings of Parliament by virtue of their right as privy councillors. Technically the woolsack is not part of the House of Lords and so any member of the Privy Council (even if they are not a peer) can sit by the woolsack in the presence of Her Majesty.
174. Spelman, *supra*, 70.
175. John Stow, *Annales, Or a Generall Chronicle of England* (London, 1631), 567.

Illustration of King Henry VIII's Parliament in 1523 in the Garter Book of Thomas Wriothesley, Garter King of Arms, in the Royal Collection, Windsor Castle. The Judges can be seen sitting by the woolsack with their scarlet hoods cast over both shoulders like a scarf.

and the "tippet" (i.e., scarf) put on, the hood was then pulled over the Judge's head and worn limp like a casting hood.[176] Regardless, it is clear that the same hood was worn by Judges in two different ways, which presumably would still have been lined hoods.[177] However, by the end of the 15th century, as the hood was growing in size, the Judges began using the smaller and less bulky unlined scarlet hood of the Serjeants-at-law, and to this day the casting-hood worn by judges remains unlined.[178]

---

176. *Ibid.*
177. Baker, *Collected II, supra*, 824.
178. *Ibid.*, 822.

There are also two sketches by the Flemish artist Lucas de Heere, in which two versions of English Judges' robes were depicted, including the casting-hood. In the version located in the British Library, one of the two Judges wears a violet robe, mantle and hood and the other Judge wears a pink or light red robe with a scarlet casting hood but without a scarf.[179] However, in the Gent version of the sketch, one Judge is wearing a robe and mantle and hood but the other Judge is wearing a robe which is incorrectly depicted as being open at the front down the whole length of the robe lined with miniver, which was not the form of dress worn during this period in the 16th century.[180]

Portrait of two Judges by Flemish artist Lucas de Heere, entitled "Corte Beschryvinghe van Engheland, Schotland, ende Irland, a short description of England, Scotland and Ireland." In this version one of the two Judges wears a violet robe, mantle and hood and the other Judge wears a pink robe with a scarlet casting hood but without a scarf. British Library MS Add.28330, folio 29 © The British ibrary Board

The Judges' Rules of 1635 required that the casting-hood be worn on the right shoulder, with its liripipe hanging down in front or tucked into the girdle or cincture, and had to be worn over the stole, as opposed to underneath the stole, as a Judge was of temporal dignity only.[181] One of the earliest examples of the casting-hood being worn in this fashion is the mutilated brass (the head is missing) of Sir John Anthony Fitzherbert, a Judge of the Court of Common Pleas, at Norbury, Derbyshire dated 1538.[182] The Judges' Rules of 1635 also provided that the casting-hood be always worn with the scarf and that it was always to be in the colour scarlet, irrespective of the colour of the robe worn. Interestingly, although the 1635 Rules refer to the scarf or stole as a "tippet", modern day Judges and writers have misinterpreted the word "tippet" to mean "casting-hood" when in fact it refers to the black scarf.[183] The Judges' Rules also stated that in the House of Lords, at the Council Table and at church during term time, the casting-hood was to be "pinned abroad towards the left shoulder", which refers to the ancient practice of Judges wearing their hoods scarf-wise or squared around the neck, with the cowl part of the hood pinned on the left shoulder.[184] However, this practice of pinning abroad the hood was discontinued by Judges some time after 1635 and the cowl part of the hood was allowed to simply fall limp behind, and there is evidence that Serjeants-at-law were wearing their casting-hoods in this manner before 1640, as can be seen in the portrait of Sir John Glanville the younger (1586-1661).[185]

---

179. 'Corte Beschryvinghe van Engheland', British Library MS Add. 28330, folio 29.
180. Rijksuniversiteit-Gent MS 2466, folio 67.
181. Hargreaves- Mawdsley, *supra*, 64.
182. Druitt, *supra*, 228.
183. The word "tippet" is one of the most confusing words used by Judges and writers in describing legal dress, as noted by one writer: "Now there never was a more confusing word than this one, in this connection. "When I use a word," said Humpty Dumpty in "Alice Through the Looking-Glass," "it means just what I chose it to mean." And to different writers "tippet" means a hood, a scarf, or a sash (or casting-hood). Since judicial costume includes all three garments, obviously it is better not to employ the word at all. So we shall refer to the garment … by its ancient and true identity of casting-hood" (Derriman, *supra*, 87).
184. Baker, *Collected II*, *supra*, 826.
185. *Ibid.*

Portrait of Sir John Glanville the younger (1586-1661), the son of Sir John Glanville the elder. Glanville the younger became a Serjeant-at-law in 1637 and subsequently Speaker of the House of Commons during the Short Parliament which sat from 13 April to 5 May 1640 when it was dissolved by Charles I. Reproduced courtesy of The Benchers of The Honourable Society of Lincoln's Inn (the Licensor). Copyright; the Licensor

Portrait of Sir Gyles Ayre (1635-1695), appointed Serjeant-at-law and a Judge of the Court of King's Bench in 1689. He is wearing the scarlet casting hood over his right shoulder, along with a voluminous full-bottomed wig that was in lay fashion during the reign Charles II. © Salisbury City Council

During the eighteenth and early nineteenth centuries there can be seen a decline in the wearing of the casting-hood by Judges, particularly for Judges on the Crown side when on circuit, who would remove the hood and mantle and instead wear the black scarf over the robe, at the same time in which the dress for *nisi prius* Judges on circuit became the black silk gown.[186] The tail of the casting-hood was usually worn beneath the scarf, and is therefore not prominently shown in some of the few portraits which depict this dress. For example, it cannot be seen in the engravings of Sir Michael Foster J of the Court of King's Bench (1745-1763) by James Basire, Sir Lloyd Kenyon CJ of the Court of King's Bench (1788-1802) by J. Chapman, and in a woodcut of Baron Parke (1834-1856) by H. Anelay.[187] However, the casting-hood can be clearly seen in the oil painting of Lawrence J by Hoppner, although this seems to be the exception rather than the norm at this time. On most occasions, it therefore seems that the casting-hood was forgotten to be worn by Judges during the eighteenth and early nineteenth centuries.

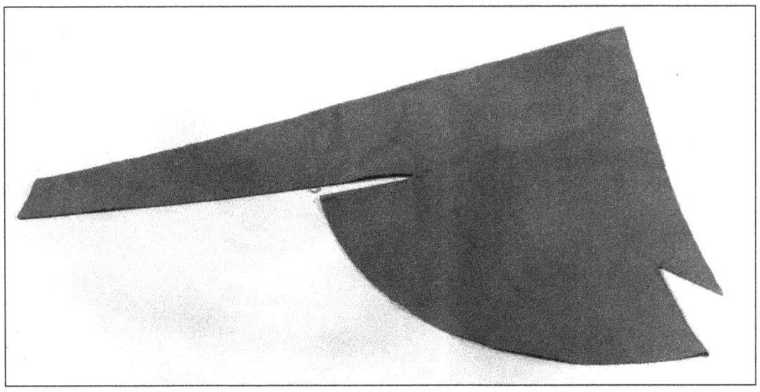

Photograph of Serjeant Gaselee's scarlet hood.

It has been recorded by contemporary observers that Lord Coleridge CJ revived the use of the scarlet casting hood at about the time that the Judges relocated from Westminster Hall to the Royal Courts of Justice at the Strand in 1883, who sanctioned that the casting-hood be worn above the scarf, meaning that the liripipe of the hood began to be worn transversely above the scarf so that it became more visible.[188] It appears that this slight change in the use of the casting-hood was a reversion to 18th century practice, though the casting-hood in some instances is shown incorrectly worn on the left side.[189]

---

186. Derriman, *supra*, 88.
187. Depicted in the Illustrated London News, 22 March 1845, 185.
188. Baker, *Collected II, supra*, 827; "Judicial Costume," *The Law Times* 103 (1897) 577; Pulling, *supra*, 227. The casting-hood can be seen in the etching of Baron Huddlestone published in April, 1884 by Horace Petherick, in the front-piece to Volume 1 of Pump Court: Baker, *ibid*.
189. There are conflicting reports on the wearing of the casting-hood over the left-shoulder by Judges in the 19th century. It has been reported by one observer that Lord Coleridge decided to wear his "gun-case" over his left shoulder in order to distinguish himself from the the puisne Judges (F. E. Sawyer, *Notes & Queries - 6th series* 9 (1884) 465). However, another contemporary observer states the exact opposite in that Lord Coleridge authorised the use of the "scarlet sash, to be worn over the right shoulder, while puisne judges were authorised to wear it over the left shoulder, attached to the hood at the back" ('Judicial Costume' (1897) 103 *The Law Times* 577). In any event, the wearing of the casting-hood over the left shoulder was in clear defiance of the Judges' Rules of 1635 which explicitly states that the "scarlet casting-hood is to be put above the tippet on the right side; for Justice Walmesley and Justice Warburton, and all the judges before, did wear them in that manner; and did declare, that by wearing the hood on the right side, and above the tippet, was signified more temporal dignity; and by the tippet on the left side only, the judges did resemble priests".

The "Gun-case"

It has been suggested by some writers that the introduction of the adjusted casting-hood now worn above the scarf was actually an invention by Lord Coleridge CJ of a decorative red sash referred to by many ignorant of its origins as the "gun case", as can be seen in the following account by MacKinnon LJ:

Copy of painting of Sir Alexander Cockburn LCJ, engraved by Thomas Lewis Atkinson in circa 1871. He is wearing the robe, mantle, hood, with bands, a black girdle and a full-bottomed wig. Unlike his successor, he is not wearing the black scarf beneath the hood, which indicates that the practice of wearing the black scarf underneath the mantle began during the time of his successor, Lord Coleridge.
Attributed to the Harvard Law School Library

> When Lord Coleridge was the first Lord Chief Justice of the Queen's Bench Division he persuaded his colleagues to agree to the introduction of the strip of red cloth which starts from the right shoulder, goes diagonally across the chest towards the left hip, and is kept in that position by the cincture. So far as I know this was a pure invention for which there was no precedent of any kind. I suppose Coleridge thought it was pretty. In academic costume it might be called a liripipe. For some reason, which I have never been able to discover, judges' clerks and circuit butlers have long called this liripipe 'the gun case'.
>
> I have lately tried to discover when this Victorian excrescence was perpetrated, but I have failed. The minute books of meetings of judges of the King's Bench only go back to 1881, and contain nothing about the matter.[190]

However, the above account was later corrected by F. N. Newark who correctly affirms that this was not the invention of Lord Coleridge CJ but rather a relic of the former casting-hood, and explains why it was referred to by some as the "gun-case":

> Lord Coleridge has often been blamed for this, but there is no truth in the story. Lord Coleridge became Lord Chief Justice in 1880 and ten years before an extremely well-informed article on Judicial Costume in Leisure Hour, vol. xxvi, 707, had described the 'gun case' under that name. Furthermore, the writer of this article explains why the vestment gets its particular name. It is so called because its shape is, or was similar to that of a gun-case. It is not a strip of uniform width, but the part hanging down in front is narrower than that hanging down behind, and those who posses a canvas gun-case with the elongated pouch to hold the barrel will immediately perceive the resemblance.[191]

---

190. MacKinnon, *supra*, 31. See also F. E. Sawyer, *supra*, 465; J. C. Sikes, *Notes & Queries - 7th series* 1 (1886) 468.

191. F. H. Newark, "Notes - The Gun Case," *The Law Quarterly Review* 62 (1946) 181. Serjeant Pulling also affirms the antiq-

Copy of a painting of Lord Coleridge (1821-1894), the first Lord Chief Justice of England and Wales, showing his printed autograph below on the right, dating circa 1878. The black scarf can be clearly seen now forming part of the ceremonial costume of Judges, as it is worn underneath the hood and mantle - which marked a change in practice as to its use during Lord Coleridge CJ's chief justiceship to that of his predecessor, who clearly did not wear the black scarf with his hood and mantle. Attributed to the Harvard Law School Library

The rumours of Lord Coleridge CJ having invented the "gun-case" may also be due to the adjustment at the same time by the robe-makers of the style and length of the casting-hood itself, although the reasons for such change are not clear. In any event, the changes made to the casting-hood at this time were indefensible given that Serjeants-at-law had continued to wear the casting-hood in their true shape until the same period:

> The robe-makers at some point thereafter forgot that the tail was part of a hood and made it even longer, with an unshaped and closed back-piece instead of the ancient cowl. It is difficult to suppose that this error began until the disappearance of the serjeants at law, who had kept up the use of casting-hoods in their true shape until the Victorian period. On the other hand, the judges may have found the real thing uncomfortably lop-sided.[192]

In any event, this deformed descendent of the original casting-hood is still worn by Judges sitting in criminal matters in the High Court of England and Wales, as well as in various Supreme and District Courts in Australia and many other countries.

---

uity of the newly introduced casting-hood, stating that "[t]he scarlet casting-hood, now recently brought back into use by the Judges at the Nisi Prius sittings, is in accordance with the rule as to robes made in June 1635, one of which directed that "when the Judges sit upon Nisi Prius in Westminster or in London, they go in Violet Gowns and Scarlet Casting-Hoods and Tippets, upon Holy days in Scarlet" (Pulling, *supra*, 227)

192. Baker, *Collected II, supra*, 827.

Portrait of Lord Russell of Killowen (1832-1900), Lord Chief Justice from 1894 to 1900, by John Singer Sargent, dated 1899. This is one of the rare portraits of a Lord Chief Justice wearing the black robe with full hood and mantle with miniver facings. It is also one of the few portraits which shows that the scarlet casting hood being worn with the hood and mantle, a practice which was commenced by his predecessor Lord Coleridge. This practice was quite irregular, given that the casting hood was the ordinary hood taken off and suspended over the shoulder by its liripipe.
Reproduced courtesy of The Benchers of The Honourable Society of Lincoln's Inn (the Licensor). Copyright; the Licensor

Also, between 1880 and 1890, another modern practice began of wearing the casting-hood underneath the hood and mantle.[193] This practice seems to have begun by Lord Coleridge at the same time that he revived the casting-hood in 1883, for his predecessor Sir Alexander Cockburn LCJ did not wear the casting-hood underneath his hood. This practice of wearing the casting-hood underneath the hood seems to have been adopted with nisi prius black robes, for there is a portrait of Lord Russell of Killowen CJ wearing the nisi prius black robe and hood along with the scarlet-casting hood. It is not entirely clear why this modern practice arose, but is nevertheless unfortunate, as it neglects to understand the relevance of the casting-hood, as it seems an anomoly that the Judges should wear two hoods at the same time.[194] However, it is not clear whether the casting-hood is still worn with the full hood as the photographs of the High Court Judges in their ceremonial scarlet robes do not show them also wearing the casting-hood, which is a welcome reversion to proper practice.

193. Baker, *Collected II*, *supra*, 816.
194. *Ibid.*

Portrait by Jozsi Arpád Koppay (1859-1927) of Lord Astbury (1860-1939), showing the scarlet casting hood worn over the right shoulder is clearly visible underneath the hood with its deformed "liripipe" hanging down below the knees and, along with the black scarf, is now invariably worn underneath both ceremonial and working day dress of High Court Judges, which is an anomaly given that it seems irregular that a Judge should wear two hoods at the same time, and the scarf was meant to replace the hood and mantle for warmth.
With kind permission of The President and Fellows of Trinity College, Oxford

THE BLACK SCARF

In addition to the casting-hood, the Judge would also wear a black scarf (also referred to as a 'stole'[195] or 'tippet'[196]) around the neck, similar to that worn by the Christian clergy, and it is said that it symbolises the power of a Judge to try ecclesiastical causes.[197]

The stole (derived from the Latin "*stola*"[198]) is derived from the ecclesiastical vestments of a priest, and has been long used by Kings during their investiture ceremonies.[199] The scarf when worn would hang down suspended from the neck and the two ends of it were serrated.[200] The scarf of a Chief Justice would be of satin or velvet material, whereas that of a puisne Judge would be made of taffeta.[201]

Portrait of Sir John Fortescue depicted wearing a scarlet robe open from the neck down and lined with coloured fur, with a black scarf around the neck hanging down to the waist. The existing portrait of Fortescue CJ is a copy of the original and dates to the 16th century. Reproduced courtesy of The Benchers of The Honourable Society of Lincoln's Inn (the Licensor). Copyright; the Licensor

195. Derived from the Latin "*stola*" (Planche, *supra*, 486). See also Derriman, *supra*, 86.
196. In the Judges' Rules of 1635, the scarf is referred to as a "tippet", which is the correct use of the term. It is unfortunate that the term "tippet" is now used by Judges and writers to refer to the scarlet casting-hood which is incorrect.
197. Newark, "Judicial Robes," *supra*, 208. The stole is even referred to by Chaucer in his Cantebury Tales: "Forth cometh the Priest with stole about his neck".
198. The term *stola* historically referred to the long tunic worn by Roman women, with Planche noting that the "transference of the name to so dissimilar an article of costume is a useful caution against hasty conclusions from merely verbal evidence" (Planche, *supra*, 487).
199. Planche, *supra*, 486. As to the connection between the stole and the investiture of Kings, Planche remarks that "Walsingham, in his account of the coronation of Richard II, mentions that the king was invested first with the tunic of St. Edward and then with the dalmatic, "projecta circa collum ejus stola." Henry IV is described as having been arrayed at the time of his coronation as a bishop that should sing mass, with a dalmatic like tunic and a stole about his neck. ... The investing with a white stole, "in modum crucis in pectore," is particularly mentioned in several foreign ceremonials. Goldastus in the 'Constitutiones Imperiales,' speaking of Maximilian, king of the Romans, says, "induebatur cum sandalis et stola alba in modum crucis in pectore" (*ibid.*)
200. Hargreaves-Mawdsley, *supra*, 63.
201. Newark, *supra*, 208. Cf. Derriman who states that the scarf was made of "broad black silk": Derriman, *supra*, 86.

One of the earliest illustrations of a stole being worn by a Judge is the now destroyed portrait of Sir John Fortescue, Lord Chief Justice of the Court of King's Bench (died circa 1477/1479), in which he is depicted wearing a scarlet robe open from the neck down and lined with coloured fur, with a black scarf around the neck hanging down to the waist. The existing portrait of Fortescue LCJ is a copy of the original and dates to the 16th century.

Illustration of King Edward I's Parliament in the Garter Book of Thomas Wriothesley, Garter King of Arms, in the Royal Collection, Windsor Castle. Royal Collection Trust / © Her Majesty Queen Elizabeth II 2018

The black scarf can also be seen in the illustration in the Wriothesley manuscript of the Parliament of King Edward I drawn in 1523, where the third Judge from the left seated on the front woolsack with his back to the King is wearing a black scarf over his shoulder, though it is unclear whether in fact the scarf was worn by Judges during the reign of Edward I as this is not a contemporaneous drawing having been drawn over 200 years after Edward Longshank's reign. A question arises as to whether the stole and casting-hood were historically worn together at the same time, as is the case presently.[202] The portrait of Sir John Fortescue described above does not depict him wearing a casting-hood or coif, though the painting is not contemporary and dates from the early 16th century. However, the portrait of John Southcote J of the Court of Queen's Bench (1563-1584) shows him wearing the scarlet robe, black cincture and black scarf, with the liripipe of the scarlet casting-hood covering the upper right-hand side of the black scarf, which may be an artistic error as part of the scarf ought to be visible under the casting-hood.[203]

By the eighteenth century, it appears that Judges on the Crown side when on circuit discarded the hood and mantle and wore the black scarf instead, as can be seen in the engravings of Sir Michael Foster, Sir Soulden Lawrence and Baron Parke, but it is unclear whether the casting-hood was also worn at the same time.

The black scarf is now always worn irrespective of the occasion, even when the mantle and/or hood is worn, which is clearly an anomaly given that the scarf was worn as part of a Judge's undress and was meant to replace the hood and mantle for warmth.[204] It seems that this practice began during the chief justiceship of Lord Coleridge who, along with reintroducing the casting-hood, also began the practice of wearing the casting-hood and scarf underneath the hood on all occasions, as can be seen in his portrait by E. U. Eddis in 1878.

---

202. Baker, *Collected II, supra*, 824.
203. *Ibid.*
204. Derriman, *supra*, 87.

Right. Engraving of Sir Michael Foster (1689-1763), a Justice of the Court of King's Bench from 1745 to 1763, showing the black scarf being worn over the scarlet robe (without the hood or mantle), which indicates that this was the less formal dress worn outside of Westminster Hall for judges on the Crown side who would abandon the mantle and hood and instead wear a black scarf whilst on circuit. It also shows that, by the middle of the eighteenth century, the scarlet casting-hood had been forgotten by Judges and was not re-adopted until the late nineteenth century. From Michael Dodson's *The Life of Sir Michael Foster, Knt: sometime one of the judges of the Court of King's Bench and Recorder of Bristol* (1811)

Above. Engraving of Sir James Parke, Baron of the Court of Exchequer, wearing what appears to be undress for circuit, namely a scarlet robe, black girdle, a black scarf which is tucked underneath the girdle, bands and a full-bottomed wig. Illustration for *The Illustrated London News*, 22 March 1845. © Look and Learn / Illustrated Papers Collection / Bridgeman Images

Above. Portrait of John Southcote J of the Court of Queen's Bench (1563-1584) showing him wearing the scarlet robe, black cincture and black scarf, with the liripipe of the scarlet casting-hood covering the upper right-hand side of the black scarf, which may be an artistic error as part of the scarf ought to be visible under the casting-hood. With kind permission from Lord Petre

Right. Portrait by Herbert James Gunn (1893-1964) in circa 1946 of Lord Goddard (1877-1971), Lord Chief Justice of England and Wales from 1946 to 1958, wearing the scarlet robe, hood and mantle faced with miniver, along with the SS collar, white bands, a full-bottomed wig and a pair of white gloves in hand, which is the current ceremonial dress of the Lord Chief Justice of England and Wales. Note the black scarf which is now invariably worn underneath the ood, which is an unfortunate anomaly given that the scarf was traditionally worn as part of a Judge's undress and was meant to replace the hood and mantle for warmth. Note also the miniver lining which has now extended to almost the bottom of the robe. With kind permission of The President and Fellows of Trinity College, Oxford

Vanity Fair watercolour of Mr Justice Darling (later Lord Darling), dated 8 May 1907, wearing the current working-day dress of a High Court Judge during a criminal sitting, namely a scarlet robe faced with miniver, black scarf, black girdle and scarlet casting hood, plain bands and a bench wig. National Portrait Gallery, London

CINCTURES AND GIRDLES

The cincture and girdle[205] have formed part of a Judge's dress from at least the mid 15th century. It is a rope-like vestment which encircles the body above or around the waist and was originally used by the Ancient Romans who wore it to hold their tunica in place.[206]

The traditional girdle worn by Judges represents the ecclesiastical girdle or cincture worn by the Christian clergy, which was said to resemble the ancient Levitical vestment which was later to be adopted by the Christians.[207] This resemblance between the ancient judicial girdle and ecclesiastical girdle can be clearly seen in early portraits of Judges.[208] The girdle was said to be a symbol of priestly or royal dignity and chastity.[209]

The cincture was of some black material such as silk of taffeta and was worn by Judges on all occasions.[210] During the 15th century, there was no standard practice as to the wearing of the cincture by Judges, for the brasses and effigies show Judges either wearing none of them, or simply wearing girdles, rosaries, belts and even daggers or purses. The portrait of Sir James Dyer CJ of the Court of Common Pleas (1559-1582) depicts a a narrow black girdle which is knotted in front, and in a later portrait of Sir John Powell J of the Court of Common Pleas can be seen a rounded and knotted girdle.[211]

By 1600, it had become the norm for a plain black girdle or cincture to be knotted in front and by the time of King Charles I it had become customary to tie the girdle into a bow.[212] The change in the style of tying the girdle can

205. The terms "cincture" and "girdle" refer to the same item and are interchangeable terms, both having been used to refer to the same thing by Judges and writers.
206. It has also been said that the girdle was worn by some Kings and other great personages in the East: Wharton B. Marriott, *Vestiarium Christianum: The Origin and Gradual Development of the Dress of Holy Ministry in the Church* (London: Rivingtons, 1868) 213.
207. The religious nature of the girdle and its use by the Christian clergy is apparent by its adoption as a religious symbol due to the early Christian followers' literal interpretation of the Christian Holy Writings, for example "Righteousness shall be the belt around his waist, and faithfulness the belt around his loins" (Isaiah 11:5) and "Let your waist be girded and your lamps burning" (Luke 12:35). By the early 8th century, when the Romans abandoned the long tunica, the Deacons of the Eastern Church adopted the girdle, which was said to resemble the ancient Levitical vestment: "in the eighth or ninth century, the idea of an intended resemblance in detail between the Christian and Levitical vestments was first broached, the Girdle, naturally was either not worn at all (with the *tunica talaris* it was not necessary), or, when worn, was not visible, and was thought of only as a matter of convenience. In none of the early monuments of the West before A.D. 800, is any trace of it to be seen. But in the East we have mention of a Girdle as worn by deacons, early in the eighth century" (Marriott, *ibid*, 213-214).
208. Derriman, *supra*, 88.
209. Marriott, *supra*, 213. It has further been noted that "Christ referred to the girdle as a symbol of preparation and readiness for service (Luke 12:35-38). St. Paul referred to it as a symbol of truth (Ephesians 6:14). The girdle of the monastic habit, knotted three times at the ends, symbolizes the three vows of poverty, chastity and obedience. The girdle became a Christian symbol of chastity, possibly derived from the ancient Jewish custom of women wearing ornate girdles symbolic of their virtue (Proverbs 31). Some traditional clergy still use an old vesting prayer when putting on the girdle which says, "Gird me, O Lord, with the girdle of purity, and quench in me the fire of concupiscence that the grace of temperance and chastity may abide in me." Stephen E. Moore, *Church Words: Origins and Meanings* (Forward Movement Publications, 1996) 54.
210. Hargreaves-Mawdsley, *supra*, 64; Newark, "Judicial Robes," *supra,* 209.
211. Derriman, *supra*, 88.
212. Hargreaves-Mawdsley, *supra*, 60.

be seen in two portraits of Sir John Popham CJ of the Court of King's Bench (1592-1607): the first portrait, described above depicts a narrow black girdle knotted in front, whereas a subsequent portrait depicts him wearing a girdle which is tied up into a bow.[213]

Portrait of Sir John Popham, Lord Chief Justice of the Court of King's Bench (1592-1607), showing the mantle fastened to his right shoulder and a narrow black girdle knotted in front. His sleeves have not been customarily folded back which shows the inner miniver lining.
© National Portrait Gallery, London

213. There a two versions of this later portrait of Sir John Popham, the one pictured in this book is by George Perfect Harding (1779-1853) and is a copy of the original. The other version is either an original or older copy of the original and depicts the tied knot slightly differently with the mantle fastened to the right rather than in the middle, indicating that Harding's portrayal of the mantle is inaccurate.

Although the cincture continues to be worn by Judges to this day, it has dramatically widened in width, looking more like a black strap or sash wrapped around the waist than the traditional silk girdle which could be easily tied or knotted together and is now more properly described as a cummerbund or sash than a cincture or girdle.[214] The current girdle worn by Judges is fastened with an imitation knot and is worn over the ends of the black scarf and over the casting-hood.[215]

A subsequent portrait of Sir John Popham depicting him wearing a girdle which is tied up into a bow. Note also the mantle which is now fastened at the centre underneath the chin and pulled back on both sides. The miniver lining can be clearly seen inside the wide sleeves. The black hat is not part of the habit and was simply part of the lay fashion of the time. © National Portrait Gallery, London

214. See e.g., the dress requirements of Judges of the District Court of Western Australia in Practice Direction GEN 1 of 2009 'Court Attire', where the dress requirements of Judges sitting in criminal and ceremonial occasions is described as "Navy gown with purple bands, red sash and *black cummerbund*, jabot or bands, without wig", emphasis added.

215. Derriman, *supra*, 88.

Portrait of Sir John Pratt (1657-1725), Lord Chief Justice of the Court of King's Bench, attributed to Micahel Dahl, (1656-1743), in circa 1718-1725. He is wearing a natural coloured full-bottomed wig which was in lay fashion at the time, and the black girdle is still quite narrow and can be easily tied up in a knot. © National Trust Images

Portrait of Sir William Lee (1688-1754), Lord Chief Justice of the Court of King's Bench (1737-1754), by C.F. Barker after John Vanderbank in 1845, based on an engraving in 1738. The black girdle had clearly widened into a black cumerband. © National Portrait Gallery, London

Oil painting on canvas by Thomas Hudson (1701-1779) of the Earl of Hardwicke (1690-1764), Lord Chancellor from 1737 to 1756. Dating circa 1750.

CHAPTER 3

Other Items of Court Dress

In addition to the traditional habit of a Judge described earlier, there were many other items of court attire that were worn by both the Bench and Bar, including gowns of silk, stuff and damask, and a variety of neckwear and headgear which gradually evolved over the centuries to the present court attire. The distinctive dress of the Bar is also discussed, given the interconnectedness and commonality of the various items worn by both Judges and practitioners in court.

CHANCERY JUDGES' BLACK AND GOLD GOWN

Since the later sixteenth century, the Lord Chancellor and the Master of the Rolls have worn an elaborate black flowered damask gown with gold lace.[1] The fashion of decorating gowns with "guards" or bands of colourful material dates to about 1500 and the guards of gold lace began to be used by eminent and wealthy office holders in the middle of the 16th century.[2] An early portrait of Sir Robert Broke, Speaker of the House of the Commons, dated 1554, portrays him wearing such a gown, and it appears that the first Lord Chancellor to wear such a gown was Sir Christopher Hatton, as can be seen in a portrait dated 1587.[3]

Following Hatton LC's adoption of this style of dress, all subsequent Lord Chancellors to the present day have adhered to the black and gold gown without exception, even though the fashion of wearing such robes disappeared from wider use during the reign of Charles I.[4] Another early portrait of this distinctive attire can be seen in the portrait of Sir Francis Bacon dated circa 1618 located in the National Portrait Gallery. Most official portraits of the Lord Chancellors depict them in these distinctive robes and - since the late seventeenth century - wearing the full-bottomed wig.

Following the passage of the *Judicature Acts*, the Lords Justices of Appeal and President of the Probate, Divorce and Admiralty Division (now Family Division) of the High Court began to wear these ceremonial robes.[5] The Chancellor of the High Court (formerly known as the Vice-Chancellor of the High Court)[6] also wears the same ceremonial dress as worn by the Master of the Rolls and the President of the Family Division of the High Court.

Note: illuminated letter from page 29.

1. *Court Dress*, *supra*, Derriman, *supra*, Appendix, 2.2.3. 160.
2. *Ibid.*
3. Lord Chancellor from 1587 to 1591.
4. Derriman, *supra*, 161.
5. These robes were previously worn by the Lords Justices of the former Court of Appeal in Chancery, as well as by Privy Councillors and Chancellors of the Exchequers, which means that the Lords Justices are also wearing these robes by virtue of their status as privy councillors: *ibid*, 177.
6. Not to be confused with previous office of Vice-Chancellor which was established in 1813 and disappeared with the retire-

Above. Portrait of Sir Francis Bacon (1561-1626) as Lord Chancellor, one of the earliest images of a Lord Chancellor wearing what appears to be the black flowered damask gown with gold lace gown. He is also wearing the large Elizabethan ruffs and a large hat which were in lay fashion at the time and never viewed as being legal dress. Portrait by George Perfect Harding. © Parliamentary Art Collection

Below. Portrait of Francis North, (later Lord Guildford) as Lord Keeper of the Great Seal by John Riley (1646-1691) circa 1682 at the time of his appointment as Lord Keeper of the Great Seal, which explains why he is wearing the elaborate Chancery black and gold gown, which has remained practically unchanged to this day and is still worn by the Lord Chancellor, Master of the Rolls and Lords Justices of Appeal, among others. © National Portrait Gallery, London

ment of Sir James Bacon V-C in 1886. It is believed that the Vice-Chancellor wore a similar gown but that it was made of blue damask rather than black flowered damask: *Consultation on Court Dress*, *supra*, Appendix, 2.3.3.

Oil painting by Jonathan Richardson of the Earl of Cowper (1665-1723), Lord Chancellor from 1705 to 1710, and again from 1714 to 1718.

Full-length portrait of Lord Talbot (1685-1737), Lord Chancellor from 1733 until his death in 1737. He is depicted wearing the black flowered damask gown with gold lace gown and holding the Lord Chancellor's purse with his left hand, beside a table, in an interior. By John Vanderbank the younger (1694-1739), circa 1735.

Portrait of the Earl of Eldon (1751-1838) Lord Chancellor (1801-1806, 1807-1827), who famously sought permission from the King to remove his wig when in court, which was refused. Oil painting by William Owen. © Parliamentary Art Collection

Full-length portrait of Lord Thurlow (1731-1816) Lord Chancellor (1778-1792). Oil painting by George Romney. © Parliamentary Art Collection

Portrait of the Earl of Birkenhead (1872-1930), Lord Chancellor from 1919 to 1922, wearing the elaborate chancery gown, with laced jabot and cuffs. Oil painting by Harrington Mann. © Parliamentary Art Collection

Portrait by Eden Upton Edis (1812-1901) of Lord Chelmsford (1794-1878), Lord Chancellor from 1858 to 1859. © Abingdon-on-Thames Town Council

The Rt. Hon. Elizabeth Truss MP outside the Royal Courts of Justice before being sworn in as the first woman Lord Chancellor on 21 July 2016.
© Josh John

The Rt. Hon. David Lidington MP before being sworn in as Lord Chancellor on 17 June 2017.
© Crown Copyright

Above. The Rt. Hon David Lidington MP on his way to the Royal Courts of Justice to be sworn in as Lord Chancellor on 17 June 2017. The mace bearer leads the procession, followed by the purse bearer.
© Josh John

The Lord Chancellor David Lidington greeting the Lord Chief Justice and Master of the Rolls, showing the back of the black and gold gown.
© Josh John

BLACK SILK GOWN

The origins of the black silk gown - worn by Queen's Counsel and Judges over court dress - are unclear, though it has been suggested that the plain black gown was worn by men of dignity during Elizabethan and Jacobean times.[7] Originally, the first King's Counsel were the King's Serjeants[8] who wore the same habit of a Serjeant-at-law.[9] By the Restoration, however, King's Counsel assumed an elaborate gown decorated with lace and tufts which was made of black flowered damask and was worn over a black velvet court coat and gold brocade waistcoat.[10] By the beginning of the eighteenth century (and possibly earlier), the more elaborate tufted gown became the ceremonial dress for Queen's Counsel, who had by that time adopted the current black silk gown as their working-day dress which has remained unchanged to this day.[11] The black silk gown is quite simple in its appearance and style, being a plain black gown with a large cape collar and long hanging sleeve panels from above the elbow, with two long silk streamers inside the gown which hang from the collar.[12] There is an old professional tradition that the black silk gown was adopted by the Bench when the Royal court went into mourning following the death of Queen Mary II in 1694.[13] However, no direct contemporary source has verified this old professional tradition.[14] However, it can be seen that prior to the death of Mary II, Queen's Counsel had adopted the more elaborate tufted gown which was made of black flowered damask, but after her death were wearing plain silk gowns.[15] The black silk gown was also adopted by Serjeants-at-law at around the same time, and Serjeant Pulling has also referred to this tradition as follows:

---

7. Hargreaves-Mawdsley, *supra*, 86.

8. A King's or Queen's Serjeant was a Serjeant-at-Law appointed by the Crown as a legal adviser to the Sovereign and his or her government, similar to the Attorney General, and would represent the Crown in court, acting as prosecutor in criminal cases and as representative in civil cases, and would have higher powers and ranking in the lower courts than both the Attorney General and Solicitor General: Pulling, *supra*, 40.

9. *Court Dress, supra*, Appendix, 3.4.1. Queen's Counsel were originally created during the reign of Queen Elizabeth I as assistants to the Attorney General and Solicitor General and did not come into prominence until around 1604 when they were appointed from amongst the barrister who were favoured by the King; and unlike the order of Serjeants-at-law, Queen's Counsel are not a separate order and the title of "Queen's Counsel" is merely an honorary title bestowed by the Crown on experienced and leading barristers: W.S. Holdsworth, History of English Law, xii, p 5; Hargreaves-Mawdsley, p 85. The first Queen's Counsel appointed was Sir Francis Bacon in 1597 by way of an honour by Queen Elizabeth I which gave him precedence at the Bar, and he was subsequently formally appointed by King James I in 1603 by way of Letters Patent which afforded him the title "King's Counsel", along with an annuity of 40 pounds, which at that time was a considerable sum: *ibid*, Derriman, *supra*, 58. The text of the Letters Patent named Bacon as "*Consiliarium nostrum ad legem, sive unum de Consilio nostro erudito in Lege*" (i.e., "one of our Counsel Learned in the Law"): Derriman, *ibid, supra*.

10. The black velvet court coat was a special type of tailcoat which had elaborate buttons, gauntlet cuffs and braid: PJ Healy, "Of Wigs, Wig Bags and Rosettes", *Brief*, 21.

11. *Court Dress*, 3.4.1.

12. Murray B. Blok, "A Brief History of Court Attire," *The Advocate* (Vancouver) 64 (2006) 65, 71.

13. George Ruggle, *Ignoramus*, ed. E. Hawkins (London, 1787) 57. See also Derriman, *supra*, 65.

14. Sir John Hamilton Baker, *Collected I* (Cambridge University Press, 2013) 138. Some writers have claimed that this tradition began following the death of Queen Anne in 1714 (*see e.g.*, Inderwick, *supra*, 122), which is clearly incorrect.

15. Pulling, *supra*, 233. In Ruggles's *Ignoramus*, it has been reported that "[t]he gown now used is undoubtedly not that be-

[o]n most occasions Serjeants, like the Queen's Counsel, use only the black Court dress and silk gown which came into fashion at the end of the seventeenth century, when all the Judges and Serjeants of the Law, and all the members of the Legislature, assembled at Westminster Abbey in full mourning costume to attend the funeral of the departed Queen [Mary II].[16]

Late 17th century engraving of Sir Geoffrey Palmer (1598-1670) by Robert White after Sir Peter Lely, showing him wearing the tufted gown which has six horizontal rows of lace on the sleeve above the elbow, each row having three tufts. Attributed to the University of Leicester

The tufted gown continued to be the ceremonial robe of Queen's Counsel until the 1920s when it fell into desuetude, but is still worn by the Common Crier and the Common Serjeant of the City of London.[17] In any event, by the 18th century the black silk gown had become the working dress of Chancery Judges[18] and, later, by the common law Judges sitting at *nisi prius* when on circuit, though it is not entirely clear what was the practice of Judges in *nisi prius* sittings for some are depicted wearing black silk gowns while others wear the traditional *nisi prius* robes. By the same time the black silk gown had also become the distinguishing dress of Queen's Counsel, which has resulted in the well-known legal expressions "Silk" and "taking silk" (which have been used by lawyers at least since 1857 and 1875 respectively) being clear references to a Barrister who has been appointed Queen's Counsel or - in some jurisdictions - Senior Counsel.[19]

In addition to the black silk gown, Queen's Counsel also wear a black velvet tailcoat and waistcoat, knee breeches, buckled shoes, lace stock and cuffs, full-bottomed wig and white gloves held limp in hand.[20] During periods of court mourning, Queen's Counsel wear a stuff gown of the same pattern as the silk gown, but given that stuff is much cheaper than silk, stuff gowns are commonly worn by Queen's Counsel in both the English High Court, Crown Court and Court of Appeal of England and Wales.[21]

---

longing to their profession. The ancient gown was probably of cloth, and was undoubtedly faced with black velvet, and had on it tufts of silk down the facings and on the fronts of the arms. This is still the proper dress and recognised as such; for it is observable that on Birth Days the King's Counsel appear at Court, in gowns exactly answering this description, and this continued invariably to be the constant dress of an advocate till the death of Queen Mary in 1694, at which time the present gown was introduced as mourning on the occasions, and having been found more convenient and less troublesome than the other, has since been continued" (*Ignoramus*, ed. E. Hawkins (1787), p 57).

16. Pulling, 235, *supra*.

17. Blok, *supra*, "65, 71, 76. The official dress of the Common Serjeant is the black tufted and guarded gown with barrister's wig and bands and a full-bottomed wig and laced jabot on ceremonial and state occasions: Derriman, 187, *supra*.

18. It is because of this fact that the black silk gown are sometimes referred to as "the Chancery gown": E. K. Williams, "Judicial Robes," *Advocate* 10 (1952) 109.

19. J. C. Jeaffreson, *A Book about Lawyers* (New York: G. W. Carleton & Co, 1867), ii. 9; Baker, *Collected I*, *supra*, 139; Derriman, *supra*, 65.

20. Derriman, *supra*, 64.

21. *Court Dress*, *supra*, Appendix, 3.4.3; Derriman, *supra*, 65.

Portrait of John Meller (1665-1733), Master of the High Court of Chancery, by Charles Jervas (1675-1739) and Thomas Gainsborough (1727-1788), showing the black silk gown worn over a court coat, with wide bands and a full-bottomed wig of the natural style worn during the early to mid eighteenth century.

Portrait of Charles John Darling QC (1849-1936), later appointed Lord Darling, by Charles Wellington Furse in 1890, wearing the black silk gown, over a court coat, plain bands and a bar wig - the current dress worn by Queen's Counsel and Senior Counsel today.
© National Portrait Gallery, London

Oil painting on canvas of The Right Hon. Charles Yorke (1722-1770) by Thomas Hudson (1701-1779), circa 1756. The second son of the 1st Earl of Hardwicke, he was appointed Solicitor-General in 1756, Attorney General in 1765, and Lord Chancellor, like his father before him, in 1770, but died on the day after his acceptance of the appointment. This portrait was probably painted to commemorate his appointment as Solicitor-General in 1756 and shows him wearing what appears to be the elaborate gown decorated with lace and tufts which was made of black flowered damask and was worn over a black velvet court coat and gold brocade waistcoat. © National Trust Images

Above. Full-length portrait of Sir Dudley Ryder (1691-1756), Attorney General (1737-1754) by James Cranke. He is wearing the tufted gown made of flowered damask, which formerly was the ceremonial gown worn by Queen's Counsel and Law Officers of the Crown until circa 1921. Reproduced courtesy of The Benchers of The Honourable Society of Lincoln's Inn (the Licensor). Copyright; the Licensor.

Right. Portrait of James Mingay by Charles Howard Hodges, after George Romney mezzotint, published 1791. He is wearing the elaborate gown decorated with lace and tufts which was made of black flowered damask and was worn over a black velvet court coat over a gold brocade waistcoat. Attributed to the Rijksmuseum

Photograph of the Common Crier on 30 March 2015, following the dissolution of Parliament, reading out a copy of the Royal Proclamation summoning a new Parliament and requiring an election, on the steps of the Royal Exchange, having been it handed to him by the Common Serjeant of the City, ahead of it being also read out in the London boroughs. The Common crier is wearing the elaborate black gown decorated with lace and tufts which is made of black flowered damask and is worn over a black velvet court coat, with laced cuffs and jabot and a barrister's wig. Contributor: Stephen Chung / Alamy Stock Photo

Commemoration of the establishment of the Integrated Single Centre for Crime at Liverpool Crown Court on 8 December 2015. The Lord Chief Justice of England and Wales, the Rt. Hon. the Lord Thomas of Cwngiedd CJ, who is wearing the black silk gown over a court coat and waistcoat, with the SS collar, bands and a bench wig, with His Honour Judge Goldstone QC, Honorary Recorder of Liverpool, who is wearing a scarlet robe with black facings and a black scarlet hood, and Mr Justice Holroyde, Senior Presiding Judge for the North West also wearing a black silk gown. © Liverpool Echo

JUNIOR BARRISTERS' GOWN

The current open gown worn by junior barristers "was not at first a 'habit' of prescribed pattern", and was derived from the lay dress of Tudor times.[22] Unlike Serjeants-at-law, who wore elaborate parti-coloured and rayed robes closed at the front, with corresponding hoods lined with lambs' wool and a white coif, the junior or utter (i.e., outer) barristers were not permitted to wear such elaborate dress, and until the late thirteenth century wore, instead, an ankle-length robe which was closed at the front and belted at the middle and was parti-coloured with one side being plain cloth and the other side being rayed cloth of another colour, without any hood or coif.[23] Examples of the barristers' parti-coloured robes can be seen in the Inner Temple illuminations.

By the time of King Henry VII (1485-1509), an open gown without sleeves had replaced the closed ankle length robe in general society, meaning that barristers, whose dress at this time reflected the lay fashions of society, simply followed suit.[24] Early examples of this can be seen from the brasses of William Eyre in a civilian gown (dated 1507) at Great Cressingham, Norfolk and Robert Southwell in a civilian fur-lined gown (dated 1514) at Barham in Suffolk.[25] Although by the sixteenth century the barristers' gown had become darker and muted (or sad) in colour, a set colour or pattern of barristers' robes had not yet come into the vogue, as can be seen in the following observation of Sir William Dugdale, who observed that the members of the Middle Temple during the Tudor period had:

> no order for their Apparell; but every man may go as him listeth, so that his Apparell pretend no lightness or wantonness in the wearer; for, even as his Apparell doth shew him to be, even so shall he be esteemed among them.[26]

With the advent of breaches, boots, cloaks and other fripperies in the latter part of the sixteenth century, the Inns of Court[27] issued a raft of regulations prohibiting the wearing by barristers of such items, and between 1580 and 1600 all four Inns of Court has formally required their respective members to wear the gown on all occasions, including in public.[28] As a result of these prohibitions on elaborate dress, the young barristers of the time explored oth-

22. Baker, *Serjeants-at-Law*, *supra*, 82.
23. Baker, *Collected II*, *supra*, 859.
24. Hargreaves-Mawdsley, *supra*, 88.
25. Druitt, *supra*, 232-233.
26. Dugdale, *Origines Juridicales*, *supra*, 197.
27. There are four Inns of Court: Lincoln's Inn, Inner Temple, Middle Temple and Gray's Inn: Derriman, *supra*, 15.
28. For example, in 1635 the Lincoln's Inn had "ordered that yf from henceforth any gent. Of this societie shall in meale times come into the Hall with any other upper garment than a gowne, hee shalbee ipso facto suspended from being a member of the Societie": W. P. Baildon, ed., *The Records of the Honourable Society of Lincoln's Inn: The Black Books, Vol. II from AD 1586 to AD 1660* (London: Lincoln's Inn, 1898) 325. In the same text it has also been noted that in 1610 "by Advise of all the Judges of England, it is ordered that no Utter Barrister or yonge gent. Of this House shall goe booted or with his rapyer under his gowne in the House or City of London or suburbs thereof, upon payne to be put out of commons; and the same order and payne for such of the Utter Barristers that walk in the House without

er ways in which to elaborately style themselves, and began to decorate their gowns with lace, velvet and wings on their sleeves,[29] much to the dislike of Chief Justice Wray of the Court of King's Bench (1574-1592) as reported in the following account by Mr Secondary Kempe in October of 1602:

> Mr Kempe in the King's Bench reported that in tymes past the counsellors wore gowns faced with satten, and some with yellowe cotten, and the benchers with jennet furre; nowe they are come to that pride and fa[n] tastickness that every one must have a velvet face, and some soe tricked with lace the Justice Wray in his tyme spake to such an odd counsellor in this manner: *Quomondo intrasti, domine, non habens vestem nuptialem?* Get you from the barre, or I will put you from the barr for your folish pride.[30]

Posthumous engraving of Richard Graves (died 1669), a bencher of Lincoln's Inn, by George Vertue in circa 1720, showing him wearing the mourning gown with a hood on the left shoulder, which is one of the earliest extant illustrations of the stuff gown now worn by the junior Bar. © National Portrait Gallery, London

It is by this time the gown of utter barristers most likely comprised of "a plain, standard pattern of gown which was generally recognised as duly modest."[31] By the beginning of the seventeenth century, different styles had emerged for the gowns of utter barristers, readers of the Inns of Court, benchers and King's Counsel. The standard gown of the utter bar was ankle-length and pleated, with "the sleeve cut square at the bottom. It was edged at the front and bottom with velvet. On the upper sleeve was a vertical slit, running from the centre of the arm-slit to the point of the shoulder, but sewn or hooked close; this slit, and also the horizontal arm-slit, were edged all round with velvet about one inch wide."[32] It was famously described by Sir Henry Chauncy, who was called to the bar in 1656, as:

> a Noble Robe, fac'd down before, guarded with two welts of Velvet on the Sleeves extended from the Shoulder to the Elbow, and another on the border of it, like the Gards, which the Romans used to distinguish the different Degrees of Men among them.[33]

---

their gowned eyther in terme or vacation" (*ibid*, 132); Charles Henry Hopwood, Middle Temple Records Volume I (London: Butterworth & Co, 1904), 269, no. 4; Reginald James Fletcher, ed., *The Pension Book of Gray's Inn* (*Records of the Honourable Society*) *1569-1669*, (London: Chiswick Press, 1901) 148; F. A. Inderwick, *A Calendar of the Inner Temple Records* Vol. I. (London: Stevens & Sons, 1896) 438-439.

29. The use of wings on barristers' sleeves was prohibited in 1584 and in Middle Temple also prohibited the use of velvet on gowns worn except by benchers: Dugdale, *Origines Juridicales*, *supra*, 191.

30. John Bruce, ed., Diary of John Manningham of the Middle Temple and of Bradbourne, Kent, Barrister-at-law, 1602-1603 (Westminster: J. B. Nichols & Sons, 1868) 45.

31. Baker, *Collected II*, *supra*, 861.

32. *Ibid*, 862. The vertical strips of velvet on the upper sleeve identified the wearer's rank: *ibid*.

33. Sir Henry Chauncy, quoted in *ibid*, 864. The earliest illus.

Towards the latter part of Queen Elizabeth I's reign, distinctive long welts had developed on the upper part of the sleeve, as can be clearly seen in the portrait of William Burton dated 1604. Even more clearer illustrations of utter barristers wearing the "Noble Robe" can be seen during the reign of King Charles I, such as the portrait of Sir Bulstrode Whitelocke (dated 1634) a posthumous painting of Robert Ashley (dated 1641) commemorating his bequest of books to the Middle Temple Library, a painting of William Denny (died 1642) and an oil painting of Edward Finch, amongst others.[34] Thus, from 1600 to 1685 it is clear that the "Noble Robe" was the principal gown worn by utter barristers, although during the Interregnum (1649-1660) barristers did not wear an official costume.[35] However, everything changed with the death of King Charles II in 1685. Following his death the whole royal court - including the Bar - went into mourning and began wearing mourning dress. Some commentators had incorrectly claimed that the Bar began wearing the mourning gown upon the death of Queen Mary II or Queen Anne,[36] but these are clearly legal folklore and "garbled tradition",[37] for there is clear evidence that the mourning gown was adopted by the Bar much earlier in 1685 upon the death of Charles II.[38]

The mourning gown universally adopted by the Bar in 1685 is the current gown worn by junior barristers today. It is a full gown made of a lighter woolen material called "stuff" which is pleated at the yoke (like an academic gown) and has wide bell-shaped sleeves which were caught up with three buttoned tapes over the elbow.[39] However, not everyone approved of the change. Some contemporaries, such as Sir Henry Chauncy who, after noting how the "Noble Robe" survived the English Civil War while others were forced to discard their "habits", lamented the change from the "Noble Robe" of cloth and velvet to the stuff gown:

> [B]ut 'tis great Pity, and it seems very ominous that these learned Men should now decline this Noble Robe and wear a scandalous Livery which resemble those that Bearers usually wear at Funerals, as though the Law lay a dying: However it is greatly hoped, That that worthy Patron of the Law, Sir John Holt, the present Lord Chief Justice, will thoroughly reform this ill practice, and that none of the Reverend Sages of the Law will suffer those Gentlemen to share in the profit and advantage of that Profession which they scandalize

trative evidence of this gown is the effigy of George Littleton (d. 1600) at Bromsgrove, Worcestershire, and another early example of the gown can be seen in the portrait of William Burton on a panel dated 1604 which is in the possession of the Society of Antiquaries: *ibid*, 862-863.

34. *Ibid*, 863.

35. Inderwick, *The King's Peace*, *supra*, 203.

36. *See e.g.*, Ruggle, *Ignoramus*, *supra*, 5n.

37. Baker, *supra*, 865.

38. *See e.g.*, Narcissus Luttrell, *A Brief Historical Relation of State Affairs from September 1678 to April 1714* (Oxford: Oxford University Press,1857), 299-300.

39. Baker, *Collected II*, *supra*, 857.

40. Sir Henry Chauncy, quoted in *ibid*, 864.

Portrait of Sir Bulstrode Whitelocke (dated 1634) by an unknown artist showing him wearing the "Noble Robe" of old. This portraits shows the velvet welts picked out with delicate pipping, and there is a short vertical slit where the velvet welts touch the elbow. NPG 4499. © National Portrait Gallery, London

> by devesting it of that Ancient Robe, and introducing an ignomimious Habit in the room of it.[40]

The then Lord Chief Justice of the Court of King's Bench, Sir John Holt, was of a similar view to that of Chauncy, for on 29 October 1697 - the first day of Michaelmas Term - it has been recorded:

> Yesterday the Lord Chief Justice Holt ordered all barristers to appear next term in their proper gowns and not in mourning ones, as they have done since the death of King Charles; otherwise [he] will not hear them; which will cost them £15 a man.[41]

The same diarist later recorded that at the next term "the barristers appeared at the king's bench in such gowns as they wore before the death of King

41. Luttrell, *supra*, 299-300.
42. *Ibid*, 336.

Portrait of William Denny (died 1642) by an unknown artist, a bencher of Gray's Inn, showing the horizontal welt above the arm but the vertical welts cannot be seen. © Norwich Civic Portrait Collection, Norwich Castle Museum and Art Gallery

Charles the 2nd".[42] However, the reversal to the "noble robe" was only temporary, the much cheaper cost of the gowns playing a large part in swaying preferences permanently towards the mourning gown.[43]

The new gown was not originally a legal gown but was commonly used in periods of mourning and had a diminutive black hood over the left shoulder. This is represented by a black triangular appendage which is suspended over the back of the left shoulder by a long black strip of stuff hanging in front of the gown. Various theories had been advanced over the centuries to explain the origins of the appendage. One well known theory is that it is in fact a remnant of a wallet or pouch into which a client could surreptitiously slip the barrister's *honorarium* without anyone noticing.[44] The inherent problem with this theory is that any attempt to deposit the money into the purse would be practically very difficult and the appendage could have been designed in much better ways if this was its true purpose.[45]

Another theory which has been advanced explaining the purpose or origins of this appendage is that it derives from the medieval chaperon, which was a band of cloth that hung from the shoulder and to which a bourrelet or padded cap was attached which hung down the back of the wearer when not in use.[46] However, the problem with this theory is that junior barristers did not wear hoods until such time as they were appointed as Serjeants-at-law, and the

43. The old gown cost approximately 15 pounds in 1697 whereas the new robe cost 25 shillings in 1718: BL MS Add 41843, fo. 62. By 1867, the cost of the same robe had increased to 30 shillings: Jeaffreson, *Book about Lawyers*, pp 9-10. Another reason for why the Bar preferred the stuff gown to the old gown was that the old gown was made of cloth or grogram would have been hot during the summer, and given that the barrister was forced to wear the gown open and over his usual coats, which meant that the stuff gown (which was more lighter) would have been more comfortable: Baker, *Collected II*, *supra*, 865.

44. *Ibid.*, 857.

45. *Ibid.*, 858.

46. Hargreaves-Mawdsley, *supra*, 90; E. MacCulloch, *Notes & Queries* - 1st series 10 (1854) 213 (1854) G. J. French, *Notes & Queries* - 1st series 10 (1854) 38.

47. Hargreaves-Mawdsley, *supra*, 89-90. The idea that the hood was a distinguishing feature of a Serjeant-at-law's dress can be seen in the following statement by a Judge during the time of King Henry VIII that the hood distinguished the Serjeants "from the residue which be studens of the lawe" (British Library MS Harley 361, folio 85v).

wearing of hats or caps had been prohibited regulations passed by the Inns of Court between 1547 and 1600.[47]

Derriman has attempted to reconcile the two theories suggesting that the origins of the appendage as being both a hood and pocket:

> The true explanation of these odd features seems to be that given by Blackham ("Wig and Gown", 1932) - namely that the fiddle-shaped appendage is a diminutive representation of the ancient hood, and the strip of cloth is the lirippium which was an important part of the hood, as it indicated by its length the rank of the wearer. The common, but fictional, explanation of the flap at the back of the gown is that it is a purse into which grateful clients could slip coins - literally behind the back of the wearer! Barristers even today do not (in theory) work for payment; they cannot sue for unpaid fees since these are held to be merely honoraria. This seems to be a relic of the days when lawyers were in the main clerics who placed their learning at the disposal of lay litigants. One writer ingeniously suggests that the reason why the pocket is behind is in order that the barrister should not see the amount of the fee and be influenced thereby in the conduct of his case! The more usual explanation of the position is that money could be placed in the pocket without being handed over openly and thus causing offence to the advocate. The flap of cloth is of a peculiar design if it were ever intended for this purpose. But Blackham points out that "as both hood and hanging sleeves were formerly used as pockets it is not impossible that the old barrister's hood provided him with a primitive pocket" - so that the "fee" explanation of the

Full-length painting of Robert Ashley (died in 1640/1641), located in the Middle Temple Library, which was painted posthumously in 1641 in commemoration of his bequest of books to the Middle Temple Library. © Middle Temple Library

48. Derriman, *supra*, 35.

appendage to which the hood has now shrunk may not be entirely without foundation.[48]

However, Sir John Baker has clearly articulated a third theory and has explained that the true origin of the black appendage is a diminutive hood that formed part of the mourning gown.[49] This is supported by the series of engravings of the funeral procession of Sir Philip Sidney in 1587 which depict the mourners in the funeral procession both wearing their hoods cast over their heads and over their left shoulder with the liripipe hanging in front.[50] The casting of the hood over the left shoulder during mourning can also be seen during the funeral procession of Queen Elizabeth I. This theory is also supported by

Engraving of the funeral procession of Sir Philip Sidney showing the mourners wearing their hoods cast over their heads with the liripipe hanging down behind.

49. Baker, *Collected II*, *supra*, 859, 867.
50. *Ibid*, 866.

the fact that the barristers always wore their hoods over their left shoulder, rather than their right shoulder. Given that Judges and Serjeants wore their casting hoods over their right shoulder, it has been suggested that the wearing of their casting hoods as such was as a sign of their temporal dignity, whereas priests wore their hoods over their left shoulders as a sign of their spiritual authority, meaning that the "vestigial hood of the barrister's gown is worn on the left to distinguish its spiritual origins in mourning from the temporal authority

Coloured engraving of the funeral procession of Queen Elizabeth I in 1603, showing the hood being cast over the left shoulder.

vested in the judge's hood worn on the right."[51]

The black mourning hood was also originally worn over the head and by 1600 it had become customary for the wearer to hang the hood limp over his left shoulder with its liripipe hanging freely in front - similar to that of a Judge's casting hood.[52] Early illustrations of the new gown can be seen in the painting of the Court of Chancery by Benjamin Ferrers dated circa 1720 which, although the barristers and serjeants are shown from the back, it can be seen that the junior barristers have on their left shoulders pleated yokes of triangular ap-

---

51. Woodcock, *supra*, 64.
52. Baker, *Collected II*, *supra*, 866.

pendages, indicating the black mourning hood. Thus, it appears that the black mourning hood was originally larger than it is at present, but smaller than the much larger and full-sized scarlet casting hoods worn by Judges and Serjeants, though both were of the same pattern.[53] In any event, it is undoubtedly clear that the black appendage is a vestigial hood which was part of the mourning dress adopted by the junior Bar in 1685 and worn by them ever since. The appendage representing the diminutive hood is now permanently attached to the back of the gown and the cowl part of the hood is sewn up along the curved edge of the hood.[54]

Other than the diminutive hood, the gown has hardly changed in size and appearance since it was adopted by the Bar following the death of Charles II. The only major change can be seen in the way the sleeves at caught up over the elbow, for since the nineteenth century there have been three buttons and tapes on the sleeves, though such items were introduced mainly for convenience and did not carry any special significance.[55]

Drawing of a junior barrister's diminutive hood. The hood is sewn up from "c" to "b" with the line between "a" and "c" kept open, with the hood suspended from "b". Based on a hood made in about 1900.
© Sir John Baker QC

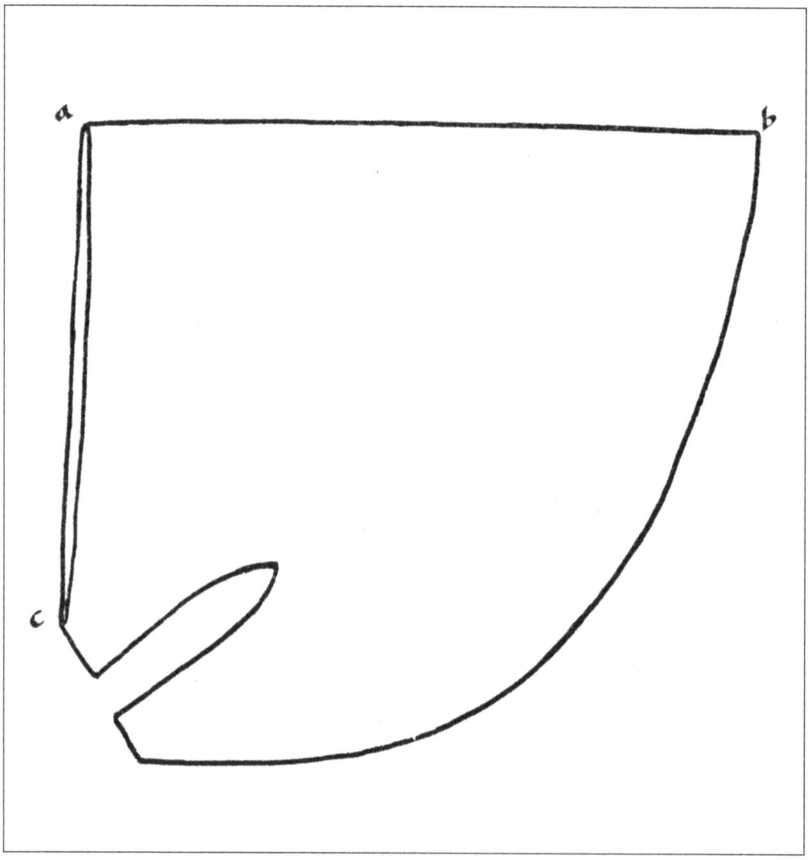

53. *Ibid*, 867.
54. *Court Dress, supra*, Appendix, 3.3.1.
55. Baker, *Collected II, supra*, 867.

To this day, the Courts - both in England and Wales, Australia and many other Commonwealth countries - have failed to specify the specific gown that is required to be worn by junior counsel in court. Although this means that members of the junior Bar could still opt to wear the more elaborate "Noble Robe" made of cloth and velvet, it would most likely provoke protests from the Bench, meaning that "usage has overridden propriety and the Bar has acquired a prescriptive right to wear stuff."[56]

COURT COAT AND WAISTCOAT

The current court suit worn by Queen's Counsel and Judges has its origins in the ordinary dress worn by gentlemen after the Restoration of Charles II in 1660.[57] In its fullest form, which is almost the same as that worn by lay gentlemen in the late eighteenth century, it consisted of:

> a black swallow-tail coat with cuffs, vest (or waistcoat) and knee breeches, worn with silk stockings and patent leather pumps with buckles. It is derived from the ordinary dress of the late eighteenth century ... In the first decade of the nineteenth century, men took to wearing trousers and a newer style of coat with turn-down collar and lapels.[58]

Although junior barristers abandoned the old form of court suits by around 1800, Judges, Serjeants-at-law and King's Counsel continued to wear the old style of court coat underneath their black silk robes, with the only change being that trousers were now worn in court for ordinary sittings while the more elaborate knee breeches and stockings left for ceremonial occasions, a tradition which has continued to this day.[59]

In 1863, a new style of court coat was invented by Frank Smith & Company (known as the "Barrister's waistcoat" or "bar jacket") which was a combination of the vest and sleeves of the court coat.[60] This ingenious combination of the two items into one meant that the Bench and Bar no longer needed to wear both the court coat and waistcoat, and by the 1950s barristers generally abandoned the sleeveless vest under a court coat, which was an open coat in a cutaway style, and wore the sleeved waistcoat (i.e., a bar jacket) instead.[61] The late Judge Paul Healy of the District Court of Western Australia has described the current working coat (or bar jacket) of Queen's Counsel currently in use as follows:

---

56. *Ibid.*
57. Paul James Healy, "Of Wigs, Wig Bags and Rosettes," *Brief* (April 2000) 20, 21.
58. *Court Dress, supra*, Appendix, 7.1.1.
59. *Ibid.*
60. *Ibid.*
61. Blok, *supra*, 74.

> "The court coat usually has a stand collar and is pigeon breasted, and is supposed to have seven buttons up the right front and seven notched or false holes up the left, the holes being three and a half inches at the bottom. It has gauntlet cuffs with three notched holes and buttons.
>
> There are supposed to be three pointed flaps on the waist scam with three buttons under each point; six buttons behind, two at the waist, two at the bottom of the skirts and two midway. The coat has a black silk lining."[62]

The traditional court coat over a sleeveless vest continues to be worn by Queen's Counsel in ceremonial occasions, by English High Court Judges sitting in the Central Criminal Court in London and by Lords Justices of Appeal sitting in the criminal division of the Court of Appeal. It is also worn by some Judges in various Australian courts, such as the Supreme Court of Tasmania. During periods of mourning, Judges and Queen's Counsel also wear mourning bands (which have a central pleat) and weepers,[63] which are white linen coverings for the cuffs of the court coat. These may also be used for private mourning. Junior barristers may also use mourning bands, but not weepers. However, the origins of these additional items worn during periods of court mourning remain unclear.[64]

NECKWEAR AND GLOVES

The neckwear of Judges never formed part of the traditional Judges' habit, and was worn by Judges in accordance with the lay fashion of the time.[65] Indeed, the earliest portraits of Judges show that the robes were closely fitted around the neck and no form of neckwear was originally worn.[66] By the 16th century, it had become customary for Judges to wear Tudor ruffs of various sizes. The ruffs eventually gave way for point lace bands or square linen collars in about 1640, which later evolved into the plain formal white bands which have now become the invariable neckwear of both the Bench and Bar.

Bands

The two stips of white linen bands currently worn by the Bench and Bar form an inextricable part of court attire, but this was not always the case. It appears

62. Paul James Healy, "The Dress of Queen's Counsel and Senior Counsel," *Brief* (November 2001) 22.
63. *Court Dress, supra*, Appendix, 7.2.1.
64. *Ibid.* Given that the last period of official court mourning was back in 1952, following the death of King George VI, the current generation of Judges and Barristers may have never worn mourning bands or weepers and it remains to be seen whether they will adopt mourning dress following the passing of Her Majesty.
65. Hargreaves-Mawdsley, *supra*, 66.
66. Derriman, *supra*, 89.

Engraving of part of the formal procession of the coronation of King James II in 1685, showing the Masters in Chancery, the King's Serjeants-at-law, the King's Attorney-General and Solicitor, followed by the King's antient sergeant and esquires. The Attorney General appears to be the only legal or judicial figure wearing or holding gloves, a practice which has been suggested to have led to the expression "the Attorney-General wearing white gloves". © British Library Board. All Rights Reserved / Bridgeman Images

that are actually derived from the square linen collars which came into vogue during the middle of the seventeenth century.[67] Various other explanations have been given for the origins of bands, as has been clearly outlined by Derriman:

> The origins of the bands is disputed. The most fantastic "explanation" is that given by Pearse ("Guide to the Inns of Court," 1855), who says they were copied from the clergy from the Jewish rabbis, and represent the two Tables of the Law - the Ten Commandments - carried from Sinai by Moses. He adds that the bands were adopted by "the early lawyers" from clerical costume. It has been claimed that the bands are relics of the amice, and Cohen says it seems likely that they "developed from the overlapping borders of the mitre, tied under the chin. Blackman ("Wig and Gown," 1932) says the bands are the ends of a soft white "jabot" or neckband worn before starched collars came into use.[68]

In any event, they were adopted by Judges in the middle of the seventeenth century and have been retained by the Bench and Bar ever since.[69] It appears that Lord Finch of Fordwich CJ of the Court of Common Pleas in 1635 was the first Judge to wear modern-day bands. Also in 1635, Bulstrode Whitelocke recorded in his diary that he was one of the first barristers to wear bands in private dress.[70] By about 1640, the wearing of plain white bands had become commonplace amongst the members of the legal profession.[71]

Originally, the bands were in the form of wide (or square) collars which were tied in the front with lace, but by the late 1680s had converted into their current form of being two rectangles of white linen tied at the throat, and have since then remained an integral element to the dress of judges and barristers, clergy, parliamentary clerks, other public officials and various university graduates and officers.[72] The transformation of the bands during the 19th century can be clearly seen in the following exposition by Sir John Baker QC:

---

67. *Ibid*, 37.
68. Derriman, *supra*, 36-37.
69. *Ibid*, 37.
70. *Court Dress, supra*, Appendix 7.1.1.
71. *Ibid*.
72. *Ibid*.

"Until around 1800 the bands were worn so as to conceal the neck-band or collar of the shirt. By 1810 they were generally tied over a white stock, which usually showed the corners of a standing collar beneath. In Victorian times, when the stock was discontinued, the usual neckwear with bands became the upright or wing collar. This collar is usually of starched linen, though impecunious barristers since the 1860s have been known to use paper substitutes. Some late-Victorian judges and counsel used a turn-down collar with bands, and there have been occasional instances in the present century. The turn-down collar is not contrary to the present dress requirements, though the dress sense of the Bench and Bar has generally kept it at bay.[73]

Jabots

By the 18th century, it had also become commonplace for Judges to wear a lace fall (or jabot) instead of bands when wearing full dress at royal courts (i.e., at court in the presence of the Sovereign), which was another innovation resulting from the lay fashions of the time.[74] In relatively modern times (although it is not clear exactly when this practice began) the laced jabot was adopted as part of the full ceremonial dress of the Lord Chancellor, Lords Justices of Appeal, Queen's Counsel and Circuit Judges, although the Lord Chief Justice of England and Wales and Judges of the High Court of England and Wales continue to correctly wear the the more traditional white bands on ceremonial occasions.[75]

More recently, a "faux" version of a wing collar with bands has been introduced which has the appearance of being white bands tied around the wing collar. This item (referred to by most as a "jabot", when in fact it is a combination of both the bands and jabot) allows the Bench and Bar to wear the jabot over normal business shirts - some even wear it over a tie which is anomalous given that the bands are in fact a form of neckwear and are worn in substitute of, and not in addition to, the business tie. The popularity of this modern "jabot" has resulted in many practitioners not knowing how to wear it, with many incorrectly wearing it over the bar jacket when in fact it should be worn underneath the bar jacket to represent the white tunic shirt worn underneath the court coat.

---

73. *Ibid*, Appendix, 7.1.3. Upon the death of a Sovereign, barristers traditionally have worn mourning bands "which have a thin longitudinal stripe on the white lawn" (Derriman, *supra*, 37). The bands were folded over on the edge and in the centre to make pleats which gave them a somewhat darker appearance. Other items of mourning dress included crape (which is a black silk used for mourning dress) which would cover the scarf, cincture and edges of the Judges' hood and "weepers" which were white lawn cuff covers which would cover the Judges' cuffs and sleeves so as to allow the Judge to use his sleeves to wipe his tears (hence, the use of the term "weeper") (Hargreaves-Mawdsley, *supra*, 68; Newark, "Judicial Robes," *supra*, 212-213).
74. Hargreaves-Mawdsley, *supra*, 66.
75. *Court Dress*, *supra*, Appendix, 7.1.2.

Gloves

Gloves had been worn by Judges and Serjeants-at-law since at least the fourteenth century.[76] Serjeants-at-law were officially presented with gloves (as well as money which was termed "regards") upon their elevation to the Order of the Coif. This can be seen in the following entry in 1495:

> Accounts of Walter Rouden, Collector of the Regard given ... to John Boteler, Richard Higham and Robert Constable, recently elected, named and promoted to the state and degree of the King's Serjeants, Michaelmas Term 11 Henry VII, 1495.
>
> Paid to each of the Serjeants by the hands by Robert Drury, then speaker of the King's Parliament for three pairs of gloves in which to place the "regards" for the Serjeants 12d.[77]

There is little historical illustrative evidence of Judges wearing or holding gloves. In an engraving of the formal procession of the coronation of King James II in 1685, the Attorney General appears to be the only legal or judicial figure wearing or holding gloves, a practice which has been suggested to have led to the expression "the Attorney-General wearing white gloves", which was still extant in the early twentieth century.[78] By the end of the sixteenth century Judges began to generally carry the gloves in hand,[79] a practice which continues to this day on ceremonial occasions such as the opening of the legal year. Interestingly, the present Lord Chancellor David Gauke (2018-) reverted to pre-sixteenth century practice by wearing his white gloves after his swearing-in-ceremony, though it is unclear why he did so as the Lord Chief Justice carried his gloves limp in hand.

Present Lord Chancellor, the Rt. Hon. David Gauke MP (2018-), at the time of his swearing-in as Lord Chancellor on 8 January 2018. He is wearing the white gloves instead of holding them in hand. © Crown Copyright

76. Hargreaves-Mawdsley, *supra*, 56. It has been suggested that during the Anglo-Saxon period, Judges were forbidden to wear gloves on the bench, possibly due to the fact that gloves were considered to be a form or bribery because of their ability to contain money: Derriman, *supra*, 94.

77. James William Norton-Kyshe, *Law and Customs Relating to Gloves* (London: Stevens & Hayens, 1901) 60-61.

78. *Ibid*, 67-68.

79. Hargreaves-Mawdsley, *supra*, 56; Dugdale, *Origines Juridicales*, *supra*, 137.

JUDGES' HEADDRESS

Unlike the robes of Judges which have remained to a large extent unaltered over the centuries, the headdress of Judges on the other hand has varied, ranging from white coifs to full-bottomed wigs and to no headdress at all. Apart from the white linen coif worn by the Serjeants-at-law, no headdresses were worn by he Bench and Bar in court in medieval times.[80]

Originally, two other forms of headdress were worn by Judges (usually over the coif), namely the black skull-cap and black cornered cap (*pileus quadratus*), although the term "black cap" is also confusingly used by writers to refer to either one or both of the two forms of black headdress.[81]

The Coif

The Coif was the *primus et precipuss* of the habit of a Serjeant-at-law.[82] It was a close-fitting skull-shaped white cap, the front corners of which were drawn down into strings which were tied underneath a person's chin, covering the wearer's brow and ears.[83] Pictorial evidence also indicates that a seam ran from the back to the front of the coif over the crown of the head.[84] As the coif was considered to be a manner of dressing or controlling the hair rather than being a form of hat, it was worn by Serjeants-at-law all the time, including in the presence of the Sovereign and was made of white silk, as explained by Sir John Fortescue (himself being a Serjeant in 1438 and then a Judge in 1442) as follows:

> Every Serjeant wears in Court a white silk coif, which is a badge that they are graduates in law, and is the chief ensign of habit with which the Serjeants at Law are distinguished at their creation. Neither shall a Judge, or a Serjeant at Law, take off the said coif though he be in the Royal Presence and talking with the King's Majesty.[85]

As stated by Fortescue above, the coif was originally made of silk[86] but it ap-

80. *Court Dress, supra*, Appendix, 6.1.

81. *Ibid*, 42-43.

82. *De Laudibus*, 124. Early accounts referred to the coif as a 'hoif' which was an English synonym of 'coif' but did not last long in general use, as explained by Sir John Baker: "by the middle of the fourteenth century the coif, or 'hoif' (the short-lived English synonym), was becoming the peculiar badge of the order of serjeants. The poem Winner and Waster mentions Shareshull and other judges in about 1352 sitting on the bench with houves, and in the 1370s Langland twice wrote of serjeants pleading at the bar in houves of silk. A few years after that, Gower spoke of an apprentice becoming a serjeant by having the coif put on his head, as if it were perhaps already a ceremony" (Baker, *Serjeants-at-Law, supra*, 69-70).

83. Woodcock, *supra*, 42.

84. Baker, *Serjeants-at-Law, supra*, 72.

85. Amos, *supra*, 191-192. See the original Latin in *De Laudibus*, 124.

86. In the 1370s William Langland twice wrote of serjeants-at-law pleading at the bar in "hoves of selke": "Conscience and the kynge in to court wente. Where hoved an hundrid in hoves of selke, Seriantz it semede that serveth at the barre, Plededen for penyes and poundes the law" (Derek Pearsall, ed., *Piers Plowman by William Langland* (York Medieval Texts, 1978), 38) and "Shal no serjaunt for that servyse were a silk houve, Ne no ray robe with rich pelure" (G. Kane ed., *Piers Plowman: The A Version* (Talbot Donaldson, 1960) 252).

Part of the formal procession for the coronation of James II: Gentlemen of the Privy Chamber; Judges; Lord Chief Justice of the Kings Bench; Lord Chief Baron of the Exchequer / British Library, London, UK / © British Library Board. All Rights Reserved / Bridgeman Images

pears that by 1600 the coif was made out of linen instead,[87] and the Judges' Rules of 1635 refer to the "coyfes of lawn".[88]

The coif underwent further changes over the sixteenth and seventeenth centuries, as has been clearly outlined by Sir John Baker:

> During the sixteenth century the coif became closer in shape to a skull-cap, with right angled front corners to which thin ties or laces were sewn. Around 1600 the ties were left off altogether, and the coif was made in the same shape as the black velvet skull-cap which almost concealed it. The skull-cap combined with the coif cleared the ears, and sometimes the front corners of the coif were folded back for greater comfort. It is possible that the combination was sometimes made in one piece, the coif being a white lawn lining and edging to the skull-cap.
>
> When wigs were introduced, the same combination of skull-cap and coif was worn at the back, though in paintings it is not always visible. ... During the eighteenth and nineteenth centuries the serjeants' insignia were gradually reduced in size by the wig-makers until, by Victorian times, the consisted merely of a two-inch circle of black silk with a crimped lawn edging. The serjeants and judges wore the coif not only on their full-bottomed wigs but also on the tie-wigs and bench-wigs worn in court. The coif was probably last worn in court in 1900.[89]

Today, the representation of the coif can now be seen in the small indentation in the crown of a judge's bench wig and full-bottomed wig - a small yet lasting and symbolic reminder of the of centuries old insignia of the Order of the Coif.[90]

---

87. In 1597, Richard Hooker wrote that "will any man think that a velvet coat is of more price than a linen coif, knowing the one to be an ordinary garment, the other an ornament which only sergeants at law do wear?": Richard Hooker, *Of the Laws of Ecclesiastical Polity in Two Volumes* - Volume II (Book V) (London: Dent, 1907), 173.

88. Cf. Dugdale who states that Serjeants-at-Law wore a coif "of white silk, or linnen" (emphasis added) (Dugdale, *Origines Juridicales*, *supra*, 136) which seems to indicate that both were worn during his time.

89. Baker, *Serjeants-at-Law*, *supra*, 73. Given that Lord Lindley, who by 1900 was Master of the Rolls and was the last serjeant-at-law to be appointed, moved to the House of Lords upon becoming a Lord of Appeal in Ordinary, and that all other serjeants had died prior to 1900, it is more probable than not the coif ceased to be worn in court after Lord Lindley's departure in 1900 (*ibid*).

90. Woodcock, *supra*, 42.

Black Cornered Cap

In the early Tudor period, both Judges and Serjeants-at-law began to wear flat black bonnets or black caps, which by Elizabethan times had transformed into a black square cap (or black cornered cap).[91] The first evidence of the use of the black cornered cap can be seen in the tomb of William Rudhall (1470-1530), a Serjeant-at-law.[93] As outlined in the Judges Rules of 1635[92], the Judges wore the black cornered cap on all occasions when in court at Westminster Hall and most portraits of Judges up until the Restoration of Charles II show the Judges wearing the black cornered cap.

The black cornered cap ceased to be worn by Judges following the introduction of wigs after the Restoration (as can be seen in the portrait of Sir John Glynne LCJ, who was Lord Chief Justice during the Protectorate and immediately after the Restoration), with the exception that on ceremonial or solemn occasions the black cornered cap was worn over the wig.[94] By the 19th century, the black cornered cap had become associated with the passing of a death sentence and was later termed the "judgment cap":

Engraved portrait of Sir Edward Coke LCJ by R. White (circa 1669) wearing the black cornered cap which is joined to the loose black skull cap over the white coif. He is also wearing large ruffs which were the lay fashion of that time from Dugdale's Chronica Series bound behind the 1671 edition of *Origines Juridiciales*. This engraving can also be found on the front-piece of Coke LCJ's own *The Third Part of the Institutes of the Laws of England; Concerning High Treason, and other Pleas of the Crown, and Criminal Causes* (1669)

> The covering of the head by the judge is a sign of mourning. The judge is supposed to be assuming the highest function of power, that is to say, taking away life, and therefore the head is covered in token of putting on the full dignity of the Crown, at the same time giving additional solemnity to the awful occasion.[95]

The black square cap continues to be carried by Judges limp in hand along with the white gloves during ceremonial occasions, such as the State Opening of Parliament in the House of Lords or during the Opening of the Law Term annual procession, and is also sometimes tucked into the girdle.[96] An early example of this can be seen in the engraving of the coronation procession of James II which clearly show the Judges holding the black cornered cap in hand.

---

91. *Court Dress, supra*, Appendix, 6.1. The black cornered cap is also referred to as the "Erasmus" cap ("Judicial Costume," *Leisure Hour, supra*, 708.
92. The Judges' Rules of 1635 state that "[t]he Judges in Term Time are to sit at Westminster in the courts ... wearing their cornered caps.
93. Woodcock, *supra*, 42.
94. *Ibid*, 43.
95. "Judicial Costume," *The Law Times, supra*, 577. Another 19th century observer has noted that "immediately after the clerk for the Crown has "called upon the prisoner" to know "why judgment of death should not be passed upon him to die according to law," the judge solemnly places the cap upon his wig, and proceeds with his sad duty" ("Judicial Costume," *Leisure Hour, supra*, 708-709).
96. Derriman, *supra*, 92.

Black Skull Cap

It is unclear when the black skull cap first began to be worn by Judges,[97] although it has been suggested that they began to be worn during the fifteenth century.[98] By the sixteenth century, most lawyers and judges had adopted the round black skull caps.[99] The black skull cap was of various sizes, sometimes small and tight and other times looser and larger and lined with scarlet.[100]

Historically, however, the black cap was always worn over the white coif by the Chief Justices when robed, while the puisne Judges would simply wear the coif.[101] Early examples of the black skull cap being worn over the white coif can be seen in the portraits of Sir Matthew Hale LCJ by JM Wright and Sir Richard Rainsford by Gerard Soest. Some later Judges (such as Denman CJ and Jervis CJ) were well-known in not wearing the black cap at all.[102]

By 1635 both the black skull cap and the black cornered had become standard part of a Judge's habit, for the Judges' Rules of 1635 included the rule that "judges in term time are to sit at Westminster in the courts ... wearing their velvet caps and coifs of lawn and cornered caps."

At the beginning of the seventeenth century, a practice began of Judges wearing the square black cap over the the black skull cap which is then placed over the coif as can be seen in the engraved portraits of Sir John Clenche (Baron of the Exchequer and Justice of the Queen's Bench) by Wenceslaus Hollar and Sir Edward Coke LCJ by R. White in Dugdale's *Chronica Series* bound behind the 1671 edition of *Origines Juridiciales*), and the portraits Sir Edmund Anderson and Sir John Popham in the National Portrait Gallery.[103] Initially, the 'combined' black skull cap was (generally) worn more closely so as to fit to the coif which in turn was to cover the Judge's ears, as can be seen in early portraits (such as the portrait engraving of Sir John Clenche). However, by middle of the seventeenth century, the black skull cap began to be more loosely worn and the coif itself had become so curtailed that it now hardly covered the Judge's ears, as can be seen in the engravings of Sir Edward Coke LCJ and Sir Robert Heath LCJ (1575-1649) of the Court of King's Bench.[104]

Portrait engraving of Sir John Clenche (1535-1607), Baron of the Exchequer and Justice of the Queen's Bench by Wenceslaus Hollar dated 1664 from Dugdale's Chronica Series bound behind the 1671 edition of *Origines Juridiciales*. Unlike Coke's later engraving, Clenche J's portrait shows the close-fitted black skull-cap covering the white coif which in turn is tightly covering his ears.

97. "Judicial Costume," *The Law Times*, *supra*, 577.
98. Hargreaves-Mawdsley, *supra*, 59.
99. *Court Dress*, *supra*, Appendix, 6.2.
100. Hargreaves-Mawdsley, *supra*, 65.
101. "Judicial Costume," *Leisure Hour*, *supra*, 708.
102. *Ibid*, 709. The 19th century American lawyer and senator, Charles Sumner, has recounted that Lord Denman CJ not only disliked wearing the black skull cap, he also disliked the wig, as he "considered the wig the silliest thing in England. I took the liberty of telling this to Justice Allan Park, who at once exclaimed that it was all of a piece with Denman's coxcombry: that he just wished to show off his own person" (Croake James, *Curiosities of Law and Lawyers* (London: Sampson Low, Rasten & Co, 1896) 593).
103. Hargreaves-Mawdsley, *supra*, 59. Although not entirely clear, it appears that the square black cap always remained separate from the black skull cap and would be able to be carried limp in hand by Judges (Baker, *Serjeants-at-Law*, *supra*, 83).
104. Hargreaves-Mawdsley, *supra*, 65.

By the time wigs had come into the vogue following the Restoration in 1660, the coif and black skull cap had diminished in size (the coif now resembling the black skull-cap in appearance), resulting in the white coif and black skull-cap transforming into a single black skull-cap (also referred to as a "black round cap") with white edging representing the coif. Judges and Serjeants began to wear this diminutive black round cap on the back of the wig or, in the case of those Judges who resisted the new fashion, over their own natural hair, as can be seen in the portraits of Sir Matthew Hale (1609-1676), Sir Thomas Jones (1614-1692) and Sir Thomas Street (1629-1696).[105]

Painting of Sir Robert Heath LCJ (by an unnamed follower of Cornelius Johnson (1593-1661) as Lord Chief Justice, showing the curtailed coif which no longer covers his ears. By permission of the Master and Fellows of St John's College, Cambridge

105. *Ibid*; *Court Dress*, *supra*, Appendix, 6.2.

Portrait engraving of Sir Robert Heath (1575-1649), Chief Justice of the Court of Common Pleas and subsequently Lord Chief Justice of the Court of King's Bench by Wenceslaus Hollar dated 1664 from Dugdale's Chronica Series bound behind the 1671 edition of *Origines Juridiciales*. As with earlier portraits, Heath LCJ is wearing large laced ruffs in line with the fashions of the day, though he would be last Lord Chief Justice to do so.

Oil painting on canvas of Sir John Glynne (1603-1666), by a follower of Sir Peter Lely (1618- 1680). This portrait was taken during the time of Oliver Cromwell, wearing a scarlet robe, hood and mantle lined with miniver, and a black skull cap over a loosely worn white coif. In 1655 he was appointed by Cromwell as Lord Chief Justice of the Upper Bench and resigned from office in January 1660 prior to the Restoration of Charles II. Note the square collars which had now replaced the large Tudor ruffs for neckwear.

By Victorian times, all that was left of the white coif and black skull cap was a 2 inch circular patch of black silk or satin surrounded by a circular edging of white frilled muslin fixed to the top of a Judge's bob wig and full-bottomed wig.[106] One such example can be seen in the portrait of Sir Thomas Reeve LCJ of the Court of Common Pleas (1735-1736) by Jacopo Amiconi, showing him wearing the black skull cap on his wig.

Portrait engraving of Sir Thomas Street J (1629-1696) of the Court of Common Pleas by R. White in 1688, wearing the smaller skull cap and coif over his own hair. Although by this stage most lawyers and Judges had adopted a natural coloured wig of some sort, Street J continued to wear his own natural hair till the end and was the last known Judge of his time to do so.

A painted oval half-length portrait of Sir Thomas Jones (1614-1692), after Wolfgang William Claret (1665-1706). On 29 September 1683 he succeeded Francis Pemberton as Lord Chief Justice of the Court of Common Pleas. In 1686 he was dismissed for refusing to declare in favour of the royal dispensing power. In 1689 he and Pemberton were committed to custody by Parliament for a breach of privilege in the previous two reigns, but were released when Parliament was prorogued. He is wearing the black cap over the white coif over his natural hair, and was one of the last Judges to not adopt the fashionable wig. © National Trust Images

106. *Ibid.*

Remnant of the Coif-skull-cap

Portrait of Sir Thomas Reeve CJ of the Court of Common Pleas (1735-1736) by Jacopo Amiconi (circa 1730-1736), showing the diminished skull-cap worn over the wig, the latter almost covering it. Attributed to the Athenaeum

Following the enactment of the *Judicature Acts*, Judges were no longer required to be Serjeants-at-law prior to assuming judicial office.[107] This significant reform meant that the white coif was no longer required to be worn by Judges. However, in memory of the coif, a small circular depression on the crown of a Judge's bench wig and full-bottomed wig (which housed the small black patch of silk with white edging symbolising the coif-skull-cap) was retained as a last remnant of the coif and skull-cap. This circular depression was designed to enable Serjeants-at-law to wear wigs while at the same time retaining at least a resemblance of the coif-skull-cap.[108] Today, the black cornered cap is carried limp in the hand, along with a pair of white gloves.[109]

Tricorne Hats

The three-cornered (or "Tricorne") hats which Judges traditionally carried with them during ceremonial occasions, but seldom wore, appears to have been a custom derived from France during the mid to late seventeenth century - at about the same time that the periwig displaced caps.[110]

The tricorne hat can be seen worn by the Judges over their full-bottomed wigs sitting in Westminster Hall in the etching and engraving of the interior of Westminster Hall, entitled "First Day of Term," circa 1745, and it has been suggested that the Judges wore the tricorne hat instead of the black cornered cap in order to conform with the provisions of the Judges Rules of 1635 which required that Judges wear the black cornered cap when sitting in Westminster Hall.[111] The tricorne hat was last worn by English Judges during the opening of assize.[112]

A Judge's Tricorne Hat.
© Sir John Baker QC

107. Section 88 of the Judicature Act 36 & 37 Vict. c. 66 provided that "no person appointed a Judge of either of the said Courts shall henceforth be required to take or to have taken the degree of Serjeant-at-law".
108. Windeyer, *supra*, 401; *Court Dress*, *supra*, Appendix, 6.2.
109. *Ibid.*
110. Windeyer, *supra*, 399.
111. Derriman, *supra*, 93.
112. *Ibid.*

Painting by Dance of Charles Pratt, 1st Earl Camden (1714-1794), Lord Chancellor from 1766-1770, wearing the tricorne hat over his full-bottomed wig, along with the elaborate gown of black flowered damask and gold lace, and elaborately laced jabot and cuffs.

Two photographs of Sir Samuel Griffith CJ in ceremonial attire (date unknown), most likely during the time of his appointment as Chief Justice of the Supreme Court of Queensland. Note that he is holding the tricorne hat, and is wearing buckled shoes and black tights, which is an adherence to the dress of a Judge of the High Court of England and Wales. Attributed to the State Library of Queensland

The Wig

The wig or periwig[113] was never considered part of the traditional ensemble of a Judge. In fact, they are a relatively new addition to the forensic garb of Lawyers and Judges. They have a separate history to that of the Habit of a Judge and were simply adopted up by both the Bench and Bar in the late 17th century in order to keep up with the fashions of the time. Over the centuries, this distinctive piece of headdress has now come to symbolise more than anything else the legal profession and judiciary:

Painting of King Charles II (1630-1685) by John Michael Wright (1617-94) in circa 1676. Charles II is wearing his parliamentary robes over the Order of the Garter robes, along with the Crown of State, the Sword of State and the Garter Collar with the Great George. He has the new Orb in his left hand and the new Sceptre in his right, both of which were made for his coronation. He is seated under a canopy of state embroidered with the Royal Coat of Arms, in front of an armorial cloth of honour, with a tapestry depicting the Abduction of Romulus and Remus. He is wearing a large natural coloured wig, which was in vogue in France and, following his Restoration, the wig was adopted in England. Royal Collection Trust / © Her Majesty Queen Elizabeth II 2018

113. The term "wig" derives from the French word "perruque", which underwent "a variety of Anglicisations and corruptions through the sixteenth and seventeenth centuries; these include 'perewincle' (1580; nothing to do with the flower periwincle, whose name has a different derivation), 'perug' (1581), 'per-wyke' (1588), 'perewincke' (1597) and the more usual 'perewig', 'perriwig' or, the most commonly seen, 'periwig' and 'peruke'. (The word is thought ultimately to derive from the Latin pilus, meaning a hair)" Woodcock, *supra*, 10.

> When compared to the gown and the robe, the wig is a relative newcomer to the traditions of the Bench and Bar. However, in adopting the wig in the manner that it did, the profession was following a tradition as old as that of wearing the robe. As it had done with the coif centuries earlier, the profession assiduously created exclusivity and distinctiveness by continuing to wear a style of headdress that had dropped out of fashion. The legal profession could thereby proclaim a special social status for its fraternity. The success of this adopted newcomer is such that the wig—in particular, the full-bottomed wig—has attained the same status as the red robe in judicial iconography.[114]

The wig was first introduced from France into England after the Restoration during the reign of King Charles II in 1663.[115] Although initially disapproved by the judiciary (notable among them being Sir Matthew Hale and Sir Thomas Street, who refused to adopt the new fashion and continued to wear the coif and skull cap over their natural hair till the end of their lives), the wig was gradually adopted by both the Bench and Bar in the 1680s, and most judicial portraits after 1685 appear to depict the Judges wearing wigs, though initially in their natural colour.[116] Soon thereafter the wig became larger and more stylised, and such a change can be clearly seen in the succeeding portraits of the notorious Lord Jeffreys:[117] in his earliest portrait he is portrayed with his own hair; as Recorder of London (circa 1680) he is depicted in a dark wig; as Lord Chief Justice (circa 1683) he is portrayed in a longer wig which is lighter in colour; and finally as Lord Chancellor (circa 1685) he is depicted wearing a very long full-bottomed wig.[118] These successive portraits indicate the advanc-

---

114. J. G. McLaren, "A Brief History of Wigs in the Legal Profession," *International Journal of the Legal Profession* 6/2 (1999) 241.

115. The wig first began its ascendancy as a fashionable item of dress in France in 1624 after King Louis XIII went prematurely bald and wanted to disguise his baldness with a wig; and was later popularised by his successor King Louis XIV (1646-1716): *ibid*, 242-243. See also Sir Bernard Sugerman, "The Wearing of the Wig," *The Australian Law Journal* 47 (1973) 39, 40. The earliest date of the adoption of the wig in England can be seen in the diary entries of Samuel Pepys (1633-1703), who wrote in his diary on 9 May 1663 that he "did try two or three borders and periwigs, meaning to wear one; and yet I have no stomach for it, but the pains of keeping my hair clean is so great" (*Diary of Samuel Pepys*). Six months later (on 2 November 1663), Pepys records in his diary that he had heard the Duke of York (i.e., the future King James II) say that he was going to wear a periwig, which prompted him to have his head shaved the next day: "without more ado I went up [to the periwig maker] and there he cut off my hair, which went a little to my heart at present to part with; but, it being over, and my periwig on, I paid him 3 for it; and away went he with my own hair to make up another…" (*ibid*).

116. *Court Dress, supra*, Appendix, 5.1.1; Sugerman, *ibid*. Initially, Judges wore wigs of the same colour of their own natural hair, which was sometimes made from the hair of him who wore it and other times combined with a lock of growing hair at the Judge's forehead, and so it was difficult to precisely identify whether the Judge in question was wearing a wig or simply their own natural hair: *ibid*.

117. Lord Jeffreys was a notorious figure during the later Stuart period. A recent article has referred to the Lord Chancellor as follows: "Jeffreys exemplified the degeneracy of the Bench under the later Stuarts. Prior to his appointment as Lord Chancellor, he gained notoriety as Chief Justice for his superintendence of the special commission erected to try and punish participants in the Monmouth Rebellion. Later termed the "Bloody Assizes", Jeffreys' tour of duty in the west was characterized by gross denials of procedural fairness and mass executions. Lord Campbell records that, when he came to Dorsetshire, "Bills of indictment for high treason were found by the hundred, often without evidence, the Grand Jury being afraid that, if they were at all scrupulous, they themselves might be brought in 'aiders and abettors.'" Hundreds were sent to the gallows and, of those that were spared, many were sent to the West Indies as slaves, to the personal profit of Jeffreys and other officials" (C. Langford, "The Prerogative Writs and the origins of English administrative law," *Australian Law Journal* 88 (2014) 567, 586-587).

118. *Court Dress, supra*, Appendix, 5.1.1.

es in fashion and may also indicate how the more larger the wig indicated the greater the station or position of the wearer.[119]

This larger and more extravagant natural wig later became known as the "full-bottomed wig" or the "full-bottom":

> These early wigs, like their French originals, aimed towards naturalism. They were parted in the centre, were flat on top and descended into a cascade of curls in blond, brown or black (the colour favoured by the King). They came to be known as Full-bottomed Wigs or Full-bottoms and their bulk and size grew greater and their appearance more artificial, as the seventeenth century wore on.[120]

An early portrait of Lord Jeffreys (by John Michael Wright) portrayed with his own hair in circa 1675, NPG 6047. © National Portrait Gallery, London

119. *Ibid.*
120. Woodcock, *supra*, 12-13.

Lord Jeffreys (after John Michael Wright) as Recorder of London (circa 1680) depicted in a dark coloured wig.
NPG 56 © National Portrait Gallery, London

Lord Jeffreys in later years ... c. 1685 Painting by an unknown artist after Riley of George Jeffreys, 1st Baron Jeffreys (1648-89), Lord Chancellor.
© Parliamentary Art Collection

During the reign of King William III and up until the early eighteenth century, the Judges wore large dark-coloured wigs, as can be clearly seen in the portrait of Sir John Holt LCJ (1642-1710) painted by Richard Van Bleeck in circa 1700, which was in the ordinary lay style of the time, which by this time become so large that Judges began the practice of almost always carrying the cornered cap in their hands.[121]

In 1705, however, wigs began to be powdered in white and grey and covered with pomade and meal, and by the mid 1750s this had become universal custom.[122] At this point in time, the wigs were of no official significance to the habit of a Judge, with Judges simply following contemporary fashions.[123] By 1720, however, when it had become more fashionable for smaller wigs to be worn in general society,[124] the Judges at this point decided to retain their larger wigs which, although by now had gone out of general fashion, were deemed necessary by Judges to be retained in order to maintain their dignity, as one eighteenth century writer has noted:

---

121. Hargreaves-Mawdsley, *supra*, 67.
122. *Court Dress*, *supra*, Appendix, 5.1.1; Hargreaves-Mawdsley, *supra*, 67.
123. *Ibid.*
124. *Ibid.*

Portrait of Sir John Holt (1642-1710), Lord Chief Justice of the Court of King's Bench (1689-1709), by Richard van Bleeck (1670-1747) dating circa 1700. The robe is now opened just underneath the waist, with deeper miniver cuffs and a broader black girdle, with wide bands (still resembling the square collars from which they derived from) worn at the neck, with the mantle now clearly fastened at the centre which is turned back to show the miniver lining. The distinctive black wig is of the natural style worn by gentlemen of that period, and the cornered cap is no longer worn but held in his right hand.

> It was observed, that a peruke procured many persons a respect, and even veneration, which they were strangers to before, and to which they had not the least claim from their personal merit. The judges and physicians, who thoroughly understood this magic of the wig, gave it all the advantage of length as well as size.[125]

Initially, when the wig came into vogue in the seventeenth century, the full-bottomed wig was worn by both Judges and all members of the Bar (i.e., utter barristers, Queen's/King's Counsel and Serjeants-at-law), a practice which continued until the late eighteenth century.[126] This can be clearly seen in the painting of the Court of Chancery by Benjamin Ferrers dated circa 1720 which shows the Judges and most of the Bar wearing the full-bottomed wig, although a few junior barristers are depicted wearing the slightly shorter wig known as the "campaign wig".[127]

At around the same time (i.e., circa 1720), a large white or grey wig began to be worn which was not very high at the crown and which had lappets falling forward over each shoulder with a queue falling on the back - which from around 1720 began to be recognised by the public as the distinctive headgear worn by Judges and Serjeants-at-law, and which was the precursor to the modern full-bottomed wig.[128] Although most Judges adopted this latest form of wig, some Judges as late as 1758 kept on wearing the more traditional black wigs and voluminous wigs of the ordinary lay style of the time of William III, as can be seen in William Hogarth's famous 1758 oil-on-canvas painting and print entitled *The Bench*.

Thus, between 1720 and 1760 the Judge's wig became a badge of office as a result of the Judges' continuing use of a lay fashion which had gone out of

125. David Hughson, *London: Being an Accurate History and Description of the British Metropolis and its Neighbourhood to Thirty Miles Extent, from an Actual Perambulation*, Volume IV (London: Stratford, 1807), 566.

126. *Court Dress*, *supra*, Appendix, 5.3.1.

127. *Ibid*. The "Campaign Wig" (also known as the "Travelling Wig") was one of a variety of styles and names of wigs which began to take hold from the latter part of the seventeenth century, and differed from the full-bottomed wig by gathering "together the hair at the back and side of the wig into two great twists, tapered at the back and side into two knotted tails, for a more manageable style" (Woodcock, *supra*, 14).

128. Hargreaves-Mawdsley, *supra*, 67. Early evidence of this type of wig being associated with the judiciary can be seen the

common use.[129] This distinctive type of full-bottomed wig with a trim crown and puffed-up large lappets falling forward over the Judge's shoulders can be clearly seen in the portraits of Lord Mansfield (in his portrait by Reynolds in 1756), Lord Ellenborough CJ and Sir Charles Abbott CJ of the Court of King's Bench, which depicts them wearing the same sized wig as that depicted in Hogarth's *The Bench*, though with a trimmer crown and less bushy, (though puffed up), lappets without the large curls from top to bottom, as can be seen in older portraits in the late seventeenth and early eighteenth centuries.

The Court of Chancery by Benjamin Ferrers (died 1732) dated circa 1720 which shows the Judges and most of the Bar wearing the large full-bottomed wig, with large lappets falling on each shoulder and the queue or tail falling behind their backs. A Serjeant-at-law can be seen from behind wearing the full-bottomed wig on top of which a black velvet skull-cap is worn which has entirely obscured the white edging of the cap symbolising the coif. The white edging, however, can be clearly seen on the black caps worn by the other two Serjeants sitting in the middle of the painting, which show the coifs as having a straight lower edge. A junior barrister standing at the bottom left-hand side of the painting is wearing the slightly shorter " campaign wig" distinguishable by the knotted tails on both sides of the wig.
Contributor: Art Collection 2 / Alamy Stock Photo

---

essay written in *The Guardian* on 1 September 1713 by the poet and dramatist John Gay (1685-1732), who observed that "the Full bottom formally combed all before, denotes the Lawyer and Politician" (John Gay, "Sciences of *Poetry* and *Dress*," *The Guardian*, no. 149, 1 September 1713).

129. *Ibid.*

William Hogarth's print entitled "The Bench" dated 1758. This print depicts four Judges sitting in the Court of Common Pleas (from left to right: William Noel, Sir John Willes CJ, Henry Bathurst (later Earl Bathurst LC), and Sir Edward Clive, who is dozing on Bathurst J's shoulder). Above them is the Royal Coat of Arms, which Hogarth has deliberately partly covered so that only part of the motto of the Order of the garter "Honi soit qui mal y pense" (namely, "mal y pense" which loosely translates as "thinking evil" or "evil thinks") can be seen above the Judges. The large full-bottomed wigs worn by the Judges reflect the voluminous style of wig worn by Judges in the late seventeenth century. Sir Edward Clive's dark coloured wig reflects the lay fashion during the reign of William III. The black skull-cap can also be clearly seen on three of the four Judges. Contributor: Lebrecht Music and Arts Photo Library / Alamy Stock Photo

Portrait of Sir Laurence Carter (1672-1745), Baron of the Exchequer (1726-1745) After Jonathan Richardson the Elder (c.1663-1745), wearing the ceremonial scarlet winter robes adopted by Barons of the Exchequer and a large wig similar in the style of the wigs which were worn by Judges up until the late 1720s. © Baron Carter, Baron of the Exchequer After Jonathan Richardson the Elder Leicester Arts & Museums Service

William Murray, first Earl of Mansfield (1705-1793), circa 1793, from the original of Sir Joshua Reynolds / engraved by H.T. Ryall. Attributed to National Library of Australia

Colour engraving of Edward Law, 1st Baron Ellenborough (1750-1818), Attorney-General (1801-1802) and then Lord Chief Justice (1802-1818), by G Parker After Sir Thomas Lawrence. Lord Ellenborough is shown wearing the style of full-bottomed wig adopted by Judges in the mid eighteenth century: a trimmer crown with straighter (i.e., less bushy), falling lappets on either shoulder. A facsimile of his signature is below the engraving. © Daniel Yazdani

Painting of Sir John Taylor Coleridge (1790-1876) by Margaret Sarah Carpenter (1793-1872). Coleridge is wearing the nisi prius violet robes and hood faced with changeable taffeta, white bands and full-bottomed wig which does not yet have the "doormat effect" look of an equal number of curls on each side. This robe was also worn by some Judges in Australia during the nineteenth and twentieth centuries. Reproduced by Permission of the Provost and Fellows of Eton College

By the 1780s, however, Judges began to wear smaller wigs for ordinary sittings (instead of the full-bottomed wig) and adopted the then latest fashion of the short wig which had one vertical curl at the back above two queues which hung down behind, later to be known as the "Bench wig" or the "Bob wig".[130] The change from the full-bottomed wig to the shorter bob wig was partly due to the cumbersome and heavy nature of the full-bottomed wig.[131] The full-bottomed wig continued to be worn by Judges sitting en banc in Westminster Hall and in criminal trials until the 1840s.[132] Since then, the full-bottomed wig has been reserved by Judges for only formal and ceremonial occasions, such as the State Opening of Parliament in the House of Lords, the first day of the legal term and whenever in the presence of the Sovereign.[133]

By the 1770s, barristers had adopted the latest fashion of wig by wearing either the bob wig without side curls or a tie wig with two or three horizontal rows of buckled curls along both the back and sides of the wig, the latter replacing the former by the end of the eighteenth century.[134] An early portrait of this new curled tie wig can be seen in the portrait of the legal antiquary Francis Hargrave (1741-1821) dating circa 1772.[135] Hargrave's attire is almost indistinguishable from the attire worn by barristers today.

Etching in black on white wove paper of Lloyd Kenyon, 1st Baron Kenyon (1732-1802), by engraver was William Holl the Elder (1771-1838) and the print was published in August 1804, after an original portrait made by George Romney in 1792, no longer in existence. There is a copy of part of it, (oil on canvas, 1839-1840), in the National Portrait Gallery London by William Davidson (active 1813-1843) and Sir Martin Archer Shee (1769-1850). The wig has still not yet acquired the formalised "doormat" pattern of modern day full-bottomed wigs. © Aberystwyth University School of Art Museum and Galleries

The wig rapidly went out of common use during the reign of King George III and by the end of the eighteenth century the only people who continued to wear the wig were the Bench and Bar, Bish-

130. *Ibid*, 68.
131. "Judicial Costume," *Leisure Hour*, *supra*, 709.
132. *Court Dress*, *supra*, Appendix, 5.2.1.
133. "Judicial Costume," Leisure Hour, *supra*, 709. By around 1780, barristers had also abandoned the full-bottomed wig on all but ceremonial occasions and instead began to wear either the bench wig or tie wig, the latter of which is now worn by all barristers (i.e., Queen's Counsel and junior barristers) on ordinary occasions in court. The full-bottomed wig continued to be worn by Queen's Counsel on ceremonial occasions such as the first day of the legal year, and when appearing in the Chamber of the House of Lords, though the sight of barristers appearing at the bar of the House of Lords has virtually disappeared following the transfer of the Lords of Appeal in Ordinary to the newly established Supreme Court of the United Kingdom situated across the road from Westminster Parliament in Middlesex Guildhall in October 2009.
134. Barristers continued to wear wigs with triple queue at around 1750, as can be seen in Hogarth's Second Stage of Cruelty engraving dated 1751. By 1780 it became fashionable for wearing wigs with two or three horizontal curls running around the sides and back of the wig, which was adopted by the Bar and has remained in this style to this day: Hargreaves-Mawdsley, *supra*, 91.
135. *Court Dress*, *supra*, Appendix, 5.3.1.

ops,[136] certain municipal officers, parliamentary clerks[137] and coachmen.[138] It has been reported that, around this time, Lord Eldon (while Chief Justice of the Court of Common Pleas) sought permission from George III to remove his wig upon leaving the courts and that his request was in fact ultimately refused:

> Lady Eldon's good taste and care for her husband's comfort, induced Lord Eldon, soon after his elevation to the pillow of the Common Pleas, to beg the king's permission that he might put off his judicial wig on leaving the courts, in which as Chief Justice he would be required to preside. The petition did not meet with a favourable reception. For a minute George III hesitated; whereupon Eldon supported his prayer by observing, with the fervor of an old-fashioned Tory, that the lawyer's wig was a detestable innovation - unknown in the days of James I and Charles the Martyr, the judges of which two monarchs would have rejected as an insult any proposal that they should assume a head-dress fit only for madmen at masquerades or mummers at country wakes. "What! what!" cried the king, sharply; and then, smiling mischievously, as he suddenly saw a good answer to the plausible argument, he added - "True, my lord, Charles the First's judges wore no wigs, but they wore beards. You may do the same if you like. You may please yourself about wearing or not wearing your wig; but mind, if you please yourself by imitating the old judges, as to the head - you must please me by imitating them as to the chin. You may lay aside your wig; but if you do - you must wear a beard.[139]

---

136. Bishops were granted permission by King William IV to abandon the wearing of wigs in the 1832: David Pannick, *Judges* (Oxford, 1988). Some physicians continued to wear their wigs as a mark of their profession from 1800 until approximately 1820: Phillis Emily Cunnington & Catherine Lucas, *Costume for Births, Marriages and Deaths* (New York: Barnes & Noble, 1972) 306. The Bishops continued to wear their episcopal wigs in the House of Lords until 1830 when Charles James Blomfield (1786-1857) the Bishop of London sought permission from William IV for the Episcopal bench to discontinue the practice of wearing the wig, though as late as 1858 the then Archbishop of Canterbury John Bird Sumner (1780-1862) presided over the marriage of Princess Victoria, the Princess Royal and Frederick III of Germany wearing a wig (Woodcock, *supra*, 35).

137. As for parliamentary clerks, whilst the Clerks at the Table of the House of Lords continue to wear the wig and court dress on all occasions in the House of Lords, the Clerks at the Table of the House of Commons discontinued the wearing of the wig and court dress in March 2017, reverting to a gown over which male Clerks now wear ordinary rather than wing collars and dark suits and female Clerks the equivalent, while retaining white bow ties in the case of men and bands for women. However, the Clerk of the House of Commons continues to wear the wig and court dress on ceremonial occasions such as the State Opening of Parliament (see the letter from the Clerk of the House of Commons, David Natzler, to Charles Walker OBE MP, Chair of the House of Commons Procedure Committee dated 6 February 2018). In Australia, the dress of parliamentary clerks differs not only in each state and territory but also in each of the lower Houses and upper houses of Parliament in each state and territory: for example, in Western Australia, the clerks of the Legislative Council and the Usher of the Black Rod wear court dress (without the wig), whilst the clerks of the Legislative Assembly and Serjeant-at-Arms simply wear normal business attire. At the Commonwealth level, whilst the clerks of the House of Representatives wear an academic gown over ordinary dress, the clerks of the Senate simply wear normal business attire.

138. Sugerman, *supra*, 39.

139. John Cordy Jeaffreson, *A Book About Lawyers* (New York: G. W. Carleton & Co, 1867) 180.

It is important to note, however, that Lord Eldon was not the only contemporary to dislike wearing the wig. Indeed, in 1823, Edward Nares (the son of a Judge of Common Pleas and grandson of a Master of the Rolls) wrote the following:

> Wigs are now reduced in this kingdom to mere marks of distinction; our Bishops and our Judges are almost the only persons who wear them; except the Barristers when attending our Courts of Law, who only huddle them on over their own hair, so as to make them look for all the world like the beperiwiged chimney-sweeps, that we see about the streets on May day. To our Bishops and Judges however they continue, if I may so say, appropriate marks of dignity, gravity and importance. The wonder is, that this should be so, considering the history of wigs. In former days, so little were they thought to be the emblems of gravity and dignity that the primitive Quakers seem to have found less to object against titles than against wigs.[140]

Portrait of Francis Hargrave (1741-1821), dated circa 1772, showing the latest fashion of wig by wearing a Tie Wig with two or three horizontal rows of buckled curls along both the back and sides of the wig. This style of wig, along with the bands and black stuff gown, are almost identical to the dress worn by junior barristers today.
Image courtesy of the Hyder Collection, University of Texas School of Law Foundation

Up until the early nineteenth century, wigs were required to be maintained almost on a daily basis by greasing them with a thick, scented ointment known as "pomatum" as well as powdering them with white flour as they were originally made of black horse hair.[141] An anonymous Victorian observer has described this difficult process of maintaining these old wigs:

> These wigs, until recently, were made of thin horsehair, plentifully greased, and powdered thickly with flour. They required to be greased, curled, and powdered every week or fortnight, and soon got into a dirty and offensive condition if neglected.[142]

Fortunately, things improved on 14 March 1822 when a Humphrey Ravenscroft (a third generation wig maker) obtained a patent for a particular Tie Wig that no required to be greased or powdered with white flour.[143] This new "forensic wig" was now made of white horse hair and no longer needed to be curled, thus retaining its style for an indefinite period, with the patent itself stating that the curls of this new Tie Wig:

> are constructed on a Principal to Supersede the Necessity for Frizzing, Curling, or Using Hard Pomatum, and for forming the Curls in a Way not to be Uncurled, and also for the Tails of the Wig not to require Tying in Dressing; and, further, the Impossibility of any Person Untying them.[144]

---

140. Edward Nares, *Heraldic Anomalies or Rank Confusion in our Orders of Precedence with Disquisitions moral, philosophical, and historical, on all the existing Orders of Society* - Volume 2 (1823) 259-260.
141. Woodcock, *supra*, 40.
142. "Judicial Costume," *Leisure Hour*, *supra*, 709.
143. Woodcock, *supra*, 40.
144. Una Campbell, *Robes of the Realm: 300 Realms of Ceremonial Dress* (London: Michael O'Mara Books Limited, 1989) 27.

Regarding the development of the full-bottomed wigs, by the beginning of the nineteenth century, full-bottomed wigs had gone through further, albeit slight, modifications, in that the puffed up lappets had reduced in size and were no longer large and puffy but rather had become flattened in appearance, with early signs of rows of curls on each side of the lappets, particularly on the top half of the lappets, as can be seen in the portraits of Sir John Richardson (1771-1841), a Judge of the Court of Common Pleas (1818-1824), by Thomas Phillips (1770-1845), and Sir William Seymour (born 1793), a puisne Judge of the Supreme Court of Bombay, by Thomas Phillips (1770-1845).[145]

Portrait of Sir John Richardson (1771-1841), a Judge of the Court of Common Pleas (1818-1824), by Thomas Phillips (1770-1845) in circa 1818-1824, wearing the scarlet robe, hood and mantle faced with miniver, a black cincture worn around the waist, holding a black cornered cap limp in hand and wearing wide, fine see through bands, and a full-bottomed wig. The style of the full-bottomed wig show the origins of the later style of full-bottomed wig worn by Judges today: the top half of the lappets on each shoulder show a number of fine even curls, which Ravenscroft a decade or so later adopted to create the current full-bottomed wig with its lappets having a clear "doormat effect" look.

145. It has been indicated by some sources that Sir William Seymour was Chief Justice of the Supreme Court of Bombay (see e.g., National Portrait Gallery, London: https://www.npg.org.uk/collections/search/person/mp127114/sir-william-seymour [11 March 2018]), whereas in fact he was merely a puisne Judge and was appointed to the Supreme Court of Bombay on the same day as his judicial brother Sir James Dewar who was appointed as Chief Justice of Bombay on 11 September 1829 (*The Asiatic Journal and Monthly Register for British and Foreign India, China, and Australia*, Volume 1, Parbury, Allen, and Company, 1830, p 238). There is also record in hansard confirming that Seymour was appointed as a puisne Judge and not as Chief Justice, in 1829: "In the mean time [sic] the King has, on my recommendation, made your Advocate General, Mr. Dewar, Chief Justice. I advised this appointment, because that gentleman appears to have shown ability and discretion during the late conflict with the Supreme Court, and because he appears to take a right view of the law, and to be on terms of confidence with you. … The Puisne Judge appointed in the room of Sir C. Chambers is Mr. William Seymour, of the Chancery Bar. The Lord Chancellor has a very good opinion of him, and generally, I think, he appeared to have higher claims than any other candidate. He is a gentleman in his manners, and a man of cultivated mind. He seems to have right notions of his duty, and of the law which has been so strangely misinterpreted. He will rather support Government than use the authority of the Supreme Court as a means of raising opposition. At least, if he is not all this, I have been deceived in him. He will embark in less than two months. He will probably be knighted before he sails; and as it will not be right that the Chief Justice alone should not be knighted, we must consider in what manner that can be best effected. I believe it may be done by patent; but my present idea is to empower you, as Governor, to confer the honour of knighthood on Mr. Dewar" (House of Commons, *Debates*, 4 March 1830, vol 22 cc. 1293-1294).

This slight, yet significant, evolution in the style of the full-bottomed wig eventually culminated in Ravenscroft's newly patented full-bottomed wig in 1835 which made further stylistic changes to the early nineteenth century style wig. For following the success of the newly patented "forensic wig", Humphrey Ravenscroft then undertook the even greater task of improving the much larger full-bottomed wig, a process which culminated in a report by Ravenscroft to the Lord Chancellor and other senior Judges which was published on 1 January 1835. In recommending the new wig in his report, Ravenscroft outlines how the new full-bottomed wig has been remodelled by him so that, inter alia, the large flaps or lappets over each shoulder now had a uniformity of curls going all the way to the bottom of the lappets, giving its modern "doormat effect" look which all Judges' wigs now have:

Portrait of Sir William Seymour (b. 1793), a puisne Judge of the Supreme Court Bombay, by Thomas Phillips (1770-1845), though sometimes incorrectly identified as Chief Justice of Bombay, which he was not. By permission of the Provost and Fellows of Oriel College Oxford

> The Patentee most respectfully submits his new and improved Full-Bottom Wig, which has been re-modelled and executed on an entirely new principle, the Flaps or Wings having the same uniformity of curl as the Body of the Wig, and by their peculiar construction they retain the powder and pomatum, which will not fall out in wearing, neither will they soil or powder the silk gowns or robes in the manner the common Full-Bottom Wigs usually do …
>
> The Patentee … will guarantee that the hair of the Full-Bottom Wig shall retain the same uniformity of curl all over, so long as they can possibly be worn and dressed; and also, that the powder and pomatum will not fall through the Flaps or Wings; and, what is of infinite advantage, they will not in the slightest degree oppose the organ of hearing, …[146]

Most Judges thereafter adopted the newly patented full-bottomed wig with its modern "doormat effect" and without a queue or tail at the back of the wig, although some Judges and Barristers as late as 1877 continued to grease and powder their old style wigs,[147] which can also be seen in the portrait of the opening of the Royal Courts of Justice at the Strand by Queen Victoria in 1882.

146. Campbell, *supra*, 28. Initially, though, some Judges resisted the newly innovated forensic and full-bottomed wigs created by Ravenscroft. For example, Sir James Alan Parke refused to even see his own son at the bar when he appeared before him in the newly patented forensic wig: "A few years ago, when an invention came out by means of which wigs were made with the appearance of being powdered and yet without powder, and without the consequent dirt, Park resisted the change as an innovation on the constitution; and he actually refused to recognise his own son at the bar when he appeared in one of the new fangled wigs" (James, *supra*, 593).

147. Woodcock, *supra*, 46. A Victorian observer has noted that "[l]atterly, patent wigs have been in use, made of thick white horsehair, and these are much preferred, as they are light, clean, and cheap, require no dressing, and their wearers are not called upon to to pay hair-powder duty to the Inland Revenue. The old wig, however, with its greasy and floury accessories, still maintains its sway with a considerable portion of the English Bench and Bar" ("Judicial Costume," *Leisure Hour*, *supra*, 709).

Photographs of the three justices who presided over the famous Tichborne Claimant case, Mr. Justice Mellor, the Lord Chief Justice of England, Sir Alexander Cockburn and Mr. Justice Lush. Photograph taken circa 1874. Lush J's wig is in the style worn by a majority of Judges up until the mid eighteenth century, with larger lappets, and, along with the even curls on both lappets, seem to be combination of the new and old style of full-bottomed wigs which were no longer worn in the twentieth century.

Portrait of Gordon Hewart (1870–1943), 1st Viscount Hewart, Lord Chief Justice of England (1922–1940) by John Saint-Helier Lander (1869-1944), showing the new style of full-bottomed wig as designed by Ravenscroft, with its "doormat effect" look. This is the current dress of the Lord Chief Justice of England and Wales on ceremonial occasions, though traditional white bands are worn instead of the laced bands which can be seen worn by Viscount Hewart CJ.

Thus, by the middle of the 19th century, three standardised forms of wig had emerged which (apart from certain stylistic changes) had become specifically associated with the judiciary and legal profession, all three of which are still in modern use:[148]

An anonymous Judge by an unknown artist, showing the new style of full-bottomed wig as designed by Ravenscroft, with its "door-mat" effect look. The Judge is also wearing white bands and a black silk gown and court dress, which is the ceremonial dress worn by Queen's Counsel today. © Aberystwyth University School of Art Museum and Galleries

1. The Tie Wig (or Barrister's wig) which has a "frizzed crown, beneath which are ranged three horizontal rows of seven cylindrical buckles, then one row of four buckles, one upright perpendicular buckle at the top of the neck, then a final row of two buckles beneath which hang two looped tails",[149] which is worn by Queen's/Senior Counsel and junior Barristers;
2. The Bob Wig (or Bench wig) which has both a frizzed crown and sides without any rows of buckles or curls (except one vertical curl at the back) with a single small horizontal buckle on each of the two short tails hanging at the back, which is worn by Judges in criminal matters in England and Wales and in civil and/or criminal matters in most jurisdictions in Australia and many other Commonwealth and former Commonwealth countries; and
3. The full-bottomed wig, with a frizzed crown and twenty curls on each lappet and without a queue at the back, which is worn on ceremonial occasions by judges and counsel in England and Wales and in some jurisdictions in Australia (such as New South Wales) and various other Commonwealth and former Commonwealth countries.

In July 1868, Sir James Wilde[150] (who was the presiding Judge in the probate case of *Kingdon v Rookes*) took the then unusual step of removing his wig in court for two days during a heatwave, and permitted Counsel to do the same,[151] which attracted comment from the press at the time.[152] Sir Robert Collier[153] - a former Solicitor-General who was Counsel for the Plaintiffs in this case before Wilde J[154] - was also reported to have proposed from the Bar the abandonment of wigs altogether.[155] It was reported in one newspaper that from the Bench, Sir James Wilde said that:

> he had set the example of leaving off the wig in consequence of the unprecedented heat of the weather, as he thought there were limits to human endurance. Sir Robert Collier expressed a wish that this precedent might be followed, and hoped that the obsolete institution of the wig was coming to an end—a hope in which many members of the Bar heartily concur.[156]

---

148. *Court Dress*, *supra*, Appendix, 5.1.3.
149. Woodcock, *supra*, 40.
150. Later Lord Penzance (1816-1899).
151. The temperature on 23 and 24 July 1868 was reported as 90 degrees Fahrenheit and several deaths were reported each day from sunstroke: *see The Times*, 24 July 1868, 5d, lla and 12a; The Times, 23 July 1868, 5f.
152. *See e.g.*, "Miscellaneous," *The Leeds Mercury*, Saturday, 1 August 1868; "Notes by the Way," Nottinghamshire Guardian, Friday, 31 July 1868; "News," *The Chelmsford Chronicle*, Friday, 24 July 1868, 4; "Law Intelligence," *Daily News*, Thursday, 23 July 1868.
153. Later Lord Monkswell (1817-1886).
154. "Court of Probate and Divorce," *The Exeter and Plymouth Gazette*, Thursday, 31 July 1868, 3.
155. "Miscellaneous," *supra*; *The Times*, 24 July 1868, *supra*; *The Times*, 23 July 1868, *supra*. The *Daily News* at the time also expressed a similar view, and "hoped that the laudable practice now introduced may be continued. The legal costume, minus the wig, is sufficiently grave and dignified, but if some sort of head gear is thought desirable (as no doubt it is) something a little less ludicrous than the one now rejected might now be invented" "Law Intelligence," *supra*.
156. *Ibid.* In another article it was reported that: "Sir Robert Collier, the ex Solicitor-General, does not believe in the dignity

However, this radical change met with little support from either the Bench or Bar, but it has been a common practice since then for wigs to be removed by both the Bench and Bar during hot weather.[157]

The decision of *R v Whittaker*[158] resulted in the wearing of the wig being officially sanctioned by the courts. In this case, a Barrister appeared at the Bar without a wig and gown, resulting in the presiding Judge stating that he neither saw nor heard the Barrister, which began the convention that a Judge will indicate to Counsel who are inappropriately dressed by saying to them that he or she cannot "see" them.[159] *R v Whittaker* is now cited as authority in *Halsbury's Laws of England* for the general rule that Barristers are required to wear robes (or "court dress"[160]) when appearing in open court whenever the Judge is robed.[161]

The bare patch on the crown of the bench wig and full-bottomed wig was designed to accommodate the necessity of Serjeants-at-law who were appointed Judges to wear their coif.[162] A little circle of white lawn representing the Serjeants' coif was affixed in the patch, and a small black circle was superimposed on the white circle to indicate the black velvet skull cap which was also worn by Judges over the white coif at the time of the introduction of the wig.[163] However, after the enactment of the *Judicature Acts* of 1873 and 1875, Judges were no longer required to have been Serjeants-at-law prior to judicial appointment and the patch system was no longer required, though a depression was left in the crown of the judicial wig which has been retained to this day.[164] A Victorian observer has left a rather interesting account of the symbolic depression on the crown of a Judge's wig:

> But though the full-bottom wig was certainly covering enough, and to spare, for the judges and serjeants, the coif was still deemed indispensable, and as no ordinary skull-cap could cover the gigantic wig, the coif at once dwindled down to a flat piece of black silk, the size of a five-shilling piece, edged with a muslin frilling; and the adornment … is still used by all judges appointed before the passing of the Judicature Act, 1875, which Act swept away the old custom of appointing serjeants, and removed coif and serjeants' tippet from

---

conferred by the forensic wig. On the morning after Sir James Wilde had invited the bar to lay their wigs aside on account of the heat, the learned member for Plymouth expressed a hope that there was an end to that "obsolete institution." On Friday, however, the judge of the Divorce Court intimated that as the weather had become cooler he wished counsel to resume their wigs. This they accordingly did": "Notes by the Way," *supra*.

157. *Court Dress*, *supra*, Appendix 5.1.2. One example of a modern Judge following the example of Sir James Wilde was Judge David Miller who also expressed similar sentiments to that of Sir Robert Collier: "[I]n my court in warm weather … neither advocates nor myself wear wigs. I have decided that comfort should take precedence over tradition. There have been no untoward effects. In my view the appearance of the advocates, of both sexes, is improved and the dignity of the court in no way diminished. May I suggest that, if wigs are no longer worn, the only losers will be the wig-makers." Letter to the *The Times*, 21 August 1995, 15.

158. (1844) 8 JP 390.

159. McLaren, *supra*, 245. The case of R v Whittaker is also "authority for the proposition that Counsel are not heard in sittings in open Court unless fully robed" (Martin, *supra*, 8).

160. The term "Court Dress" in this instance refers to "wigs, gowns, wing collars and bands or collarettes": see Court Dress: Revised Guidance from the Chairman of the Bar Council of England and Wales, Desmond Browne QC, 2 June 2009; and *Halsbury's Laws of England*, Volume 66 (2015) para 909.

161. *Halsbury's Laws of England*, *ibid.*

162. Derriman, *supra*, 91.

163. *Ibid.*

164. *Ibid.*

Watercolour of the House of Lords by Joseph Nash, showing the Judges' full-bottomed wigs (which can be clearly seen at the centre) as they watch Queen Victoria seated in the House of Lords during the State Opening of Parliament in 1857
© Parliamentary Art Collection

> all future judges. The very peculiar appearance of this little silk patch, buried amidst the horsehair of the judicial wig, may be illustrated by an incident which occured before the late Mr. Justice Willes. Two soldiers, being tried for robbery before him, made some extremely humorous remarks, one of which so tickled the learned judge that he suddenly bent his head over his note-book to conceal his laughter. The moment his coif became visible, from his position, to the prisoners before him, one of them exclaimed, with apparent astonishment, "Hallo Bill! What's that hole on the top of old beak's head? "Oh," growled out the other, " why it's the hole where the old beggar's brains have gone out of, to be sure![165]

On 28 March 1922, a resolution was passed by a majority of Judges of the King's Bench Division permitting newly admitted women to wear wigs, the resolution stating that women barristers "are to wear barristers' wigs which should completely cover and conceal the hair."[166] More recently, Sikh barristers and Judges have since the 1960s been permitted to wear their religious turban instead of the wig in court and on ceremonial occasions.[167]

Moving forward over three centuries after the Restoration the Bench and Bar continue to wear it in our courts to this day, showing how the wig, which was merely a lay fashion adopted by the Bench and Bar in the late seventeenth century, later became an intricate part of court attire and a symbol of the legal profession.[168]

Photograph of the full-bottomed wig of The Hon. Thomas Ryan, a former Justice of the Supreme Court of Queensland. With kind permission from the Supreme Court Library of Queensland

165. "Judicial Costume," *Leisure Hour*, *supra*, 709.
166. MacKinnon, *supra*, 32. It has been recorded that Darling J moved an amendment to the resolution so as to force women barristers to wear a biretta instead of a barristers' wig which was seconded by Horridge J but was ultimately defeated by nine votes to two votes (*ibid*).
167. Woodcock, *supra*, 42.
168. Derriman has suggested that "[t]he retention of the wig as part of the barrister's official costume must be ascribed mainly to the traditional conservatism of the profession, though it undoubtedly has a levelling effect - and a dignifying one - on the variety of faces whose owners plead in our courts" (Derriman, *supra*, 37-38).

Judges in their their full-bottomed wigs, sitting on the woolsack, watching the The Queen deliver her speech from the Throne at the State Opening of Parliament in November 1967. To the left and right can be seen the Prince of Wales and the Princess Royal both seated on either side. Royal Collection Trust / © Her Majesty Queen Elizabeth II 2018

Below. Almost 50 years later, the Judges in their their full-bottomed wigs, sitting on the same woolsack, watching the Lord Chancellor Michael Gove deliver the prepared speech to The Queen at the State Opening of Parliament on 18 May 2016. To the left can be seen the Prince of Wales and the Duchess of Cornwall seated. To the right can be seen standing Lady Susan Hussey, the Queen's Lady-in-Waiting. © House of Lords 2018 / Photography by Roger Harris

Her Majesty The Queen sitting between the former Lord Chief Justice, Lord Judge, and former Lord Chancellor, the Rt Hon Kenneth Clarke CH, QC, along with Sir John Thomas (later Lord Thomas of Cwmgiedd CJ) then President of the Queen's Bench Division sitting on the far left and Lord Neuberger of Abbotsbury (former Master of the Rolls) sitting on the far right, at the opening of the Rolls Building on 7 December 2011.
Contributor: PA Images / Alamy Stock Photo

CHAPTER 4

Court Dress in England and Wales

As has been noted earlier, the ceremonial and working day dress of Judges in England and Wales varies according to the level of appointment and the occasion and are of great antiquity. Prior to the reforms to working day dress of English Judges which came into effect on 1 October 2008, the occasions for the use of the various robes was as follows:

Lords of Appeal in Ordinary	Do not robe to sit judicially. For ceremonial occasions inside the House of Lords: the customary scarlet robe trimmed with ermine of a peer with the rank of a baron For ceremonial occasions outside of the House of Lords: Black court tail coat and waistcoat with stripped trousers (mourning dress)
Lords Justices of Appeal	Ceremonial dress: Black court tail coat and waistcoat; knee breeches with steel buckles, black silk stockings and court shoes with steel buckles, lace jabot and lace sleeve ruffles, black damask robe embroidered with gold lace, full bottomed wig, white gloves. Sitting in the Court of Appeal: Black court coat and waistcoat, black silk gown, plain bands and short bench wig
High Court Judges	Ceremonial dress: (i) Michaelmas and Hilary terms: Black knee breeches with steel buckles, black silk stockings and court shoes with steel buckles, scarlet robe of cloth, hood and mantle trimmed with miniver, black scarf, girdle, white bands, full bottomed wig, with black cap and white gloves in hand

Note: illuminated letter from page 66.

High Court Judges	(ii) Easter and Trinity terms: the same as above except that the scarlet cloth robe is trimmed with taffeta or silk Working dress varies according to Division: (i) Queen's Bench Division: Sitting in the Crown Court (crime) and on Red Letter Days during Michaelmas and Hilary terms: scarlet robe trimmed with miniver, black scarf and girdle, scarlet casting-hood, plain bands and bench wig Sitting in the Crown Court (crime) and on Red Letter Days during Easter and Hilary terms: the same as above except that the scarlet robe is trimmed with taffeta or silk Working dress varies according to Division: (i) Queen's Bench Division: Sitting in the Crown Court (crime) and on Red Letter Days during Michaelmas and Hilary terms: scarlet robe trimmed with miniver, black scarf and girdle, scarlet casting-hood, plain bands and bench wig Sitting in the Crown Court (crime) and on Red Letter Days during Easter and Hilary terms: the same as above except that the scarlet robe is trimmed with taffeta or silk Sitting in the High Court (civil) during Michaelmas and Hilary terms: black robe of cloth trimmed with miniver, black scarf, scarlet casting-hood and girdle, plain bands and short bench wig Sitting in the High Court (civil) during Easter and Trinity terms: violet robe of cloth trimmed with taffeta or silk, black scarf, scarlet casting-hood and girdle, plain bands and short bench wig Sitting in the Divisional Court or in the Court of Appeal: Court coat and wasitcoat, black silk gown, plain bands and short bench wig (i) Chancery Division Sitting in Court: court coat and wasitcoat, black silk gown, plain bands and short bench wig On Red Letter Days during Michaelmas and Hilary terms: scarlet robe trimmed with miniver etc same as worn by Judges of the Queen's Bench Division On Red Letter Days during Easter and Trinity terms: scarlet robe trimmed with silk etc same as worn by Judges of the Queen's Bench Division

High Court Judges	(i) Family Division Sitting in Court: court coat and wasitcoat, black silk gown, plain bands and short bench wig When trying civil cases on circuit (nisi prius) during Michaelmas and Hilary terms: black robe of cloth trimmed with miniver etc same as worn by Judges of the Queen's Bench Division When trying civil cases on circuit (nisi prius) during Easter and Trinity terms: violet robe of cloth trimmed with silk etc same as worn by Judges of the Queen's Bench Division When trying criminal cases and on Red Letter Days during Michaelmas and Hilary terms: scarlet robe trimmed with miniver etc same as worn by Judges of the Queen's Bench Division Sitting in crime and on Red Letter Days during Easter and Trinity terms: scarlet robe trimmed with silk etc same as worn by Judges of the Queen's Bench Division
Circuit Judges	Ceremonial dress: Violet robe of cloth with mauve (lilac) silk facings and cuffs and corresponding hood and a mauve casting-hood, black girdle, lace jabot and lace sleeve ruffles, black knee breeches with steel buckles, black silk stockings and court shoes with steel buckles, full bottomed wig and white gloves in hand When trying civil cases in the County Court: violet robe of cloth with mauve (lilac) silk facings and cuffs and a mauve casting-hood, plain bands, black girdle and bench wig When trying criminal cases in the Crown Court: violet robe of cloth with mauve (lilac) silk facings and cuffs and a scarlet casting-hood, black girdle and bench wig

Early Proposals for Changes to Judges' Robes

In 1970 a Working Party[1] was set up in light of the Government's decision in principle to meet the cost of Judges' robes from public funds to consider, inter alia, what changes, if any, might be made in the number and variety of judicial robes, or in any of the materials of which they are made and to make recommendations accordingly.[2]

Amognst the Working Party's recommendations were that nisi prius robes of black cloth trimmed with miniver and violet cloth trimmed with silk or taffeta worn by Judges of the Queen's Bench Division and by some of the Judges of the Probate Divorce and Admiralty Division when engaged in civil work be discontinued.[3] Instead, it was proposed that, when trying civil cases, the Judges of all Divisions of the High Court should wear the black silk gown and court coat and wasitcoat of black cloth, as was worn by the Judges of the Chancery Division and Judges of the Probate, Divorce and Admiralty Division.[4] It was also recommended that a cheaper fur trimming than ermine (i.e., miniver) be used for Judges' robes.[5]

Apart from agreeing that Judges in the Divisional Court should discontinue the nisi prius robes and revert to the black silk gowns worn over court coat and waistcoat and plain bands, a meeting of the Council of Judges on 1 October 1971 reached no decision on the Working Party's recommendations.[6]

An enquiry was subsequently undertaken to ascertain what economies could be made in the cost of judicial robes, the two items under consideration being the abandonment of the scarlet mantle trimmed with miniver and the substitution of rabbit for miniver upon all or some robes.[7]

Following the commencement of this enqiury, Rees J prepared a note on the impact which decisions made laregly in order to save expense may have on the kind of robes worn by Judges as well as the occasions when particular robes are to be worn and by which Judges. He noted that if the Working Party's "recommendations were accepted and implemented it would have followed that uniformity would have prevailed among High Court Judges because all would wear scarlet when trying criminal cases and all would wear black silk gowns and court coats when trying all kinds of civil cases including divorce."[8] Howev-

1. The members of the Working Party were Ashworth J, John Stephenson J, Rees J, Judge Mais, Mr B.H. Thimont (Civil Service Department) and Mr S.P. Osmond (Lord Chancellor's Office).
2. The Hon Mr Justice Ashworth, The Hon Mr Justice John Stephenson, The Hon Mr Justice Rees, His Honour Judge Mais & Mr S.P. Osmond, *Report of the Working Party on Judges' Robes*, 1970, 1: Lord Chancellor's Office, LCO 66/42. Mr B.H. Thimont (Civil Service Department) did not wish to be formally associated with the Working Party's recommendations, and was not a signatory of the report, in order not to prejudice the position of the Minister underwhich he was serving in the Civil Service Department: *ibid*, 10.
3. *Ibid*, 2.
4. *Ibid*.
5. *Ibid*, 8.
6. "Judicial Robes", Lord Chancellor's Office, LCO 66/42.
7. The Hon. Mr Justice Rees, Note: Judges' Robes, 19 November 1971: Lord Chancellor's Office, LCO 66/42
8. *Ibid*.

er, the following objections were made to the above proposal that all High Court Judges should wear black silk gowns and court coats when trying civil cases:

> 1. That the black nisi prius robe and the purple summer nisi prius robe have in their favour a traditional usage going back to medaeval times and were prescribed for use by Judges' Order of 1635. Also it has been suggested they have a dignity and distinction lacking in the black silk gown and court coat.
> 2. That the black silk gown anf court coat was an adoption of lay costume brought into use about 1770 and abandoned by Queen's Bench Judges in 1883 who then returned to the usage of the winter black and summer purple nisi prius robes. The Chancery Courts and P. D. & A. Courts continued to wear the black silk gown and court coat.
> 3. That it seems likely that a majority of Queen's Bench Judges would prefer to continue to wear nisi prius robes provided that sufficient economies can be made upon other items of judicial costume.
> 4. That the black silk gowns and court coat has now been adopted as the costume for all divisions of the Court of Appeal and it is desirable that a distinction should be maintained between the robes of appellate judges and judges of first instance.[9]

Given the above concerns raised by Judges as to the recommendations of the Working Party in its report, Rees J noted that the following new proposals were subsequently made:

> 1. That the winter and summer nisi prius robes (with certain modifications as to the fur to be used) should continue in use at least by Queen's Bench Judges.
> 2. That Circuit Judges should wear their purple robes with a scarlet tippet (or "gun case") instead of their purple tippet when trying criminal cases. It may also be the case that if the Queen's Bench Judges continue to wear their nisi prius robes the Circuit Judges will also continue to wear their purple robes when trying High Court civil cases including divorce.[10]

It was eventually agreed by the Judges of the Queen's Bench and Family Divisions (and later by the Chancery Division) that there should be virtually no change; that both the nisi prius winter black robes faced with miniver and summer violet robes faced with taffeta be retained and that miniver trimmings on the winter scarlet and winter nisi prius black robes also be retained.[11]

---

9. *Ibid.*
10. *Ibid.*
11. "Judicial Robes", Lord Chancellor's Office, LCO 66/42. It was reported that the proposals for the rationalisation and uniformity of robing and "were destroyed when Mocatta J resisted every reform: the judges were told by the Lord Chancellor that as they could not agree they must stay on as they were": Correspondence from P. D. Robinson to Mr Hodgson, dated 11 February 1986: Lord Chancellor's Office, LCO 66/42.

Continuing Use of Winter Scarlet Robes and Miniver Facings

A decade or so later the issue of the use of miniver for Judges' robes arose once again when in 1985 the Lord Chancellor, Lord Hailsham of St Marylebone (1979-1987), "expressed his concern, on conservalionalist grounds, at the continuing use of fur taken from stoates for the use of High Court judges' red robes", and was prepared to accept it being replaced with rabbit fur (coney) or nylon "because no conservationalist problems arise".[12] On 6 December 1985 Ede & Ravenscroft met with the Lord Chancellor and showed him ermine, coney and nylon-trimmed robes and it was noted that:

> There was no doubt but that the ermine was the most attractive. The coney, however, was perfectly acceprtable, and the Lord Chancellor saw no objection to its use on conservationalist grounds, because the rabbits were going to be eaten any way! The nylon was not attractive and the combined effect looked like a Father Christmas robe in a departmental store. The difficulty, apparently, is that there is too little demand for simulated erminem, and the nylon alternative is not designed to look like fur.

The above meeting resulted in the Lord Chancellor making the following provisional decisions:

> 1. That the best solution of all would be to abolish the winter robes altogether, on the ground that they were no longer needed now that we have central heating, and for the judges to wear the summer robes throughout the year.
>
> 2. That the Family Division and Chancery Division judges should in future only wear black silk gowns and give up the use of scarlet altogether. This would include attendance at the Abbey Service.
>
> 3. If this were impossible, serious thought should be given to abandoning the hood and the mantle, as being unduly hot and unnecessary in modern conditions ...
>
> 4. If the winter robes are to be retained, a possibility would be to say that we would only pay for coney; if a judge wanted ermine he would have to pay the additional coat himself.[13]

Ultimately, however, no changes took place and by late 1986 it was decided that the matter had been taken as far as it can and would not be pursued any further.[14] At present, therefore, the facings of Judges's scarlet robes can be miniver, rabbit (coney) or faux fur.

12. Correspondence from ADM Oulton, Lord Chancellor's Department, to Messrs Legg, Robinson & Wilbin dated 14 June 1985: Lord Chancellor's Office, LCO 66/42.
13. Correspondence from A. D. M. Oulton to Mr P. D. Robinson, 6 December 1985: Lord Chancellor's Office, LCO 66/42.
14. Correspondence from N Hodgson to Mr Potter and Sir Dereck Oulton, 21 August 1986: Lord Chancellor's Office, LCO 66/42.

Present Day Ceremonial Dress of English Judges

The full habit of an English Judge has been, and continues to be, displayed in spectacular fashion in various ceremonial and state occasions, notable among them being the Lord Chancellor's Breakfast and annual procession of Judges marking the opening of Michaelmas Term,[15] the State Opening of Parliament in the House of Lords,[16] whenever in the presence of the Sovereign,[17] and at legal church-services, though most legal church services were discontinued with the abolition of the assizes in 1971.[18]

Left. The Queen meeting the Lords Justices of Appeal at the opening of the Rolls Building in December 2011.
© Crown Copyright

Right. Her Majesty with the former Lord Chief Justice of England and Wales, Lord Judge at the formal opening of the Rolls Building in 2011.
© Crown Copyright

---

15. It appears that Michaelmas was chosen as the beginning of the legal year due to it preceding Advent, which is the beginning of the Church's year and was the beginning of the financial year during the middle ages: Derriman, *ibid*, 192. The annual procession of Judges on the first day of Michaelmas Term is of great antiquity, in which the Judges attend a procession from Temple Bar to Westminster Hall (usually by car). After the service at Westminster Abbey (which is conducted by the Dean of Westminster), the Judges attend a reception known as the Lord Chancellor's Breakfast. The procession is led by a tipstaff, who carries a staff bearing a silver-gilt crown (which was given by Lord Selborne LC upon the opening of the Royal Courts of Justice in 1883), followed by the Lord Chancellor's mace-bearer, followed by the purse-bearer, who is then followed by the Lord Chancellor and Lord Chief Justice who walk together, and they are followed by the Master of the Rolls who is followed by the Lords Justices of Appeal, then puisne judges, circuit judges, queen's counsel and junior barristers: *ibid*, 198.
16. Judges have, for centuries, sat by the woolsack in the House of Lords for the state openings of Parliament, on most occasions wearing their their scarlet robes.
17. An example of this took place during the opening of the Royal Courts of Justice in 1882 by Queen Victoria when the Judges appeared before her in their ceremonial robes. A recent example was in 2011 when the Judges of the High Court, Lord Justices of Appeal, the Lord Chief Justice, Master of the Rolls and Lord Chancellor appeared in full ceremonial garb in the presence of The Queen when Her Majesty officially opened the Rolls building on 7 December 2011.
18. Baker, *Collected II*, *supra*, 829.

Judges wearing their full ceremonial robes at the State Opening of Parliament in the House of Lords, on 18 May 2016. © House of Lords 2018 / Photography by Roger Harris

High Court of England and Wales

The full ceremonial dress of a Judge of the High Court of England and Wales comprises of knee breeches, black silk stockings, hose and buckled shoes, and plain bands worn beneath a scarlet cloth robe with matching hood with mantle trimmed with miniver, coney or faux fur, along with a black scarf, scarlet casting-hood and full-bottomed wig, while carrying a black cap and white gloves in hand.[19]

In 1985, the Lord Chancellor sought guidance on whether Judges sitting in the Chancery Division of the High Court should abandon scarlet robes for ceremonial occasions.[20] This practice had been introduced at the time of the Judicature Act of 1875 so as to emphasise that the Judges of all three of the new Divisions were of equal status.[21]

---

19. *Court Dress*, *supra*, 3.4.1; Correspodnence from G.P. Coldstream to Sir Sidney Abrahams dated 15 June 1954 enclosing Ede & Ravenscroft's "Judges' Robing List" of March 1953: Lord Chancellor's Office, LCO 66/42.

20. Correspondence from ADM Oulton, Lord Chancellor's Department, to Messrs Legg, Robinson & Wilbin dated 14 June 1985: Lord Chancellor's Office, LCO 2/6697.

21. As late as the end of the 19th century, Judges of the Chancery and Probate, Divorce and Admiralty Divisions continued to attend ceremonies at the opening of the legal year wearing black silk gowns: *ibid*, 95.

Left. Two High Court Judges arrive at Westminster Parliament to attend the State Opening of Parliament in the House of Lords on 18 May 2016. They are wearing the scarlet robe, hood and mantle faced with miniver, black girdle and black scarf and full-bottomed wig, holding their white gloves and black caps limp in hand.
© House of Lords 2018 / Photography by Roger Harris

Below. Start of the Legal Year on 3 October 2016. High Court Judges looking resplendent in their scarlet winter robes and full-bottomed wigs as they process from Westminster Abbey to Westminster Parliament. A service in Westminster Abbey is conducted by the Dean of Westminster to mark the start of the legal year. Judges, law officers, Queen's Counsel, government ministers and lawyers attend the service.
Contributor: Paul Marriott / Alamy Stock Photo

Lord Chief Justice of England and Wales

The ceremonial dress worn by the Lord Chief Justice of England and Wales is the same as that worn by High Court Judges (as described above) with the addition of the SS collar worn over the mantle,[22] and a train which is borne by a clerk when he walks down the procession.[23] The hood of the Lord Chief Justice has two silk bows on the shoulders in order to keep the collar in position.[24]

Lord Irvine of Lairg, the Lord Chancellor (centre) with Lord Woolf (left), who was sworn in as Lord Chief Justice of England and Wales, and Lord Phillips of Worth Matravers, who was sworn in as Master of the Rolls, in Court 4, Royal Courts of Justice, London on June 6, 2000. Contributor: PA Images / Alamy Stock Photo

Opposite, bottom. Swearing-in ceremony of the the new Lord Chancellor, the Rt. Hon. David Gauke MP on 18 January 2018 at the Royal Courts of Justice. Standing next to him are the Lord Chief Justice Lord Burnett (2017-) and the Master of the Rolls, Sir Terence Etherton MR (2016-). Contributor: PA Images / Alamy Stock Photo

22. The SS collar is worn by the Lord Chief Justice of England and Wales on ceremonial occasions. Part of the regalia of the Chief Justices of the Court of King's Bench and Common Pleas and Chief Baron of the Court of Exchequer was a gold livery collar known as a Collar of Ss or "esses". This nomenclature derives from the form of the links in the chains which appears as, or similar to, the letter "S". By no later than the last quarter of the 16th century, the SS collars were accepted as being the personal property of the office holders rather than being an "office-loom". Lord Coleridge CJ, who was the last holder of the office of Chief Justice of the Court of Common Pleas, retained his collar, which then passed to each Baron Coleridge by succession. Lord Coleridge CJ, however, was lambasted by one Judge for retaining the SS collar: MacKinnon, *supra*, 31.
23. Derriman, *supra*, 170.
24. *Ibid*.

From left to right: Sir Anthony Clarke MR (later Lord Clarke of Stone-cum-Ebony), Lord Falconer of Thoroton LC, Lord Phillips of Worth Matravers CJ and Sir Igor Judge (later Lord Judge CJ), at the Royal Courts of Justice, for the swearing in ceremony of Lord Phillips as Lord Chief Justice on 3 October 2005. Contributor: PA Images / Alamy Stock Photo

Top, left. Lord Alverstone CJ (1842-1915), later appointed Viscount Alverstone, and Lord Chief Justice from 1900 to 1913, approaches Westminster Abbey as part of the Judges' procession from the Royal Courts of Justice, for the annual religious service to mark the beginning of the legal year on 12 October 1911. Contributor: Chronicle / Alamy Stock Photo

Left. Former Lord Chief Justice of England and Wales Lord Thomas of Cwmgiedd CJ (2013-2017) at the annual procession of Judges for the Opening of the new term at Westminster on 1 October 2013. Contributor: WENN Ltd / Alamy Stock Photo

Top, right. Lord Lane (1918-2005), Lord Chief Justice of England and Wales (1980-1992), with his train-bearer, at the annual procession of Judges during the Opening of the Law Term in circa 1990. Contributor: Sally and Richard Greenhill / Alamy Stock Photo

The Lord Chancellor and Court of Appeal of England and Wales

For ceremonial occasions, the Lord Chancellor, the Master of the Rolls, the President of the Family Division and the Chancellor of the High Court, as well as the Lords Justices of Appeal,[25] wear a black damask robe trimmed with gold lace with lace bansa, frill and ruffles, a court coat, waistcoat and knee breeches of black cloth, together with a wig bag (or rosette), black silk stockings and gilt buckled shoes, along with a full-bottomed wig.[26] The Master of the Roll's black and gold gown has gold lace trimmings which are slightly different to those of the Lords Justices of Appeal and has a train which is borne by a clerk when he walks.[27] This form of ceremonial dress is due to the influence of the dress worn by Judges sitting in the Court of Chancery which later extended to the Lords Justices of the Court of Appeal.

Procession of the Lord Chancellor, Viscount Simonds, followed by the Master of the Rolls and other Lord Justices of Appeal, during the Opening of the Law Term on 10 October 1954. Contributor: Keystone Pictures USA / Alamy Stock Photo

Almost sixty years later, the same procession is taking place, with the Lord Chancellor Ken Clarke QC and Lord Chief Justice of England and Wales, Lord Judge and the Master of the Rolls behind them in 2012.
© Crown Copyright

25. The title "Lord Justice of Appeal" dates from 1876 when Parliament - at the behest of Disraeli - substituted this title for the earlier title of "Judge of Appeal" which dated from 1873: *ibid*, 176.
26. *Court Dress, supra*, 3.3.1; Correspodnence from G.P. Coldstream to Sir Sidney Abrahams dated 15 June 1954 enclosing Ede & Ravenscroft's "Judges' Robing List" of March 1953: Lord Chancellor's Office, LCO 66/42.
27. Derriman, *supra*, 175.

County Court and Crown Court

On ceremonial occasions, Circuit Judges of both the County Court and Crown Court wear a violet robe faced with lilac, a lilac casting hood worn over the left shoulder, underneath a matching violet hood faced with lilac, as well as knee breeches, stockings and buckled shoes with a lace jabot (it was agreed in 1971 that bands not be worn with the jabot)[28] and a full-bottomed wig and white gloves in hand.

County Court and other Judges processing from Westminster Abbey to the House of Lords on 3 October 2016. Contributor: Paul Marriott / Alamy Stock Photo

28. It has been reported that at the opening of the new Law Courts in Maidstone, Kent in February 1984, the Lord Chief Justice commented that the Circuit Judges present seemed to him to be incorrectly dressed because they were wearing both the jabot and bands, which had become a common practiice at the time; however, a the Lord Chancellor approved a reminder be sent to Circuit Judges in late 1985 that the recent practice of Judges wearing both jabot and bands is unjustified and that bands should not be worn by Circuit Judges on ceremonial occasions: Correspondence from T. S. Legg to the Lord Chancellor, dated 25 November 1985, Lord Chancellor's Office: LCO 66/42.

County Court Judges in their violet robes and hoods faced with lilac, with black girdles and lilac casting-hoods underneath the hood at the annual Opening of the Law Term procession in 2012. © Crown Copyright

Recorders

On ceremonial occasions, the Recorders of each city wear broadly the same robe of scarlet, similar to that worn by High Court Judges, but with a different cut and black velvet facings for both the robe and hood.[29] They also wear a black velvet casting-hood worn over the left shoulder in the same fashion as that of a Circuit Court Judge.

County Court Judges in their violet robes and hoods faced with lilac, with black girdles and lilac casting-hoods underneath the hood, behind the Honorary Recorders in their scarlet robes and hoods with black facings, at the annual Opening of the Law Term procession on 2 October 2017. Contributor: See Li / Alamy Stock Photo

29. *Ibid*, 185; Correspondence from the Rt. Hon. The Lord Thomas of Cwmgiedd to the writer, 11 September 2017.

Supreme Court of the United Kingdom

Prior to the abolition of the appellate committee of the House of Lords, the Lords of Appeal in Ordinary wore ordinary day dress during hearings and mourning dress on ceremonial occasions. However, on upon the transfer of the Law Lords into the new Supreme Court of the United Kingdom in October 2009, the now Justices of the Supreme Court decided to continue to wear ordinary business dress during normal sittings and would wear ceremonial robes of black damask with gold lace similar to those worn by the Lords Justices of Appeal (but with a flap at the back of the robe which pictures the symbol of the Supreme Court) on ceremonial occasions such as the opening of the Legal Year, the State Opening of Parliament in the House of Lords and at the swearing-in of a new Justice of the Supreme Court.

The basis for the adoption of the ceremonial gown upon the creation of the Supreme Court of the United Kingdom was due to the former Lords of Appeal in Ordinary undertaking their judicial functions as a committee of the House of Lords, rather than as a separate court and this change in attire reflected that fact:

> The creation of the Supreme Court as a court, as opposed to a Committee of the Upper House of Parliament, made it appropriate for justices to have bespoke ceremonial robes in common with other supreme courts.
> They belong to the court, not the justices, and have been designed to last at least 50 years, making a unit cost of around £200 a year.[30]

Justices of the Supreme Court of the United Kingdom attending the Judge's service this morning to mark opening of the Michaelmas Law Term on 1 October 2009. © Crown Copyright

30. "£140,000 bill for Supreme Court robes judges will hardly wear," Daily Mail, 13 December 2009, <http://www.dailymail.co.uk/news/article-1235344/140-000-Supreme-Court-robes-judges-hardly-wear.html> (accessed 14 June 2018).

In terms of the appropriate court dress worn by the Bar when appearing in the Supreme Court, it was announced on 21 November 2011 by the President of the Supreme Court, Lord Phillips of Worth Matravers P, that advocates appearing before the Court or the Judicial Committee of the Privy Council may, by agreement, dispense with any or all of the elements of traditional court dress:

> The Justices agree that this development would further underline the Court's commitment to providing an appropriate environment for considered discussion of legal issues, and is in line with the Court's goal to make this process as accessible as possible.
>
> The Justices of the Court do not wear legal dress themselves and have decided not to impose this obligation on advocates appearing before them. In future, provided that all the advocates in any particular case agree, they may communicate to the Registrar their wish to dispense with part or all of court dress. The Court will normally agree to such a request.[31]

Reforms to Working Day Dress of English Judges in 2008

On 12 July 2007, the former Lord Chief Justice of England and Wales, Lord Phillips of Worth Matravers CJ (later Senior Lord of Appeal in Ordinary and President of the Supreme Court of the United Kingdom) announced changes to the working day dress of Judges in England and Wales, which was initially meant to come into effect on 1 January 2008,[32] but was postponed to come into effect on 1 October 2008.[33] In announcing the changes, Lord Phillips of Worth Matravers said:

> At present High Court judges have no less than five different sets of working dress, depending on the jurisdiction in which they are sitting and the season of the year. After widespread consultation it has been decided to simplify this and to cease wearing wigs, wing collars and bands in civil and family jurisdictions. While there will never be unanimity of view about court dress, the desirability of these changes has a broad measure of agreement.[34]

A new civil robe - designed by fashion designer Betty Jackson CBE - was introduced which replaced the traditional robes worn by Judges in the civil and family divisions in open court. The new robes also have coloured tabs at the neck which indicate the rank of a Judge, namely gold for the heads of the Division and Lords Justices of the Court of Appeal; red for Judges of the High Court; pink for members of the High Court Masters Group (which includes

---

31. Supreme Court of the United Kingdom, Revised guidance on court dress at the UK Supreme Court, Press Notice No 12/2011, 12 November 2011.
32. Judicial Communications Office, Lord Chief Justice announces reforms to court working dress, Press Release, 12 July 2007.
33. Practice Direction (Court Dress) (No 5) and Amendment No 20 to the Consolidated Criminal Practice Directions (Court Dress), issued by Lord Phillips of Worth Matravers on 31 July 2008.
34. Judicial Communications Office, Lord Chief Justice announces reforms to court working dress, Press Release, 12 July 2007.

the Masters of the Chancery and Queen's Bench Division, District Judges of the Principal Registry of the Family Division,[35] Bankruptcy Registrars and Costs Judges and blue for District Judges.[36] However, Circuit judges, in accordance with their wish, continue to wear the same violet robe faced with lilac with a black girdle and lilac casting hood but without the wig, wing collar and bands.[37]

There was no change to the dress of Judges sitting in criminal proceedings, other than that the scarlet robes faced with taffeta was no longer required to be worn during the summer and that the scarlet robe faced with miniver can now be worn throughout the year by Judges trying criminal cases at first instance, although the summer robes can still be worn.[38] The Judges continue to wear the black silk gown over court dress with bands and a bench wig in the Criminal Division of the Court of Appeal as well as in the Central Criminal Court.

Lord Phillips of Worth Matravers CJ (as he then was) trying out the new civil robes for the press, which replaced the traditional black and violet nisi prius robes on 1 October 2008. He is standing next to the designer of the new robes, Betty Jackson. The coloured labels which resemble the white bands indicate the seniority of the Judge (red representing a Judge of the High Court of England and Wales.
Contributor: PA Images / Alamy Stock Photo

35. The then President of the Family Division, Sir Mark Potter, provided additional guidance for Judges sitting on family cases that are conducted in private directing that "there is good reason that a gown should not be worn by any of the judges listed in the said paragraph 2 when the judge is sitting in family proceedings [and in the Court of Protection], otherwise than in open court": Judicial Communications Office, Practice Direction handed Down for Court Working Dress, Press Release, 31 July 2008, p 4.

36. Practice Direction (Court Dress) (No 5) and Amendment No 20 to the Consolidated Criminal Practice Directions (Court Dress), issued by Lord Phillips of Worth Matravers on 31 July 2008, at para [3].

37. *Ibid*, at para [2].

38. *Ibid*, at para [5]. A new paragraph I.1.2 was inserted in the Consolidated Criminal Practice Direction handed down by the former Lord Chief Justice Lord Woolf on 8 July 2002 stating that "High Court Judges hearing criminal cases shall wear the winter criminal robe year-round. Scarlet summer robes are no longer issued or worn" (*ibid*, at para [6]). However, this was replaced by Part A.2 of Division XII of the consolidated *Criminal Practice Directions 2015* [2015] EWCA Crim 1567 which provides that "High Court Judges hearing criminal cases may wear the winter criminal robe year round. However, scarlet summer robes may be worn." Thus, the option of wearing either the winter or summer scarlet robes remains in place.

District Court Judges wearing their new robes with blue tabs indicating that they are District Court Judges, at the opening of the law term ceremony in 2012. © Crown Copyright

However, even though the reforms provided that scarlet robes faced with miniver would be retained for Judges sitting in criminal trials and on Red Letter Days, the accompanying illustration published in the Judiciary website confusingly shows a Judge wearing the summer scarlet robes faced with taffeta (the wearing of which was no longer compulsory from October 2008), though without the scarlet casting hood (which has not been abolished).[39] Furthermore, former Lord Chief Justice of England and Wales, Lord Thomas of Cwmgiedd CJ (2013-2017), continued to wear the scarlet robes faced with taffeta on ceremonial occasions, such as during the swearing-in ceremony of Lord Chancellor Lidington in 2017.[40]

39. This can be seen in the following link: Court Dress - Examples, Courts and Tribunals Judiciary, <https://www.judiciary.uk/about-the-judiciary/who-are-the-judiciary/court-dress/examples/> (accessed on 5 June 2018).

40. Given that the Lord Chief Justice's robes were inherited from previous Lord Chief Justices, he therefore has the advantage of wearing the summer scarlet robes faced with taffeta in hot weather: Correspondence from the Rt. Hon. The Lord Thomas of Cwmgiedd to the writer, 11 September 2017.

Lord Thomas of Cwmgiedd CJ (far right) wearing the traditional scarlet robes, hood and mantle faced with shot grey taffeta at the recent appointment ceremony of the new Lord Chancellor, the Rt. Hon. David Lidington MP (centre) on 19 June 2017, and on the left stands the Master of the Rolls, Sir Terence Etherton. This form of dress was, prior to October 2008, worn by all High Court Judges presiding over criminal matters during the summer.
© Crown Copyright

Thus, the current use of the ceremonial and working day robes of Judges in England and Wales is as follows:

Justices of the Supreme Court	Do not robe to sit judicially. For ceremonial occasions: black damask robe embroidered with gold lace over normal or mourning dress
Lords Justices of Appeal	Ceremonial dress: Black court tail coat and waistcoat; knee breeches with steel buckles, black silk stockings and court shoes with steel buckles, lace jabot and lace sleeve ruffles, black damask robe embroidered with gold lace, full bottomed wig, with white gloves in hand. Sitting in the Court of Appeal (Criminal Division): Black court coat and waistcoat, black silk gown, plain bands and short bench wig Sitting in the Court of Appeal (Civil Division): the new civil robe of blue cloth with faux fur trimmings down the robes and on the cuffs with two gold tabs at the neck, without a wig
High Court Judges	Ceremonial dress: Black knee breeches with steel buckles, black silk stockings and court shoes with steel buckles, scarlet robe of cloth, hood and mantle trimmed with miniver, black scarf, girdle, white bands, full bottomed wig, with black cap and white gloves in hand Working dress according to Division: (i) Queen's Bench Division: Sitting in the Crown Court (crime) and on Red Letter Days during all terms: scarlet robe trimmed with miniver (or silk), black scarf and girdle, scarlet casting-hood, plain bands and bench wig Sitting in the High Court (civil) during all terms: the new civil robe of blue cloth with faux fur trimmings down the robes and on the cuffs with two red tabs at the neck, without a wig (ii) Chancery Division Sitting in Court: the new civil robe of blue cloth with faux fur trimmings down the robes and on the cuffs with two red tabs at the neck, without a wig On Red Letter Days during all terms: scarlet robe trimmed with miniver etc same as worn by Judges of the Queen's Bench Division

High Court Judges	(iii) Family Division Sitting in Court (including when trying civil cases on circuit (nisi prius)): the new civil robe of blue cloth with faux fur trimmings down the robes and on the cuffs with two red tabs at the neck, without a wig When trying criminal cases and on Red Letter Days during all terms: scarlet robe trimmed with miniver etc same as worn by Judges of the Queen's Bench Division
Circuit Judges	Ceremonial dress: Violet robe of cloth with mauve (lilac) silk facings and cuffs and corresponding hood and a mauve casting-hood, black girdle, lace jabot and lace sleeve ruffles, black knee breeches with steel buckles, black silk stockings and court shoes with steel buckles, full bottomed wig and white gloves in hand When trying civil cases in the County Court: violet robe of cloth with mauve (lilac) silk facings and cuffs and a mauve casting-hood, plain bands, black girdle, without wig, wing collar and bands When trying criminal cases in the Crown Court: violet robe of cloth with mauve (lilac) silk facings and cuffs and a scarlet casting-hood, black girdle, wing collar and bands and bench wig
District Judges	Ceremonial dress: the new civil robe of blue cloth with faux fur trimmings down the robes and on the cuffs with two blue tabs at the neck, with a barrister's tye wig Sitting in open court: same as above, without the wig
Masters and Registrars	Sitting in open court: the new civil robe of blue cloth with faux fur trimmings down the robes and on the cuffs with two pink tabs at the neck, without a wig

The Rt Hon. the Lord Burnett of Maldon PC (1958-), current Lord Chief Justice of England and Wales (2017-), wearing the traditional habit of a High Court Judge, namely the scarlet robe, hood and mantle faced with miniver, black girdle, black scarf, white bands, white gloves and a full-bottomed wig, along with the SS chain. This scarlet robe, hood and mantle have been worn by Lord Chief Justices, practically unchanged, since at least the fourteenth century, highlighting the continuity of English Judges' robes.
Contributor: PA Images / Alamy Stock Photo

Present Dress Policy of the English Bar

As for the current dress policy of the English Bar, it was announced on 2 June 2009 by the Chairman of the Bar Council, Desmond Browne QC, that, following the issuing of Practice Directions by the Lord Chief Justice of England and Wales on 31 July 2008, the Bar Council carried out two surveys of the legal profession along with the Specialist Bar Associations prior to indicating its strong preference for the maintenance of the prevailing position with respect to when and where court dress (i.e., wigs, gowns, bands and wing collars) should be worn.[41]

The Revised Guidance provided that court dress was to be worn by counsel in the Court of Appeal, the High Court (Chancery Division trials and appeals, Queen's Bench Division trials, the Administrative Court on all occasions, and during contested divorce and nullity petitions in the Family Division of the High Court). Court dress is also worn in all trials in, and appeals from trials to, the County Court, in the Crown Court (apart from bail applications heard in chambers) and on all occasions when the liberty of the subject is involved except in the Magistrates Court.[42]

Thus, the English Bar continue to wear court dress, including the wig, in the High Court and Court of Appeal of England and Wales, even on occasions when Judges wear their new civil robes without a wig, with such policy being approved by the then Lord Chief Justice:

> I welcome and approve the guidance which the Bar Council has published today on court working dress, to run in parallel with the changes to judicial court working dress that take effect on 1 October this year. I am grateful to the Bar for having reached agreement with the Law Society and Institute of Legal Executives before producing their guidance.[43]

41. Court Dress: Revised Guidance from the Chairman of the Bar Council of England and Wales, Desmond Browne QC, 2 June 2009, p 1.

42. *Ibid*, 2-3. In this guidance, "business suits" means dark coloured formal non-court dress, "Court dress" means wigs, gowns, wing collars and bands or collarettes, "trials" includes any final hearing of a Part 7 Claim, Part 8 Claim or a Petition pursuant to the *Civil Procedure Rules 1998*: *ibid*.

43. Judicial Communications Office, Practice Direction handed Down for Court Working Dress, Press Release, 31 July 2008, 1.

Right. Opening of the law year procession at Westminster Abbey on 10 October 1957. Miss Rose Heilbron Q.C. (later a Judge of the High Court) can be seen on the left with other Queen's Counsel in procession from the Abbey to the House of Lords - after attending the Judge's service this morning to mark opening of the Michaelmas Law Term. Contributor: Keystone Pictures USA / Alamy Stock Photo

Below. Almost 60 years later, Queen's Counsel make the same procession in the same ceremonial attire to mark the opening of the law term on 2 October 2017. Contributor: Gavin Rodgers / Alamy Stock Photo

The Judges of the Supreme Court of New South Wales continue the tradition of wearing the scarlet robes and hoods faced with miniver and full-bottomed wigs. This photograph was taken of the swearing-in ceremony of current Chief Justice the Hon. Tom Bathurst AC at the Banco Court, Queen's Square, Sydney, on 1 June 2011

CHAPTER 5

Court Dress in Australia

Adoption of Court Dress in Australia

Court dress in Australia was one of the many customs and practices of England which was inherited in Australia at the time of British colonisation in 1788 and thereafter.[1] As was the case in England, the manner in which the Bench and Bar dressed in a court during the early decades of the colony was, and has always been ever since, overwhelmingly a matter of custom and tradition.

Sir Victor Windeyer (1900-1987)[2] has stated that the adoption of court dress by the legal profession in Australia was due to the fact that the early Barristers were from the English Bar and therefore simply continued to wear the customary dress of their office in colonial Australia, a practice which has continued to this day:

> The wearing of wigs and gowns by the Bar began in New South Wales in the 1820s, and was firmly established by the announcement in 1834 of the Imperial Government's approval of the rule made by the judges of the Supreme Court for the separation of barristers from attorneys. Those then called to the Bar had all been called in England. They were thus entitled to wear the costume of their office. As it was to be a long time before solicitors would be heard in the Supreme Court, a wig and gown became, as in England, the dress required for audience in court and the exclusive garb of those lawyers entitled to be heard. In the Port Phillip District, before the separation of Victoria from New South Wales, the same practice prevailed.[3]

The formal adoption of English legal dress in Australia can be seen in the adoption by early Australian courts of the English principle that a barrister is both invisible and inaudible if appearing before the court improperly robed. Indeed the principle underlying the decision of Lord Coleridge in *R v Whitaker*[4] to refuse to see or hear Counsel unless fully robed and bewigged can be seen in the decision of *The Queen v Matthews*,[5] which is Australian authority for the proposition that a Judge can refuse to hear Counsel if in breach of the decorum of his or her court.[6]

Note: illuminated letter from page 66.

1. Windeyer, *supra*, 402.

2. Justice of the High Court of Australia from 1958 to 1972.

3. *Ibid*. This can also be seen in the following early account by C. J. Baker, a barrister of the Inner Temple, who visited Sydney and Melbourne in 1841 and noted that in court proceedings in Melbourne "wigs and gowns are worn, and proceedings generally are conducted in the same way as at home" (C. J. Baker, *Sydney and Melbourne* (London, 1845), 33).

4. (1844) 8 JPJO 390.

5. (1887) 8 LR (NSW) 45.

6. (1887) 8 LR (NSW) 45 at 52 per Sir G Innes J: "It seems to me that it is only in reference to acts of misconduct or breaches of decorum that the Judge has a right to refuse to hear counsel. It is obvious that such a principle is well founded." A modern example of the application of this principle can be seen in the Supreme Court of Victoria where a Judge refused to hear Counsel who had appeared before him wearing wigs after the Chief Justice had issued directions to Judges to discontinue wearing wigs in court.

Usages relating to court dress have over time been laid down in rules and procedure by the courts themselves but have rarely been the subject of legislative interference. One of the rare legislative interventions occurred in 1975, when the Commonwealth Parliament, by the then section 97(4) of the *Family Law Act 1975* (Cth), forbade Judges and Counsel to wear robes in matrimonial causes.

In *Russell v Russell*,[7] the High Court of Australia considered whether s 97(4) of the *Family Law Act 1975* (Cth) was valid with respect to State courts exercising federal jurisdiction. Chief Justice Barwick and Justice Gibbs (who were in the minority) concluded that s 97(4) was invalid because it interfered with the organisation of the courts and did not relate merely to practice and procedure in the exercise of federal jurisdiction. As to the matter of court dress generally, Barwick CJ stated the following:

> The robing of the judge is not required by any State statutory law, but is part of the traditional inheritance of the State court as a court in the common law tradition. … in my opinion, neither the validity nor the regularity of what the court does would be affected by the wearing of or the dispensation with, judicial robes. …
>
> It seems to me that s 97 does not form part of the process of investing jurisdiction in State courts. I am quite clear that the section, in so far as it purports to command the court in the matter of dress, either of the judge or of counsel, is beyond the power of the Parliament. It is, in my opinion, inherent in the concept of a court that it can decide for itself how its members will be attired, and what dress it will expect of those who are to appear before it as representatives of parties. This is not a matter which, in my opinion, goes to the nature of the jurisdiction of the court, nor to the manner of the exercise: it is not relevantly part of the rules of procedure for the hearing of a matter. In my opinion, the command attempted to be given by s 97(4) can be disregarded. It is for the State courts to decide for themselves whether their judges will or will not robe, unless the State legislature should otherwise provide. …
>
> I should add expressly, lest it should not be appreciated that I have implicitly said so, that the wearing of robes and the place and nature of the place where the court sits are not, in my opinion, in any relevant sense part of the rules of practice or procedure of the court in exercising its jurisdiction in the hearing and decision of a case. They relate to the court's own organization and not to the procedure to be adopted in determining a matter.[8]

Justice Gibbs was of a similar view, also in dissent:

> The judges of the Supreme Courts, when sitting in court, traditionally wear robes. Some persons consider that robes are outmoded and should be dispensed with; others regard them as a valuable symbol of the antiquity of the honourable traditions of the law and as a means of adding to the dignity of

7. (1976) 134 CLR 495.
8. (1976) 134 CLR 495, 505-506.

> proceedings that are of their nature serious and important. We are not required to join in this controversy. It would not matter if we thought that judges could perform the duties of their office equally well if they were unrobed or that matrimonial proceedings would more appropriately be conducted in an informal atmosphere by judges wearing informal dress. The question to be decided is to be determined by a consideration of the Constitution, and not by our opinions on matters of policy of that kind. If the Parliament considers that matrimonial jurisdiction should be exercised by judges who do not robe, it can create a federal court in which the wearing of robes is proscribed - as it in fact has done. If it chooses to invest a State court with jurisdiction, it has no power to direct the judges of that court to depart from their existing standards of judicial dress. The question may be thought to be of no great importance, but its implications are by no means insignificant. The robes worn by the judges of the Supreme Court are a mark of their status. If the Parliament could legislate as to what the judges shall or shall not wear, it could force upon a court a mode of dress incompatible with its former dignity and status. Such a law might be regarded as changing the nature or character of the court, but whether or not that view would be correct, the law would in my opinion be one with respect to the court itself. In one sense, such a law might be said to be a law as to practice and procedure.[9]

Although with the majority on the validity question, Mason J seems to have agreed with the minority that "[t]he absence of robes might well be thought to diminish the air of formality which would otherwise prevail in the proceedings."[10] However, Stephen J upheld the prohibition in s 97(4) as being incidental to investiture with federal jurisdiction and as not touching upon the *Commonwealth Constitution* or organisation of the courts:

> The requirement that robes should not be worn does not, in my view, touch upon the constitution or organization of a court. In McPherson v. McPherson (1936) AC 177, at p 198, their Lordships observed that the effect of the absence of robes was to make proceedings "in one respect less formal than those of an ordinary trial"; but robed or unrobed the tribunal in question remains unaltered in its constitution and general organization. The widespread, if not universal, absence in Australian jurisdictions of any specification, statutory or otherwise, of what robes shall be worn is indicative of how far removed is this topic from matters affecting the constitution of Supreme Courts; when, as has occurred from time to time in certain Australian jurisdictions, a radical change has occurred in the robes worn on the bench this no more effected a change in the court's constitution than did the donning of wigs by the South Australian Supreme Court bench for the first time in the 1850s or their adoption of the judicial scarlet in the 1870s: Hannan's Life of Chief Justice Way

9. (1976) 134 CLR 495, 519-520.

10. (1976) 134 CLR 495, 536. Justices Mason and Jacobs, however, upheld the provision as a matter of procedure, not affecting the *Commonwealth Constitution*, structure and organisation of the courts.

(1960), p. 101. What a bench of judges customarily wears or requires counsel to wear at any particular time forms no part of the constitution or organization of that court.

...

If one aim of the Family Law Act is, so far as possible, to dispense with formality it is, I think, properly incidental to the investing of jurisdiction in State Supreme Courts to require that their proceedings shall themselves be free of the formality which wig and gown confer. Accordingly I conclude that s. 97(4) is validly authorized by s. 77(iii).[11]

One of the few other interventions by the legislature occurred in the Australian Capital Territory, where in 2002, the Legislative Council adopted a "policy" in relation to robing in the Supreme Court, which the Court then made the subject of a practice direction.[12] This intervention was quite limited, to the effect that "When the Court robes, counsel will robe" and "Wigs are only required where one is worn by the particular Judge or Judicial Registrar." However, it included a mandatory provision (which differs from customary practice) that "when the Judge or Master removes his or her wig, counsel will do likewise".[13]

Another legislative intervention was the insertion of s 9B in the *Supreme Court Act 1986* (Vic), which provided that "All matters pertaining to the robing of Judges of the Court are to be determined by the Chief Justice after consultation with the Council of the Judges." This was inserted by s 453 (Sch. 1, item 80.2) of the *Legal Practice Act 1996* (Vic).

Prior to the decision of *Russell v Russell* there were a number of cases dealing with the issue of court dress and the effect it had, if any, on court proceedings. In *McPherson v McPherson*,[14] the Judicial Committee of the Privy Council observed that the effect of the absence of robes was to make proceedings "in one respect less formal than those of an ordinary court".[15] Later in *St Edmundsbury Diocesan Board v Clark*,[16] Sir Robert Megarry V-C stated the following:

Robes are convenient in normal circumstances as an indication of the functions of those engaged in the proceedings and as enhancing the formality and dignity of a grave occasion. In their appearance they also lessen visual differences of age, sex and clothing, and so aid concentration on the real issues without distraction. But robes are not essential, and the court may dispense with them where there is good reason. Jurisdiction is neither conferred nor excluded by mere matters of attire or locality, and I need not discuss the numberless

11. (1976) 134 CLR 495, 506, 531-532.
12. Supreme Court of the Australian Capital Territory, Practice Direction 2002/1, 27 May 2002.
13. This is the policy now adopted in Supreme and County Courts of Victoria.
14. [1936] AC 177.
15. [1936] AC 177 at 198.
16. [1973] 1 Ch 323 at 330.

occasions upon which judges have exercised a variety of judicial functions in unusual places without the aid of robes for them or for counsel, from Lord Lyndhurst LC in a box at the opera to Sir Lancelot Shadwell V-C while bathing in the Thames,[17] and Sir Samuel Evans P in a dressing-gown in his bedroom.[18]

In *Re Douglas*,[19] Young J had to consider whether the "uniformity in the legal profession", sought to be brought about by the *Legal Profession Amendment (National Practising Certificates) Act 1996* (NSW), had had the result that a very experienced New South Wales solicitor, who was to appear for an accused in the District Court of New South Wales, could do so in the dress customarily associated with a barrister. His Honour noted as follows:

> the Australian courts just adopted the English system last century and then adjusted the clothing for local requirements. When there was a change from bar ties to jabots, what seems to have happened is that the judges of the superior court as a collegiate body indicated that they would see counsel in jabots instead of bar ties and the other courts followed suit. This would seem to indicate that the power is a power in the courts, query the superior court, to be exercised by all the judges. Just how the judges internally exercise that power is a matter for them.[20]

In the twenty-first century, the Bench and Bar in all jurisdictions in Australia continue to wear court dress, in one form of another, which symbolically underlines the English antecedents and heritage of Australia's common law and administration of justice. Indeed, apart from Western Australia, Judges and Barristers throughout the country still wear the bench wig and tie wig respectively which has become the recognisable symbol of the legal profession in Australia.

However, as is the case with law reform and court practice and procedure, the rules relating to court dress vary across each of the Australian states and territories. As each state and territory court determines its own rules of court and practices, so too is the case with the question of the appropriate apparel to be worn by the Bench and Bar.

---

17. Sir Lancelot Shadwell V-C (1779-1850) was the last Vice Chancellor of England (the current office of 'Chancellor of the High Court' being a separate and statutory office created in 1970 which holder until 2005 was also known as the 'Vice-Chancellor'). Shadwell V-C was in the habit of bathing every day, irrespective of the weather, in one of the creeks of the Thames near Barn Elms, and it has been reported that during one of his regular baths he is said to have granted an injunction on one occasion in the long vacation: Roget, *History of the 'Old Water Colour' Society*, 1891, ii. 210–11.

18. Sir Samuel Thomas Evans P (1859-1918) was the last person appointed as Queen's Counsel by Queen Victoria, and was later appointed as President of the Probate, Divorce and Admiralty Division of the High Court of Justice in March 1910. According to Almeric Fitzroy, "on appointment to the Presidency of the division, he hardly knew a ship's stem from its stern, and he therefore proceeded to take a trip to Gibraltar in a P. and 0. liner and spent the whole time on the bridge, so as to familiarize himself with the terminology of the cases with which he would have to deal": *The Spectator*, 5 June 1925, p 16.

19. (Unreported) NSWSC, 1 September 1998 (BC9804579 at 5).

20. *Ibid.*

Specifically, the robing requirements for Judges sitting in the various state and territory courts in Australia vary considerably. On one end of the spectrum, for example, the Judges of the Supreme Court of New South Wales wear three sets of robes and two types of wigs depending on the occasion: scarlet robes faced with miniver and full-bottomed wig for ceremonial occasions, scarlet robes faced with silk or taffeta and bench wig for criminal matters, and a black silk robe over court dress with a bench wig for civil matters. Whereas on the other end of the spectrum, Western Australia's Supreme Court Judges simply wear a black robe over normal attire for all sittings without a wig. And somewhere in the middle of this spectrum of court dress, in Queensland the Judges of the Supreme Court wear newly created robes for ceremonial occasions but wear the scarlet robes faced with taffeta and bench wig for criminal matters.

Portrait of J. H. Bent circa 1850, who sat as a judge of the old Supreme Court in New South Wales from 1814 to 1816. Attributed to the National Library of Australia

Supreme Court of New South Wales

As New South Wales was the first British colony to be established in Australia, the history of Judges' robes in Australia also naturally derives from this fledgling colony.[21] However, it is interesting to note that early in Australia's colonial history, administrators of justice did not adhere to a number of common law customs and traditions, notable among them being the adoption of court dress. This was partly due to the fact that neither the 'advocates' or 'judges' were in fact practising lawyers or trained judges:

> the judges were not judges in the strict sense of the word, and neither were the lawyers arguing cases before them legal practitioners in any orthodox sense of the notion. Since the Australian colonies had been conceived on the other side of the world as a giant prison farm, it had not been thought important to go to too much trouble in introducing English legal 'traditions' to this barbarous place. Consequently, those charged with judicial functions were public servants without any legal training. The practitioners who appeared before them at least had the benefit of legal training, but were debarred from practice in their home country as a consequence of the conviction that had led to their being transported. In other words they were emancipists - convicts who had served their time, and now were 'free'. Whilst there are not many descriptions of the dress of these quasi-judges and these emancipist practitioners in the courts of the day, a few crude paintings of their deliberations remain. These suggest that smart, formal attire was probably a reasonable description of the form of dress adopted by 'judges' and 'advocates' in the earliest Australian courts.[22]

However, by the 1820s, New South Wales was growing and the need for a sophisticated justice system increased, English Judges and Barristers began arriving in Australia and upon arrival immediately began remodelling the law and legal procedure so as to revert to, and align with, the legal customs and traditions in England.[23] It was around this time that the early Judges in the colony of New South Wales, having mostly been appointed from England, adopted the various forms of judicial dress worn in Westminster Hall, albeit initially with much simplification.[24] The portrait of Jeffery Hart Bent, the first Judge appointed in the colony of New South Wales,[25] who from 1814 to 1816 sat as a Judge of the old Supreme Court prior to the proclamation of the Third Charter

---

21. This is particularly so given that Van Diemen's Land (i.e., Tasmania) (1825), South Australia (1834), Victoria (1851) and Queensland (1859) all gradually separated from New South Wales, meaning that the same practices prevailed throughout the various colonies.
22. Rob McQueen, "Of Wigs and Gowns: A Short History of Legal and Judicial Dress in Australia," *Law Context: A Socio-Legal Journal* 16 (1999) 31, 44.
23. *Ibid*, 45.
24. Windeyer, *supra*, 402; Sugerman, *supra*, 39.
25. This was the first superior court of the Colony of New South Wales and was formerly known as the Supreme Court of Civil

of Justice in 1824, wore the black silk gown and bands.[26]

Barron Field replaced Bent as judge of the Supreme Court of Civil Judicature in May 1816, and he himself was succeeded by Sir John Wylde. Although there is no pictorial evidence of what they wore in the Supreme Court, it is probable that they too wore the then customary black silk gown and bands.[27] There is, however, a later portrait of Sir John Wylde as Chief Justice of the Cape of Good Hope wearing a scarlet robe but without a bench wig.[28] At the time of the establishment of the Supreme Court in 1824, however, there were no clear rules as to the appropriate dress of Judges.[29]

In 1834 under the Third Charter of Justice the new Supreme Court of New South Wales was established, replacing the former Supreme Court of Civil Judicature.[30] The new Supreme Court saw the appointment of a new Judge, Sir Francis Forbes, who became the first Chief Justice of New South Wales. The new Chief Justice broke with tradition by dispensing with the wearing of the bench wig in Court, his wife Lady Forbes explaining in her memoirs that "he considered it unsuited to the conditions of a young community."[31] Sir Francis had previously discarded the wig when he was Chief Justice of Newfoundland and continued that new practice in New South Wales.[32]

Judicature of New South Wales. It was established by letters patent dated 2 April 1814, now known as the *Second Charter of Justice of New South Wales*. The Supreme Court of Civil Judicature was replaced by the Supreme Court of New South Wales by letters patent sealed on 13 October 1823 and proclaimed on 17 May 1824, now known as the Third Charter of Justice.

26. Of J. H. Bent, Gleeson CJ has made the following remarks: "He is generally regarded, not only as the first judge in New South Wales, but also as the worst. The one thing he had to recommend him was a spirit of independence. He gave an early display of his mettle upon his arrival in Sydney, by refusing to disembark from his ship until the Governor arranged for a proper battery of guns to salute him. He refused to pay the road toll levied on users of Sydney's main road. He said he would be damned if he would pay any illegal tax. He called the gatekeeper a scoundrel, and threatened to put him in gaol. As a result, he was charged with toll evasion, convicted by a magistrate and fined two pounds. There being no Judicial Commission in those days, the matter was left to rest there. The Court presided over by Judge Bent only ever sat to hear one item of civil business. That was an application by three ex-convict attorneys for admission to practice. The judge, who was at risk of being outvoted by the two magistrates with whom he sat, peremptorily announced that the application was refused, and that he would never preside in a court where ex-convicts were admitted to practice. Soon afterwards he was recalled to England" (The Hon. M. Gleeson, 17 May 1999 at the 175th Anniversary Dinner of the Supreme Court of New South Wales <http://www.supremecourt.justice.nsw.gov.au/Documents/Publications/Speeches/175th%20Anniversary%20Speeches/175_06_anniv_scnsw_1999.05.17_gleeson.pdf> (accessed 1 March 2018).

27. Windeyer, *supra*, 402.

28. Portrait reproduced in Malcolm Henry Ellis, *Lachlan Macquarie* (Sydney: Dymocks, 1947) 372.

29. J.M. Bennett, *Sir Alfred Stephen: Third Chief Justice of New South Wales 1844-1873* (The Federation Press, 2009), 165.

30. The Supreme Court of New South Wales is the highest State court in New South Wales. The Court now operates under the *Supreme Court Act 1970* (NSW) and the *Civil Procedure Act 2005* (NSW). The Court is divided into the Common Law Division and the Equity Division. The Common Law Division deals with civil, criminal and administrative law matters. The Equity Division hears equity, probate, commercial, admiralty and protective matters. The Court also has a Court of Appeal and a Court of Criminal Appeal.

31. Lady Forbes, *Memoirs*, quoted in C. H. Currey, *Sir Francis Forbes, The first Chief Justice of New South Wales* (Sydney: Angus & Robertson, 1968) 5.

32. J. M. Bennett, *A History of Supreme Court of New South Wales* (Sydney: Law Book Company, 1974) 31; Bora Laskin, *The British Tradition in Canadian Law* (London, 1969), 31. During Forbe's time as Chief Justice of the Supreme Court of Newfoundland neither the bench nor the bar wore wigs (the whole matter of court dress appearing to depend more on the local tastes than the strict application of the traditional English customs) and there appears to have been no special rules or regulations regarding the question of dress in that jurisdiction until legislation was enacted in 1824 which reconstituted the Supreme Court of Newfoundland in its present form: Bennett, *ibid*, 253.

It has been suggested that this striking change to court decorum was due to Sir Francis's republican beliefs. At least that was the impression of his successor Sir James Dowling, who upon disembarking from his ship on a "fearfully hot" afternoon in February 1828 to take up the role of second puisne Judge of the Supreme Court, remarked that: "I wore my robes of office and wig. The Chief Justice wore his gown and bands, but no wig", and had formed the impression that Forbes CJ had a "roundhead republican look."[33] It appears that Forbes CJ's republican views were well known in the Colony, as it has also been reported that "Mr Chief Justice Forbes is a known republican, of which, indeed, he makes no secret, but rather expresses himself proud."[34]

However, the abolition of the wig by Forbes CJ did not last for long. The decision by Forbes CJ to discard the wig angered a small group of English-called barristers practising in Sydney, led by Dr Robert Wardell and Wentworth, who led the charge to pressure Forbes CJ to resume wearing the wig. It has been accounted that Wardell attacked Forbes CJ for discarding the wig at a dinner at the home of McLeay, the Colonial Secretary, in which Forbes CJ made disparaging remarks about the gown and wig, leaving him to explain to Wilmot-Horton:

> I used, upon that occasion, the only weapon which it became me to use - ridicule is the only active impediment you can employ against impertinence - I will affirm that upon no other occasion, can I charge my memory with the sin of having slandered wigs.[35]

The face-off between Wardell and Forbes CJ caused Wardell to complain to the Colonial Office, resulting in Wilmot-Horton writing a private letter of admonition to Forbes CJ in relation to, amongst other things, "the parable of the gown and wig", to which Forbes CJ replied on 7 March 1828 that:

> The first [i.e., the gown] I had always worn, not more from the propriety of the costume than for my liking of it - republican as my taste may be supposed, it was but in keeping, that I should entertain a liking for this exterior of the Roman citizens - ... and the second [i.e., the wig], I immediately assumed on the reading of your letter ... and it will be a great consolation, when I find my brains boiling under it in the summer, to know that I am performing my duty, and silencing a great scandal.[36]

The formal oil portrait of Sir Francis Forbes which is located in the Banco Court of the Supreme Court of New South Wales shows him in a violet robe faced with grey taffeta, which was the traditional English violet robes worn in

---

33. Journal (ML A485), 25 February 1828, 65.

34. J. Maudie, *The Felony of New South Wales*, (London: Angus & Robertson, 1965) 53.

35. J. M. Bennett, ed., *Some papers of Sir Francis Forbes : First Chief Justice in Australia* (Sydney: New South Wales Parliament, 1998) 61 at 185.

36. *Ibid.* It therefore seems that the recollection of the Australian, years afterwards on 26 September 1846 at 2192, that "before Mr Justice Dowling arrived, the Chief Justice never wore a wig" was not technically correct, and that it had nothing to do with Dowling J's arrival in Sydney.

Portrait of Sir Francis Forbes by an unknown artist, located in the Banco court of the Supreme Court of New South Wales.

nisi prius during the summer.[37] He is also wearing grey cuffs, lace bands beneath a white neckerchief and a scarlet sash (as opposed to the more traditional black cincture). The scarlet sash can be explained by Lady Forbes herself, who has written in her memoirs that it was "a broad crimson sash as worn by judges in Scotland."[38] There are also reports, starting from at least 1836, of the Judges of the Supreme Court of New South Wales wearing "purple robes" on the first day of the four Law Terms.[39] It is most likely that Forbes CJ wore this distinctive dress at ceremonial or full court sittings of the Supreme Court.[40]

Forbes CJ's successor, Sir James Dowling, also clearly wore the *nisi prius* violet robes, as seen in his official portrait by J. Dennis in 1840. The portrait depicts Dowling CJ in a violet robe and hood, with a scarlet casting-hood (which is incorrectly hanging over his hood when it should in fact be underneath it, or preferably not worn at all), scarlet cincture (i.e., girdle), laced bands and a bench wig. It has also been reported back in 1832 that Dowling CJ had even considered wearing scarlet robes, in the following rather humorous account:

---

37. J. M. Bennett, *Portraits of the Chief Justices of NSW 1821-1977* (St Ives: John Ferguson, 1977) p 5.
38. Lady Forbes, Memoirs, quoted by Currey, *supra*, 5. Sir Francis Forbes was of Scots descent and so the addition of the scarlet girdle to his dress seemed appropriate: Windeyer, *supra*, 402.
39. See e.g., "Supreme Court," *Sydney Gazette and New South Wales Advertiser*, Saturday, 17 September 1836, 3; "Law Intelligence," Sydney Herald, Monday 3 June 1839, 2; "Supreme Court," Sydney Monitor and Commercial Advertiser, Wednesday, 20 October 1841, 2; "Law Intelligence," *Sydney Herald*, Tuesday 11 January 1842, 2; "Civil Side," *Australian*, Thursday 21 April 1842, 2; "Sydney News," *Maitland Mercury and Hunter River General Advertiser*, Saturday 22 April 1843, 3; "Law Intelligence," *Sydney Herald*, Tuesday 18 July 1843, 2.
40. Bennett, *Sir Alfred Stephen*, *supra*, 165.

> We perceive … that the learned Judex Mr. Dowling has doffed the purple toga, and resumed his ordinary habits. … It is rumored - but we do not believe it, that the "Honorable Mr. Dowling, Justice," - means to try next the scarlet robe and ermine! Sir John Wylde, of Cape of Good Hope, Chief Justice, assumes the Chancellorial habitments, and moreover is my-Lorded! Why not then the second puisne Judge of New South Wales!- unless it be that ignorant people now-a-days think a scarlet mantle does not always mark the wearer as wise and perfect, any more than a black and white canomical always clothes the "man of God.[41]

Portrait of Sir James Dowling wearing the black silk gown over court dress and bands, without a wig, most likely during a civil proceeding. Date of photograph of painting circa 1870. Attributed to the National Library of Australia

It appears that the practice of wearing violet robes for ceremonial and criminal sittings of the Court continued, albeit initially, during the time of Sir Alfred Stephen CJ, for it has been reported that on Stephen CJ's first court appearance as Chief Justice on 21 October 1844, following Dowling CJ's death "Their Honors appeared in their purple robes as usual on the first day of the Term. The Bench was arrayed in mourning as a tribute of respect to the late Chief Justice."[42]

However, very shortly after his appointment the practice of wearing scarlet for criminal and ceremonial sittings of the Supreme Court commenced, although it is not entirely clear when this practice was introduced in the Supreme Court. However, it has been reported that on 28 December 1846, Stephen CJ and Therry J presided over a criminal sitting of the Supreme Court in Woolloomoolloo "both of whom appeared in scarlet robes, the proper robes for Judges sitting in criminal courts, and used *for the first time in this colony today.*"[43]

---

41. *Australian*, Sydney, Friday, 16 March 1832, 3.
42. *Australian*, Sydney, 22 October 1844, 807.
43. "Sydney News," *Maitland Mercury and Hunter River General Advertiser*, Wednesday, 30 December 1846, 2 (emphasis added).

Portrait of Sir James Dowling (1787-1844) by J. Dennis in 1840, the second Chief Justice of the Supreme Court of New South Wales and the first one to wear the wig. Sir James also appears to be the last Chief Justice of New South Wales to wear the summer violet robes faced with changeable taffeta traditionally worn by Judges sitting in Common Law Courts at Westminster Hall. Attributed to the Mitchell Library, State Library of New South Wales. Located in the Banco court of the Supreme Court of New South Wales.

Portrait of Sir John Nodes Dickinson, a Judge of the Supreme Court of New South Wales (1844-1861), by William Nicholas in circa 1848. Although not entirely clear, it is most likely that the robes worn by Dickinson J were the traditional violet robes, for the violet robes were still predominantly worn by Judges in the 1840s. Attributed to the National Library of Australia

However, it was not until Stephen CJ was succeeded by Sir James Martin CJ that the violet nisi prius robes were wholly replaced by the scarlet robes faced with miniver for ceremonial occasions, a practice which continues in New South Wales to this day.[44] On this point Kirby J has noted the following:

44. Cf. Superman P who argues that the change from nisi prius robes to scarlet commenced during the tenure of Stephen CJ: "it would appear that by about the time Sir Alfred Stephen (Chief Justice 1844-1873) commenced his long reign the judges were wearing red robes and full-bottomed wigs much as at the present day": Sugerman, *supra*, 39.

Something of the vanity of the man [i.e., Sir Alfred Stephen CJ] was demonstrated when he made his first appearance as Chief Justice wearing robes of violet. These were described by the local media as 'purple' and attributed to mourning for the late Chief Justice, whom he certainly had befriended. More likely, given the interval from the latter's death, was it that Stephen was marking the new era by a conscious colour coding. It was not until Sir James Martin, the fourth Chief Justice and Stephen's successor, that the tradition of wearing scarlet robes edged with fur was initiated to establish the dress for ceremonial occasions that persists into the current era.[45]

Upon his appointment on 19 November 1873, Sir James Martin wore the scarlet robes instead of the nisi prius violet robes, as has been reported in the following article which states that he wore:

> The scarlet gown trimmed with white fur, the black sash, scarlet tippet, and ermine hood; but with the small wig, as worn in the undress. The Puisne Judges were attired in the ordinary black silk robes.[46]

By the time of the chief justiceship of Sir Frederick Darley the current practice of wearing full-bottomed wigs, wing collar with plain white linen bands or lace jabots and a scarlet robe and hood faced with miniver for ceremonial occasions was permanently introduced, and continues to this day, as can be seen in the official photograph of the current Chief Justice, the Honourable Tom Bathurst AC. Upon Darley CJ's appointment on 7 December 1886, it has been reported that all the Puisne Judges were "attired in their scarlet and ermine robes" and that Darley CJ:

> was robed in the full judicial costume, wearing scarlet gown trimmed with white fur, black sash and scarlet tippet, and full-bottomed wig. His noble, dignified, and commanding presence … was worthy of England's greatest Judges.[47]

Portrait of Sir Alfred Stephen, third Chief Justice of New South Wales (1844-1873) attributed to J. P. Knight. In this portrait Stephen CJ is depicted in a court coat with laced jabots, which most likely represented his undress which he would wear in chambers. Located in the Banco court of the Supreme Court of New South Wales.

---

45. The Hon. Michael Kirby, *Australian Bar Review Book Review*, J.M. Bennett, *Sir Alfred Stephen: Third Chief Justice of New South Wales 1844-1873* (*Lives of the Australian Chief Justices* series), 2010, 6. See: <http://pandora.nla.gov.au/pan/96901/20160929-0803/www.michaelkirby.com.au/images/stories/speeches/2000s/2010_Speeches/2447.BookReview-SirAlfredStephen.pdf> (accessed 26 November 2017).
46. *Sydney Morning Herald*, 20 November 1873, 7.
47. *Herald*, 8 December 1886, 6.

Portrait of Sir Frederick Darley, fifth Chief Justice of New South Wales (1886-1910) by Sir John Longstaff, wearing the scarlet robe and hood faced with miniver, a black girdle, white bands and a full-bottomed wig. Darley CJ's ceremonial attire set the dress policy for ceremonial occasions and is still worn by New South Wales Supreme Court Judges for all ceremonial occasions, the only change being that some Judges choose to wear a jabot instead of bands and the black scarf is worn underneath the hood. Located in the Banco court of the Supreme Court of New South Wales.

Portrait of Sir James Martin by Miss E. Bell. Martin CJ appears to have introduced the practice of wearing scarlet robes faced with miniver for ceremonial occasions, as can be seen in his own portrait. Located in the Banco court of the Supreme Court of New South Wales.

Official photograph of current Chief Justice of New South Wales, the Hon. Tom Bathurst AC (2011-), taken on 10 June 2011. His Honour is wearing the scarlet robe and hood faced with miniver, with a laced jabot and black girdle and full-bottomed wig and white gloves in hand.

At present the Judges of the Supreme Court wear scarlet robes and hoods faced with taffeta with bands or jabots (either plain or laced) and a bench wig in criminal sittings both in the Trial Division and in the Court of Criminal Appeal. Although it is not clear when exactly the scarlet robes faced with silk were adopted by Judges of the Supreme Court of New South Wales, it is quite probable that they were adopted at the same time as the scarlet robes faced with miniver began to be worn during the chief justiceship of Sir Alfred Stephen. One clear indication that the scarlet silk robes were worn by Judges in the nineteenth century can be seen at the Opening of the Law Term ceremony in 1896 when it as reported at the time that due to the February humidity, the Judges opted to wear scarlet robes faced with silk with corresponding hoods rather than the much warmer scarlet robes faced with miniver.[48]

Portrait of William Owen, Chief Justice in Equity of the Supreme Court of New South Wales, engraved by H.S. Sadd, circa 1891. Interestingly, Owen CJ in Equity is wearing a full-bottomed wig and an elaborate robe similar to that worn by the Judges in the Court of Chancery Division, namely a black damask robe with gold lace. The Chancery robe was most likely adopted due to the equity division of the Supreme Court of New South Wales being separately administered from the common law division, with separate modes of pleading and practice, until the passage of the Supreme Court Act 1970 (NSW). Attributed to the National Library of Australia

There is also evidence of early Judges sitting in the Equity Division of the Supreme Court earing the ceremonial dress associated with the Court of Chancery, namely the black damask gown with gold lace over court dress and a full-bottomed wig. This can be clearly seen in the portraits of William Owen and Charles James Manning, both Chief Judges in Equity, dating 1891 and 1896 respectively. This may have arisen due to the fact that the equity division of the Supreme Court of New South Wales was separately administered from the common law division, and has its own separate modes of pleading and practice, until the passage of the *Supreme Court Act 1970* (NSW). However, it is not clear whether this dress was ever worn in court, for a portrait of the Judges sitting en banc in the Supreme Court in 1907 depicts Sir William Owen wearing the scarlet robes rather than the chancery gown.

48. "Their Honours ... wore full-bottomed wigs, but on account of the warm weather they discarded their hitherto worn robes of scarlet and ermine for robes of scarlet silk with grey hoods" (*Evening News*, 17 February 1896, 6).

Portrait of Charles James Manning, a Judge of the Supreme Court of New South Wales from 1889 until his death in 1898, most likely taken at the time of his appointment as Chief Judge in Equity in 1896, showing him wearing the Chancery gown of black damask with elaborate gold lace, breeches and buckled shoes, with a laced jabot, court coat and waistcoat and full-bottomed wig. The Chancery gown signified his position as a Judge in the equity division of the Supreme Court. Attributed to the National Library of Australia

Portrait of the Full Bench of the Supreme Court of New South Wales in 1907. Pictured from left to right: Pring J, Cohen J, Sir William Owen J, Darley CJ, Sir George Simpson J, A. H. Simpson J and P. W. Street J.

It is interesting to note that Judges of the Supreme Court of New South Wales always wear the hood whenever they are wearing their scarlet robes (with either silk or miniver facings) on all occasions, whereas in other jurisdictions in Australia (as well as in England and Wales) the custom was for Judges to only wear the hood for ceremonial occasions. Given that it was a common practice during the nineteenth century for Trial and Appellate Judges to wear the hood in all sittings at Westminster Hall, it appears that this tradition - even though it was subsequently abandoned by English Judges - has continued on in New South Wales to this day.

The casting-hood is another item which is not worn by Supreme Court Judges in New South Wales. This may be due to the fact that the dress of Judges of the Supreme Court is based almost exclusively on the dress worn by English Judges in the middle of the nineteenth century. As the casting hood was not worn at that time - and only reintroduced by Lord Coleridge in the late nineteenth century - it appears that this particular item was not adopted by New South Wales Supreme Court Judges.

On 20 September 2007, Spigelman CJ issued a Court Attire Policy so as to ensure that counsel appearing before the Supreme Court are in the proper attire that meets the Supreme Court's expectations.[49] Amongst other things, it provides that counsel are to wear robes and wigs when appearing before a Judge in the Court of Criminal Appeal, in criminal and civil trials, sentencing hearings, delivery of reserved judgments, motions in the probate, protective and corporations lists and when appearing for directions in the probate and protective lists of the Court. The Policy also provides that for ceremonial occasions (such as the swearing-in of a new Supreme Court Judge or for the Opening of the Law Term ceremonies at the beginning of each year) barristers are to wear robes and wigs and Senior Counsel are to wear full-bottomed wigs.[50]

Regarding the Court of Appeal, however, wigs have not been worn by either Judges or counsel in the Court of Appeal since 2007.[51] In 2007, a vote was taken by Judges of the Court of Appeal and a majority of nine out of thirteen Judges voted to discontinue the practice of wearing wigs in the Court of Appeal.[52] However a similar vote by Judges sitting in the common law/equity division of the Supreme Court saw a majority voting in favour of retaining the wig for civil matters.[53] There appears to have been no attempt to change the robing policy for criminal and ceremonial occasions.[54] Thus, for civil sittings (i.e., in both the common law and equity divisions), Judges of the Supreme Court of New South Wales wear black silk gowns over court coat with bands or jabots, and a bench wig.

Photograph of Sir Kenneth Whistler Street (1890-1972), Chief Justice of New South Wales from 1950 to 1960. Attributed to the State Library of New South Wales

49. "Court Attire Policy" issued by J J Spigelman AC Chief Justice of New South Wales, 20 September 2007.

50. The writer attended the most recent Opening of the Law Term ceremonies in Sydney on Monday, 29 January 2018, which, firstly, involved a Red Mass ceremony at St Mary's Cathedral and, secondly, an Anglican service later that morning at St James Anglican Church in Sydney. The Judges were arrayed in their ceremonial scarlet robes and hoods faced with miniver and full-bottomed wigs, whilst Senior Counsel were dressed in their silk gowns over a Queen's Counsel bar jacket with either jabots or bands and full-bottomed wigs, whilst junior lawyers (including the writer) wore the barrister's stuff gown, bar jacket with either bands or jabots and a tie wig. The Judges of the Supreme Court also undertake similar Opening of the Law Term services at Jewish, Muslim and Orthodox places of worship.

51. "Court Attire Policy" issued by J J Spigelman AC Chief Justice of New South Wales, 20 September 2007.

52. "Judges ditch wigs," Lawyers Weekly, 10 August 2007 <https://www.lawyersweekly.com.au/news/861-judges-ditch-wigs> (accessed 29 March 2018).

53. *Ibid.*

54. A Court spokeswoman at the time said that "[i]n criminal matters a wig gives a judge some anonymity … it's an issue of safety and security" (*ibid*).

Photograph of Sir Philip Whistler Street (1863-1938), Chief Justice of New South Wales from 1925 to 1934, his wife Lady Street, his son Mr Justice Kenneth Street (as he then was) standing on the left and Mr E.W. Street on the right, in Mr Justice Kenneth Street's office, New South Wales, in circa. 1931. Attributed to the National Library of Australia

Justices Fullerton, McClennan and Garling sitting in the Court of Criminal Appeal on 25 June 2012 wearing the scarlet robes and hood faced with slate grey silk or taffeta and a bench wig, which is the traditional dress worn during criminal appeals (deriving from the dress worn by Judges sitting in the Court of Crown Cases Reserved). Note that each Judge wears a different type of neckwear (Fullerton J is wearing an elaborately frilled jabot, McClennan J is wearing a plain jabot, and Garling J is wearing the traditional white bands). © getty images

Judges of the Court of Appeal, from left to right, Justice Margaret Beazley, Chief Justice James Spigelman, and Justice Roger Giles deliver their findings regarding appeals by James Hardie directors in Sydney, Friday, 17 December 2010. All three Judges are wearing black silk gowns over court coats and jabots but without wigs, which has been the dress of Judges of the Court of Appeal since 2007. © AAP Image/Jon Reid

In all criminal sittings the Judges wear the scarlet robe and hood faced with taffeta, with a black girdle, black scarf, bands or jabot and a bench wig. On ceremonial occasions, the Judges wear the scarlet robe and hood faced with miniver (or faux fur) with a black scarf underneath, a black girdle, bands or jabots and a full-bottomed wig. In addition, the Judges also carry white gloves in ceremonial occasions outside of the Supreme Court, such as the annual Opening of the Law Term church ceremonies.

Above. Justices Fullerton and McClellan leave the courtroom following the delivery of the appeal judgment on 25 June 2012. The scarlet hoods faced with silk, which are worn by all Supreme Court Judges sitting in criminal matters both at first instance and on appeal, can be clearly seen in this photograph.
© getty images

Opposite, bottom. The Red Mass ceremony underway for the Opening of the Law term at St Mary's Cathedral, Sydney, on 29 January 2018.
© Daniel Yazdani

Above, left. Judges wearing their scarlet robes and hoods, with black stockings and buckled shoes and full-bottomed wigs during the annual Opening of Law term ceremony in Sydney.

Above, right. Photograph of Sir Phillip Street, Chief Justice of New South Wales, accompanied by Lady Street, during the Opening of the Law Term ceremony in Sydney in 1930. He is also wearing buckled shoes which are no longer worn by Supreme Court Judges.

Above. The Chief Justice departs St Mary's Cathedral following the conclusion of the Red Mass ceremony on 29 January 2018. © Daniel Yazdani

Below. The President of the Court of Appeal, along with the Chief Judge of the Common Law and Equity Divisions of the Supreme Court also depart the church following the conclusion of Red Mass on 29 January 2018. © Daniel Yazdani

Supreme Court and District Court Judges, Magistrates, Senior Counsel and barristers walking past St Mary's Cathedral towards the vault underneath the Church in order to disrobe.
© Daniel Yazdani

Supreme Court and District Court Judges, Magistrates, Senior Counsel and barristers walking heading towards the vault underneath the Church in order to disrobe.
© Daniel Yazdani

Judges, lawyers and members of the public at the Anglican service for the Opening of the Law Year at St James Anglican Church in Sydney on 29 January 2018.
© Daniel Yazdani

The writer standing with the Attorney General of New South Wales, the Hon. Mark Speakman SC MP at St James Church, Sydney, prior to the commencement of the Anglican service commemorating the Opening of the Law Term on 29 January 2018. The writer is wearing the barrister's stuff gown over a bar jacket and a barrister's wig. The Attorney General is wearing the black silk gown over a Queen's Counsel bar jacket and full-bottomed wig. Both are wearing the modern "jabot" which is in the form of bands but is simply strapped on at the back of the neck.
© Daniel Yazdani

District Court of New South Wales

The District Court of New South Wales has its origins in the *District Courts Act 1858* (NSW),[55] which created District Courts, as courts of records, to replace Courts of Requests and divided the Colony into Districts.[56] It appears, from the early photographs of District Court Judges, that they wore the black silk gown over court dress as worn by Judges of the County Court in the nineteenth century.

However, during the mid twentieth century - possibly after the enactment of the *District Court Act 1973* (NSW) - the District Court Judges began to wear the violet robes faced with lilac or navy blue (similar to that worn by circuit court Judges in England and Wales), along with a scarlet casting hood over the left shoulder and a black cincture with either bands or jabots. On ceremonial occasions, District Court Judges wear the same violet hoods but with lilac casting hood (instead of the scarlet casting hood), following the ceremonial dress of County Court Judges in England and Wales. The Chief Judge of the District Court also wears a full-bottomed wig while the remaining Judges of the District Court wear the bench wig.[57]

Photograph of Judge David Forbes of the District Court of New South Wales, taken in circa 1890, wearing the working dress worn by District Court Judges presiding over civil matters, namely a black silk gown, bands court coat and a bench wig. Attributed to the National Library of Australia.

The New South Wales Bar Association has issued the following guidance with respect to robing in the District Court of New South Wales:

> The District Court has announced that wigs are no longer to be worn in District Court civil matters. Although this is the official policy of the court, the policy is not mandatory upon every judge. Situations may arise where counsel may appear in civil matters before a judge who chooses to wear a wig.
>
> The association has communicated with the court, which has indicated that in these circumstances that it will not be a discourtesy for counsel to appear before the court without a wig, in compliance with the general policy of the court.
>
> Robes should be worn in any civil matter.
>
> Criminal matters: Barristers traditionally wear robes and wigs in the District Court except on chambers matters. Barristers do not wear a wig if the judge appears without a wig at the outset.
>
> Ceremonial occasions: barristers wear robes and wigs; in the case of silk, full bottomed wigs are worn.[58]

---

55. 22 Vic No 18.
56. The *District Courts Act 1858* (NSW) remained in force until 1973, although the jurisdiction of the court was increased from time to time. The *District Court Act 1973* (NSW) abolished the District Courts and Courts of Quarter Sessions and established one District Court of New South Wales, with a statewide criminal and civil jurisdiction.
57. This is due to the status of the Chief Judge of the District Court as a Justice of the Supreme Court of New South Wales, pursuant to s 15A(1) of the *District Court Act 1973* (NSW).
58. "Court Attire," *New South Wales Bar Association*, <https://www.nswbar.asn.au/coming-to-the-bar/court-attire>(accessed 1 March 2018). In the Local Court of New South Wales the Magistrates also wear black robes over normal attire, without wigs or jabots or bands, similar to Magistrates in Queensland.

Left. Photograph of the swearing in of new District Court Judge Conomos, by the Chief Judge of the District Court on 19 April 1985. They are wearing the dress worn on ceremonial occasions, namely the violet robe and hood faced with lilac (as worn by County Court Judges in England and Wales), laced jabot and wig, (the Chief Judges always wear full-bottomed wigs). Attributed to the State Library of New South Wales.

Below. The current Chief Judge of the District Court (The Honourable Justice Derek Michael Price AM), followed by other District Court Judges, following the conclusion of the Opening of the Law Term Red Mass at St Mary's Cathedral in Sydney on 29 January 2018. © Daniel Yazdani

VICTORIA

Supreme Court of Victoria

Prior to the adoption of the current judicial robes in its April 2017 sittings, the habit of Judges of the Supreme Court of Victoria very closely reflected the seasonal dress of the Judges of the High Court of England and Wales, and in particular the summer and winter scarlet robes worn by English High Court Judges. Until very recently, the robes of Judges of the Supreme Court of Victoria consisted of summer and winter scarlet robes in criminal matters, black silk gowns for civil matters and summer and winter scarlet robes and hoods for ceremonial occasions.

Portrait of Sir William à Beckett (circa 1860) by Mosley. Early accounts have the painting hanging in a prominent position in the 'old' Court house at La Trobe and Russell Streets in Melbourne. The portrait was later moved down to the Supreme Court of Victoria Library in 1884, at the same time when the portraits of Barry, Stawell and Molesworth JJ were also commissioned. Attributed to the Supreme Court of Victoria Library

Evidence suggests that the first Judge to wear scarlet and violet robes in Victoria was the Resident Judge of the Supreme Court of New South Wales for the District of Port Phillip, Sir William à Beckett.[59] It has been reported that on the "first day of the third term [i.e., 20 July 1846], his Honor took his seat in his purple robes".[60] The tradition of scarlet robes also seem to have continued by à Beckett following the founding of the Supreme Court of Victoria in 1852 and his appointment as its first Chief Justice, for his official portrait depicts him seated and wearing the full ceremonial scarlet robes and hood faced with miniver, as well as a mantle.[61] This portrait appears to be the earliest portrait of an Australian Judge wearing robes of scarlet faced with miniver. His portrait is one of the few portraits of Judges in Australia depicted wearing the mantle, which would have been exceedingly warm for a Judge sitting in a court in the Victorian summer of the mid 19th century. Following the retirement of à Beckett CJ in 1857, no other Judge in Victoria (or any where else in Australia it seems) appears to have worn the mantle as part of their ceremonial dress.

Apart from the mantle, however, there were other intricate differences in the types of dress worn by the various Chief Justices of the Victorian Supreme Court. For example, whilst à Beckett CJ and and his successor Sir William Stawell CJ wore buckled shoes (and in the case Stawell CJ, knee breeches traditionally worn in ceremonial occasions in England), other Judges (such as George Higinbotham CJ and Sir Thomas à Beckett CJ wore ordinary black trousers and shoes instead of knee breeches and buckled shoes) and by the time of the chief justiceship of Sir Edmund Herring CJ, the laced jabot began to be worn for ceremonial occasions instead of the more traditional white bands as can be seen in Herring CJ's portrait by Sir William Dargie located in the Supreme Court Library.

Photograph of Sir William à Beckett wearing a black silk gown over court dress and a bench wig, which he would have worn when presiding over civil matters in the Court. Attributed to the State Library of Victoria

59. Sir William à Beckett was Chief Justice from January 1852 to February 1857. Initially, Sir William had a busy career practising as a barrister at the Sydney bar. Prior to his appointment as Chief Justice of the Supreme Court of the Colony of Victoria, Sir William was a resident Judge of the Supreme Court of New South Wales for the District of Port Phillip from February 1846 to 1852.

60. "Judicial Intelligence," *Port Phillip Patriot and Morning Advertiser*, Tuesday, 21 July 1846, 3.

61. The painter, Mr Mosely, was selected by Sir William à Beckett himself to undertake the commission.

Portrait of Sir William Stawell (1857-1886), commissioned in 1884, two years before his retirement from judicial office, and was commissioned at the same time as those of Redmond Barry and Molesworth JJ. Sir William was appointed Chief Justice of the Supreme Court of Victoria in 1857, a position he held for a record 29 years.
Attributed to the Supreme Court of Victoria Library

Portrait of George Higinbotham (Chief Justice 1886-1892) by L Bernard Hall, which was commissioned after his death in 1893. A committee was appointed to investigate the possibility of making a portrait of Higinbotham CJ and it was decided to appoint L Bernard Hall, who later became the director of the National Gallery of Victoria.
Attributed to the Supreme Court of Victoria Library

Above left. Photograph of Sir William Stawell in his civil black silk gown over court dress and bench wig. Attributed to the State Library of Victoria

Above right. Portrait of Sir George Higinbotham wearing his civil robes and bench wig. Attributed to the State Library of Victoria

Photograph of Sir John Madden wearing his ceremonial robes (1844-1918), Chief Justice of Victoria from 1893 until his death in 1918. Attributed to the State Library of Victoria

Photograph of Sir John Madden wearing his civil robes. Attributed to the State Library of Victoria

Below left. Photograph of Sir Redmond Barry (1813-1880) a Judge of the Supreme Court of Victoria from 1852 to 1880, dated 1872. Attributed to the State Library of Victoria

Below right. Photograph of Sir Edward Eyre Williams (1813-1880) a Judge of the Supreme Court of Victoria from 1852 to 1874, dated 1872. Attributed to the State Library of Victoria

Engraving of the the trial of Ned Kelly in the Supreme Court in Melbourne, in December of 1880. The presiding Judge is wearing a full-bottomed wig, which by this time had been abandoned by English Judges as part of their working dress.

By the twentieth century the dress of the Supreme Court Judges was as follows: for criminal matters (both in the General and Appeal Divisions of the Court), the working day dress during the summer season consisted of red robes faced with silk, a black cummerband and bands or jabots and a bench wig. The dress for criminal matters during winter season consisted of the red robes faced with miniver or coney. The ceremonial dress also differed depending on the relevant season: during summer, the judges would wear a hood faced with silk over their working day criminal summer robes, while winter ceremonial robes would consist of a hood faced with fur over criminal winter robes. The dress for civil matters (both in the Court's General and Appeal Divisions) consisted of a silk gown over bar jacket and jabot or bands. There were, therefore, five sets of robes available for a Judge of the Supreme Court of Victoria to wear at any time, depending on the season and occasion.

Interestingly, on no occasion did Judges of the Supreme Court of Victoria ever wear black scarves or casting hoods over either their criminal or ceremonial robes. There is no clear explanation as to why that is the case; however, it appears that when these robes were adopted by Victorian Judges in the mid-nineteenth century, the casting-hood had not yet come back into vogue in England, and, like their judicial colleagues in New South Wales, Victorian Judges did not adopt the casting hood when it was reintroduced by Lord Coleridge CJ in the late nineteenth century.

Above. Judges of the Supreme Court of Victoria gathered in the banco court for a ceremony celebrating 150 years of the Supreme Court in Victoria. © AAP Image/Michael Clayton-Jones Pool

Below. History was made on 5 August 2002 when an all female bench presided over the Supreme Court of Victoria. From left to right: the Hon. Justice Marilyn Warren (later Warren CJ), the late Hon. Justice Rosemary Balmford and the Hon. Justice Julie Dodds-Streeton. © Paul Trezise/Newspix

The Rosette

Victoria and Tasmania are also the only jurisdictions in Australia where Judges and Queen's Counsel and Senior Counsel wear the rosette which is attached to the back of their robes behind the neck. It is unclear why they retained this custom and others have not, although the rosette is still worn by Queen's Counsel and Judges in England and Wales.[62] The rosette is also worn by Judges wearing the new Supreme Court robes.

62. It appears that the origins of the rosette come from the "wig bag" which was worn by the Bench and Bar to protect the powder from the wig soiling their silk velvet coat, for the powder would fall from the queue of the wig and damage the delicate fabric of the velvet coat (Healy, "Of Wigs, Wig Bags and Rosettes," *supra*, 21.) The name "rosette" or "rose bag" is derived from the rose-like bow which was tied to secure the queue of the wig within the wig bag, which was enclosed around the top of the queue by a drawstring which was concealed beneath a stiff black decorative bow (*ibid*). The wig bag was later moved to the back of the coat and is now worn on ceremonial occasions by the Lord Chancellor, Master of the Rolls, Lords Justices of Appeal and Queen's Counsel.

Below. Photograph of an all-female bench of the Court of Appeal. From left to right: the Hon. Justice Pamela Tate, former Chief Justice the Hon. Marilyn Warren AC, and the Hon. Justice Anne Ferguson (now Chief Justice of Victoria), presiding over a property dispute in the Court of Appeal in November 2015. © Supreme Court of Victoria

Opposite, left. Judges wearing their summer scarlet robes during a sitting of the Court of Appeal at the Old High Court No 1 in Melbourne, Victoria on 23 March 2011. Note that the Judges do not wear either the black scarf or the scarlet casting-hood, both of which are traditionally worn when the full hood is not worn. The black scarf and casting-hood appear to have never been adopted by Judges in Victoria. © Darren Tindale/Newspix

Reform

One of the reasons why the robes of Judges of the Supreme Court were simplified was to alleviate the inconvenience of Judges of the Court of Appeal from having to change from their civil robes into their scarlet robes (or vice versa) when hearing a number of civil and criminal appeals in order to wear the proper dress reflecting the particular type of appeal.

In early 2016, it was announced by Warren CJ that, in consultation with the Council of Judges of the Supreme Court of Victoria, she had resolved, pursuant to s 9A of the *Supreme Court Act 1986* (Vic), that Judges of the Supreme Court of Victoria would no longer wear wigs effective from 1 May 2016 in civil hearings and ceremonial occasions, with the exception that where a Judge presiding over a criminal jury trial considers it to be an exceptional case warranting the wearing of a wig, the presiding Judge may seek the express permission of the Chief Justice to do so.[63] However, the wig continues to be worn by some Judges sitting in the County Court of Victoria as in that Court the wearing of wigs by Counsel and Judges is at the discretion of the presiding Judge. At first, the announcement by Warren CJ caused confusion among the members of the Victorian Bar, who initially believed that the resolution only applied to Judges and did not effect Counsel. This confusion was clearly evident from a court transcript of the commencement of a Supreme Court Trial on 24 May 2016 before Bell J, who expressed his profound disappointment and feeling of disrespect at seeing Counsel appearing before him wearing wigs:

> HIS HONOUR: Mr Mighell, … the Chief Justice has directed that judges of this court are not to wig unless the circumstances are exceptional. You are not showing, and neither are your colleagues, showing the respect that I expect of the Chief Justice from you and I want to express my profound disappointment that one, two, three, four, five members of this Bar table have wigs on, though I applaud the strength of character of your junior who does not.
> MR MIGHELL: Your Honour, we - I think I speak on behalf of all of the members of the Bar table - we mean Your Honour no disrespect in wearing wigs and we will remove our wigs.
> HIS HONOUR: Well I want to make it clear to you that it's not a question of respect for me, though I do feel disrespected. Whether you intend that disrespect or not, and I accept the fact that you do not intend it and that you are wearing wigs by reason of principle, but I experience disrespect. But the more important question is how this treats the Chief Justice, not only of this court, but this State.
> MR MIGHELL: Yes, Your Honour.
> HIS HONOUR: She is the constitutional chief of the judicial system of Victoria and has directed that judges not wear wigs, and you five stand there wearing wigs, it's untenable. Now the course I will adopt in this case, and the course I will adopt in every case where this happens, is to ask for an explana-

63. Supreme Court of Victoria, Practice Note SC Gen 4 - Custom and Protocol, 30 January 2017.

Photograph of the Hon. Anne Ferguson, present Chief Justice of Victoria (2017-), with the Hon. Justice Clyde Croft, wearing the newly created robes of the Judges of the Supreme Court of Victoria. These robes are now worn on all occasions by the Judges of the Supreme Court.
© Supreme Court of Victoria

tion. I won't ask that of you, Mr Mighell, because you've already indicated that the wigs will be taken off at my request, and I so request. I'll give you time to do that in a moment. They will need to be put away as well; I don't want them to be seen by the jury at all.
MR MIGHELL: We understand that, Your Honour.
HIS HONOUR: But I make it absolutely clear that if this happens again and there is resistance to a request then I will hear counsel as to why it is that I ought not to direct as a matter of law that the wigs be taken off and I will so rule.
MR MIGHELL: Yes, Your Honour.
HIS HONOUR: I make it absolutely clear to you and to the rest of the Common Law Bar that I am of the preliminary view that I have the power to direct that wigs not be worn because the judge controls matters of practice and procedure in this court, but that's a preliminary view and I will hear counsel in relation to that matter.[64]

Following the confusion as to the appropriate dress among the Bar, the Judges of the Common Law Division issued a notice to practitioners confirming that practitioners appearing in any common law proceeding should no longer wear wigs:

> As from the 1st day of May 2016, pursuant to a determination made by the Chief Justice under s 9A of the Supreme Court Act 1986, the judges of the Common Law Division ceased wearing wigs.
>
> It is clear that the Court has an inherent jurisdiction to determine the attire to be worn by legal practitioners in court.
>
> The judges of this Division have resolved that legal practitioners not wear wigs in any Common Law Division proceeding.[65]

In March 2017, it was also announced by the Supreme Court of Victoria that, with effect from the commencement of its April 2017 sittings, the Supreme Court will adopt new judicial robes which were designed by the Judges of the Supreme Court and are to be worn in all Divisions of the Supreme Court.[66] The new attire was agreed upon by the Council of Judges and consists of an open gown made of yoke and cool wool, with the inside of the gown coloured in red and its sleeves lined in red (the red features of the gown being a tribute to the history and heritage of the Supreme Court) with a zip-up bar jacket underneath along with the traditional white bands (rather than the laced jabots) worn as neckwear. The new gowns are made of 100% Cool Merino Wool with Bemberg lining, which makes the gowns cooler, lighter, and more comfortable compared to the traditional robes. The Supreme Court has stated that the inspiration for the "elegant robes" has been drawn, in part, from the judicial robes of the Supreme Court of Ireland adopted in 2014, and that

64. Supreme Court of Victoria, Transcript, 24 May 2016, 1-3.
65. Rani Kulkarni, Associate to the Honourable Justice J Forrest, Notice to the Profession "Wearing of wigs in Common Law Division proceedings", 26 May 2016.
66. Supreme Court of Victoria, *Annual Report 2015-2016* (Melbourne: Supreme Court of Victoria, 2017) 13; Caroline Ford, "Court couture on show," *Law Institute Victoria*, <https://www.liv.asn.au/Staying-Informed/LIJ/LIJ/March-2018/Court-couture-on-show> (accessed 1 April 2018)

The Hon Marilyn Warren, former Chief Justice of Victoria (2003-2017) on 12 June 2005, wearing the winter scarlet robe and black girdle, with bands and a bench wig, without either the black scarf or scarlet casting hood which were never adopted in Victoria. She is also not wearing the hood, which was not worn in criminal sittings and only worn during ceremonial occasions of the court.

the Supreme Court of Victoria's robes have been styled in such a way so as to reflect both notions of strength and modernity.[67]

County Court of Victoria

Photograph of Judge Clive Harris, a Judge of the County Court of Victoria from 1964 to 1989, wearing the working robes of a County Court Judge, namely the black robe with purple facings and a cummerbund, bands and bench wig. Note that the casting hood is not worn by County Court Judges on any occasion.

In around 1983, the Judges of the County Court of Victoria adopted their current working robes which consist of black robes lined with purple with a black cummerbund and jabots or bands, which is based on the dress worn by Circuit Judges of the Crown Court.[68] For ceremonial occasions, the Judges of the County Court wear the same dress as well as a corresponding hood faced with purple, white silk lace cuffs worn on the wrists and white silk lace bibs worn over the jabot, which have traditionally been worn in ceremonial occasions such as the Opening of the Legal Year or the Opening of Parliament.[69]

As to the wearing of wigs by Judges of the County Court, it is currently the practice of the County Court that such decisions are at the discretion of each individual Judge whether or not wigs will be worn by the Bench and Bar, which applies to both criminal and civil sittings.[70] The County Court has issued to practitioners a "Wig Preferences" guide of Judges of the County Court which outline to practitioners whether the particular Judge before which they will be appearing observes the wearing of wigs.[71] Given that the current Chief Judge of the County Court does not wear wigs on any occasions, the Judges of the County Court do not wear wigs when the Chief Judge is presiding over a ceremonial sitting of the Court, although individual Judges may wear wigs in ceremonial farewell ceremonies when sitting alone, and on previous ceremonial occasions some County Court Judges have worn wigs while others have not.[72]

---

67. *Ibid.*
68. Correspondence from Bridie Kelly, Senior Associate to the Chief Judge of the County Court of Victoria to the writer, 4 December 2017.
69. *Ibid.*
70. *Ibid.*
71. The current "Wig Preferences" guide is dated as at 19 February 2018. The preferences of the Judges vary, from one Judge noting that he "will wear wig if hearing criminal matter", while another noting that in "a trial, the choice is left to the Senior Counsel as to whether wigs will be worn", and another Judge has noted that whilst wigs will be worn in all criminal sittings, wigs will only be worn in civil matters "only on circuit". The variation in preferences shows how, ultimately, the appropriate attire to be worn by counsel in any court is at the discretion of the presiding judge.
72. See e.g., the welcoming ceremony of Judge Andrea Tsalamandris on 18 February 2016 in which some Judges appeared with wigs (including incoming Judge Tsalamandris) while others (including the Chief Judge) did not. Wigs were also worn by Judge Michael McInerney and counsel on his farewell ceremony on 7 December 2017. The writer has seen how his Honour, upon arriving in court remarked that, "given the recent determinations across the road, and irrespective of your views on wigs, today the Bar is full topped. It may be that this is the last occasion that you will see a Victorian Court so comprised. It takes me to the movie that you all remember, "Apocalypse Now", and the role that Robert Duvall played, Lieutenant Colonel Bill Kilgore, and if I might just misquote him: "I love the smell of horse hair in the afternoon"," which resulted in laughter from the Bar. On an earlier farewell ceremony for Judge Carolyn Douglas on 13 October 2017, whilst her Honour did wear the wig the Bar on this occasion did not.

Supreme Court of Queensland

The early portraits of Judges of the Supreme Court of Queensland indicate that court dress of that period was hardly different to that worn by Judges in the twenty first century.[73] Up until August 2017, the Judges of the Supreme Court of Queensland wore scarlet robes faced with miniver along with the hood and full-bottomed wig on all ceremonial occasions both inside and outside of the court. Prior to the establishment of the Supreme Court of Queensland in 1861, there is no indication that Judges in this colony wore scarlet robes, and simply wore the chancery black silk robes, as can be seen in the drawing of Judge Lutwyche in 1859.

However, this changed with the appointment of Sir James Cockle as the first Chief Justice of the Supreme Court of Queensland. Prior to his appointment, Sir James first practised at the Middle Temple and then joined the Midland Circuit, following which he was recommended by Sir William Erle, Chief Justice of the Court of the Common Pleas, to be appointed as as Queensland's first Chief Justice. It is therefore highly likely that the arrival of Cockle CJ in Queensland also brought in the practice of wearing the traditional scarlet and violet robes faced with miniver and taffeta, as worn by Judges in the Common Law Courts at the time. By the time of the appointment of Sir Charles Lilley as Chief Justice, it had become accustomed practice of Judges of the Supreme Court of Queensland to wear the scarlet robes and hood faced with miniver, with either bands or laced jabots and a full-bottomed wig for ceremonial occasions, a practice which continued into the twenty-first century.[74]

Drawing of Judge Alfred James Lutwyche, circa. 1859. In October of 1857, Lutwyche J was appointed the first resident Judge in the then Moreton Bay district of New South Wales. He lived at Kedron Lodge, Nelson Street, Kalinga. Two months later, he became the sole Judge of the new colony of Queensland, and occupied the bench unaided until the arrival of the first Chief Justice, Sir James Cockle, in February 1863. The contemporary drawing indicates that, initially, Judges in Queensland wore black silk robes instead of the scarlet robes of later times.
Attributed to State Library of Queensland

---

73. John McKenna, *Supreme Court of Queensland: A Concise History* (St Lucia: University of Queensland Press, 2012) 52.
74. There were occasions where Judges of the Supreme Court of Queensland wore their black silk gowns and bench wigs for ceremonial occasions, such as the appointment ceremony of Macrossan CJ in 1946, and Judges of the Court of Appeal would always wear their black silk robe over normal attire even during ceremonial sittings, while their colleagues in the trial division would wear the full ceremonial dress. As of August 2017, all Judges of the Supreme Court wear the same set of robes for ceremonial occasions.

Portrait of Sir James Cockle, (1819-1895), who, on the recommendation of Sir William Erle CJ of the Court of Common Pleas became the first Chief Justice of the Supreme Court of Queensland (1862-1879). Dated circa 1870. Apart from the full hood, these robes are still worn with a bench wig by Judges of the Supreme Court in criminal sittings.
Attributed to the National Library of Australia

Portrait of George Harding, a Justice of the Queensland Supreme Court from 1879 to 1885 by Richard Godfrey Rivers. Note the decorated laced bands worn instead of the the white bands. Reproduced with the permission of the Department of Justice and Attorney-General, Queensland. © Department of Justice and Attorney-General

Portrait by Richard Godfrey Rivers of Sir Charles Lilley, (1827-1897) the second Chief Justice of the Supreme Court of Queensland, 1879-1893 (circa 1879). Reproduced with the permission of the Department of Justice and Attorney-General, Queensland. © Department of Justice and Attorney-General

Sir Samuel Griffith (1845-1920), ninth Premier of Queensland (1883-1888, 1890-1893), third Chief Justice of Queensland (1893-1903) and the first Chief Justice of the High Court of Australia (1903-1919) in ceremonial attire. This portrait shows him wearing the judicial SS collar, traditionally associated with the Chief Justices of the common law courts at Westminster.
Reproduced with the permission of the Department of Justice and Attorney-General, Queensland.

Photograph of Sir Pope Alexander Cooper (1846-1923). He was appointed Chief Justice of Queensland in October 1903 and was knighted in 1904. He was chancellor of the University of Queensland from 1915 to 1922. He is wearing the ceremonial scarlet robes and hood faced with miniver, bands and a full-bottomed wig. Attributed to the State Library of Queensland

Hugh Denis Macrossan SPJ (1881-1940) taken in circa 1934. He was appointed Chief Justice of Queensland on 17 May 1940 and died shortly thereafter on 23 June 1940. Attributed to the State Library of Queensland.

In criminal sittings, the Judges would wear the summer scarlet robes faced with taffeta (or slate-coloured silk)[75] with scarlet casting hood and black cincture (but without the mantle and hood). However, the portrait of Sir James Cockle - the first Chief Justice of the Supreme Court of Queensland - indicates that the full hood faced with taffeta facings was historically worn over the scarlet summer robes by Queensland Judges in the 19th century. These scarlet silk robes continue to be worn by Judges of the Supreme Court Queensland at criminal sittings. The traditional black cap was also used by Judges in crimi-

75. Scarlet robes faced with shot pink taffeta were also worn.

nal sittings when imposing death sentences, and accompanying white gloves were also carried by Judges on ceremonial occasions and were presented by the Crown prosecutor to a Judge at criminal sittings at which no persons were presented for either trial or sentence.[76] Although Queensland Judges have never adopted a formal mourning dress, it has been recorded that on the death of King Edward VIII in 1910 the Judges of the Supreme Court wore black robes, crepe stoles and mourning bands.[77]

Below left. The scarlet ceremonial robes of the Hon. George Lucas AC, former Justice of the Supreme Court of Queensland. With kind permission from the Supreme Court Library of Queensland

Below right. The scarlet summer robes of the Hon. Tom Shepherdson, a former Justice of the Supreme Court of Queensland. With kind permission from the Supreme Court Library of Queensland

76. B. H. McPherson, *The Supreme Court of Queensland 1859-1960 History Jurisdiction Procedure* (Butterworths, 1989) 66.
77. *Brisbane Courier*, 10 May 1910; 40 SCL 37.

There is also both written and pictorial evidence indicating that Supreme Court Judges wore the traditional violet robes faced with taffeta in criminal trials, which was based on the violet *nisi prius* robes worn by Judges of the common law courts in England pursuant to the Judges' Rules of 1635. It appears that the violet robes were adopted at the same time as the scarlet robes were, and they were certainly in the vogue during the chief justiceship of Sir Charles Lilley CJ, for it has been reported that in March 1887 Lilley CJ and Harding and Mein JJ "appeared in purple robes" in the Full Court.[78] His successor Sir Samuel Griffith CJ is also reported to have worn "purple robes" on account of it "being a robe day".[79] The media at the time seems to have been mazed by the apparent beauty and elegance of the violet robes, as can be seen in the following reporter's account in the *Courier*:

> The Chief Justice and Mr Justice Harding appeared in their summer robes of ceremony, which our dazzled reporter diffidently describes as being violet coloured silk with some trimmings, we presume, of a fashionable shade of yellow. Poor Mr Justice Pring was in the condition of a lady whose ball dress had not arrived and was compelled to appear in a plain robe.[80]

Another example of violet having been worn by Judges can, for example, be seen in a report that during a criminal trial, Sir James Blair CJ presided over a trial "wearing a wig and violet robes".[81] Another newspaper article states that in the swearing in ceremony of E. A. Douglas J on 22 March 1929, "[t]he bench was occupied by Chief Justice Blair, Mr. Justice R. J. Douglas and Mr. Justice Henchman, who wore their violet robes".[82] The violet robes were also worn by Sir William Mack, and later worn by Connolly J, and these original robes are exhibited in the Sir Harry Gibbs Legal Heritage Centre in the Queen Elizabeth II Courts of Law in Brisbane. These robes are clearly derived from the same type of garment as worn by Judges in the Queen's Bench Division. However for some reason the colour of the facings is completely different to that worn in England - it is not of changeable taffeta and is much darker in colour. The hood is also folded very oddly at the back, and the hood looks more like an English academic hood in the way that it hangs. McPherson J stated that the violet robes continued to be favoured by some Judges as preferred court dress during the summer.[83]

---

78. "Monthly Full Court", *Telegraph*, Brisbane, Tuesday, 8 March 1887, 5.
79. "Supreme Court", *Brisbane Courier*, Wednesday, 6 December 1893. The reference to "robe day" is the first day of one of the four law terms in which Judges wore either scarlet or violet robes, a tradition that was adopted by the Queensland Judges well into the 20th century, for in 1904 it was reported that as the sitting of the Full Court "fell on one of the robe-days of the Court ... the Judges wore their purple robes" ("The Full Court", *Brisbane Courier*, Wednesday, 16 March 1904, 4). The reason for this colourful tradition was also clearly mentioned in the *Brisbane Courier* in 1926: "Judges of the Full Court yesterday were resplendent in purple robes. There are still four robe days in Queensland, the colours worn bring scarlet, purple, or black. In England, there are four law terms, called Hillary, Easter, Trinity, and Michaelmas, at the opening of which robes are worn. It is only on robe days that barristers can be admitted to the English courts. In former times a similar rule was in existence in Queensland, but now barristers can be admitted in any sitting of the Full Court" ("Robes Day", *Brisbane Courier*, Wednesday, 10 March 1926, 6).
80. *Brisbane Courier*, 25 February 1881; 10 Thorr 5a.
81. *Courier Mail*, Brisbane, Friday, 3 November 1939, 1.
82. *Telegraph*, Brisbane, Friday, 22 March 1929, 2.
83. McPherson, *supra*, 67.

The violet robes worn by Sir William Mack and later by the Hon. Justice Connolly. These robes are based on the violet robes worn by Judges in the Queen's Bench Division of the English High Court, though the colour of the facings is different and not in the form of changeable taffeta as described by the 1635 Judges' Rules. With kind permission from the Supreme Court Library of Queensland

In civil sittings, the Judges would wear the black silk gown over a court coat, bands or jabots and a bench wig, similar to that traditionally worn by the Chancery Division of the High Court. However, it appears that this dress was also worn by Judges on ceremonial occasions (such as the swearing in of a Judge) or in criminal proceedings, as can be seen in the photograph of the swearing-in of Macrossan CJ in 1946. It was also practice for the Judge to remove his wig once the Court had convened in premises in the tropical north of Queensland where court sittings took place in rooms that were not air-conditioned.[84]

The robes of the Judges of the Court of Appeal were adopted in 1991 upon the establishment of the Court of Appeal, and consists of a Queen's Counsel gown over ordinary dress.

Until August 2017, the Chief Justice and Judges sitting in the Trial Division of the Supreme Court of Queensland would wear the scarlet robes and hood faced with miniver, bands or jabots and a full-bottomed wig for ceremonial occasions. However, on 14 August 2017, it was announced by the Supreme Court of Queensland that, from 19 August 2017, the Judges of the Supreme Court of Queensland will no longer wear the traditional ceremonial robes or full-bottomed wigs on any ceremonial occasions.[85] Thereafter a new set of robes (which are based on, and very similar to, the new robes adopted by the Judges of Supreme Court of Victoria) will be worn by all Judges of the Court (including Judges of the Court of Appeal)[86] on occasions such as the swearing in of a new Judge, a farewell to a retiring Judge or other ceremonial sittings (such as Church sittings).[87]

---

84. *Ibid.*

85. Supreme Court of Queensland, "Supreme Court adopts a New Robe", Media Release, 14 August 2017.

86. Prior to the changes, Judges of the Court of Appeal would wear their own gowns when members of the General Division of the Supreme Court would wear their own ceremonial robes. Although similar, one major difference between the new Queensland and Victorian robes is that whilst the Victorian robes' sleeve linings are separated (with one row at the end of the sleeves and two rows connected further up the sleeve), the three rows of red linings on the sleeves of the Queensland robes are connected together at the end of each sleeve. It is unclear why there is a difference in the linings of the two robes.

87. Supreme Court of Queensland, "Supreme Court adopts a New Robe", Media Release, 14 August 2017.

A sitting of the Full Court circa 1938. Note that the senior presiding judge is wearing violet robes faced with taffeta and full-bottomed wig, while the other two Judges are wearing black silk gowns and bench wigs.

It appears that the change in attire for ceremonial occasions may have been partly due to the discomfort by some of the Judges of the Supreme Court of Queensland in having to wear the heavy robes, and this reason can be gleaned from the recent speech of Holmes CJ to the newly appointed Queen's Counsel and newly admitted barristers at the annual Christmas Greetings in the Banco Court:

> Christmas Greetings have become all the merrier for us Judges because of our new ceremonial robes. They may not be quite as entertaining to look at as full-bottomed wigs and fur trimmed red robes with innumerable bits and pieces attached, but they are a great deal simpler and more enjoyable to wear. I think we all feel the Christmas spirit that little bit more for actually being comfortable as we sit here.[88]

Although there have been no changes to robing practice in the Court of Appeal, Trial Judges will maintain the choice of either wearing the new robe in either the civil or criminal jurisdictions or continue to wear the traditional scarlet robes in criminal matters and the black robes in civil matters.[89] Otherwise, the conventions have remained the same, and the Supreme Court has

88. The Hon. Catherine Holmes, "Presentation of Queen's Counsel; recognition of newly -admitted barristers; and traditional exchange of Christmas Greetings Banco Court Wednesday 13 December 2017, 9.15am" <https://archive.sclqld.org.au/judgepub/2017/holmes131217.pdf> (accessed 19 March 2018)
89. Supreme Court of Queensland, "Supreme Court adopts a New Robe", Media Release, 14 August 2017.

not required that the Bar make any changes to the way in which they have traditionally robed.[90] On all occasions when the Court sits en banc, or when the Court is admitting new practitioners, counsel should continue to robe and Queen's Counsel and Senior Counsel may continue to wear full-bottomed wigs.[91] It is also customary practice in this jurisdiction that when a Judge removes his or her wig it is an invitation, but not a demand, for counsel to do likewise, and this was clarified in the following announcement by the President of the Queensland Bar Association, Christopher Hughes QC:

> It is the position of the Bar Council that the removal by a Judge in Court of his or her wig does not amount to a command for counsel, in the Court to do likewise, rather it is in the nature of only an invitation to do so.
>
> I have discussed the matter with the Chief Justice and she agrees with this protocol.
>
> The Chief Justice also acknowledges, of course, that this tradition is overruled by the practice of particular Courts, such as the Queensland Court of Appeal and the High Court of Australia, in which counsel are required to wear wigs although the members of the Court do not.[92]

Justice Neal William Macrossan (1899-1955) being sworn in as Chief Justice of Queensland by Justice Brennan on 23 April 1946. Attributed to the State Library of Queensland

90. *Ibid.*
91. The Judges of the Supreme Court of Queensland first wore their new robes at the farewell ceremony of Byrne SJA on 17 August 2017 - the very day that the changes came into effect. The members of the bar all wore wigs as per custom.
92. "Wearing of Wigs," *Queensland Bar Association* <https://www.qldbar.asn.au/#/president-message?messageId=43> (Assessed 23 November 2017).

Photograph of the Hon. Catherine Holmes, current Chief Justice of Queensland (2015-) presiding over the presentation of Queen's Counsels' Commissions in the Banco Court of the Supreme Court in Brisbane, Queensland on 14 December 2016. © Photo by Claudia Baxter/ Newspix

Photograph of the Governor of Queensland (and former Chief Justice of Queensland) His Excellency the Honourable Paul de Jersey AC, QC with the current Chief Justice of Queensland, the Honourable Catherine Holmes and the President of the Court of Appeal, the Honourable Justice Walter Sofronhoff at the Opening of the Law Term church ceremony in Brisbane in February 2018. This was the first occasion in which the Judges of the Supreme Court of Queensland wore their new ceremonial robes at the annual church ceremony. The Judges continue to wear their traditional scarlet robes and bench wig during criminal sittings of the Court. Photo supplied by Government House Queensland

District Court of Queensland

Photograph taken on 11 July 2011 of Justice Kerry Cullinane, a former Justice of the Supreme Court of Queensland, wearing the working robe of a Judge of the Queensland Supreme Court in criminal sittings, namely a scarlet robe faced with changeable taffeta (here the facings are shot pink taffeta), a black girdle, black scarf and scarlet casting hood, along with bands and a bench wig.
© Evan Morgan / Newspix

Up until 1994, the Judges of the District Court of Queensland wore the traditional black silk robes and bench wig, similar to that worn by Circuit Judges at the Central Criminal Court.[93] Upon the appointment of Chief Judge Shanahan as Chief Judge of the District Court on 18 July 1994, new violet robes based on the robes worn by Circuit Judges in the Crown Court and Judges in the District Court of South Australia were introduced for criminal and ceremonial occasions, although the black robes are also worn on certain ceremonial occasions (see for example at the opening of the Queen Elizabeth II Courts of Law where the Chief Judge of the District Court wore the black robes and a bench wig at the ceremonial opening of the new building).[94] The black robes continue to be worn by Judges in civil sittings, while

Below. At the ceremonial opening of the Queen Elizabeth Courts of Law in Brisbane in 2012. Note the Chief Judge of the District Court (sitting second from left), wearing the black silk gown and bench wig, instead of the violet robes. With kind permission from the Supreme Court Library of Queensland

93. D. Beanland, *A Court Apart: The District Court of Queensland* (Supreme Court of Queensland Library, 2009) 221.
94. *Ibid.*

Judges have the choice to wear either he violet or black robes and wig in criminal sittings.[95] However, the wig and robes may, at the discretion of the Presiding Judge, be dispensed with on certain occasions by both the Bench and Bar, such as when questioning a child in a hearing:

Photograph of His Excellency the Governor of Queensland, the Judges of the Supreme and Federal Courts, followed by Judges of the District Court of Queensland, Magistrates and Queen's Counsel at the Opening of the Law Term church ceremony in Brisbane in February 2018. Photo supplied by Government House Queensland

> The Chief Judge has requested that when children are being questioned, robes and wigs be dispensed with, however she cannot compel any individual judge to follow this practice and some may still follow the old traditions. I can recall a child of around 10 being asked who she thought the barristers were and she said "they look like penguins". One little boy thought that the Judge's robe meant that he was a karate expert, and there are many examples where children have thought that the Judge was a witch or a priest. One of my female colleagues had the ego boosting experience of being mistaken for the Queen by a little girl.[96]

95. *Ibid*, 222.
96. Speech by Judge JM Robertson, "Children as Witnesses," Paper delivered at Child Witness Support Conference, Brisbane 7 June 2007.

SOUTH AUSTRALIA

Supreme Court of South Australia

The adoption of court dress in South Australia during the early nineteenth century was not without controversy. In March 1839, Sir Charles Cooper, along with his sister Sarah Ann, arrived in Adelaide to take up his position as South Australia's second appointed judge. However, from the time of his appointment until 1850 Cooper J was the only judge in South Australia.[97] Upon his arrival in South Australia, Cooper J immediately broke with tradition by sitting in court without a wig or gown.[98] This appears to have not been a shock to the South Australian legal fraternity, for at that time, most of the legal practitioners in South Australia had been trained as attorneys or solicitors in England who did not wear any form of court dress.[99]

In May 1846, two English barristers, Messrs Wilkins and Stephen, appeared before Cooper J in full court dress as worn by the English Bar, whereas their learned friends on the other side of the bar table appeared without wigs, as was the custom in South Australia at the time.[100] The local paper reported that "though it certainly reminds us of the Courts at home, being dispensed with by his Honour and the Colonial Bar it is hardly in the best taste to wear."[101] Upon seeing them so arrayed, Cooper J told them that:

> If anyone is justified in wearing a wig, it is myself; for in summer I am tormented with the flies settling on my bare head. But I fear that, if I were to adopt it, I should be still more fatigued than I am already by the long sittings which I frequently have to endure.[102]

Following the appearance of Wilkins and Stephens in traditional court dress, a few months later another English barrister attempted to emulate the same form of dress, only this time to be rebuked by Cooper J:

> When … JW Nicholls, who was also an English barrister, appeared in a wig, the judge inquired whether he wore the wig because he supposed it a necessary part of his costume as a barrister. Nicholls said he wore it as a mark of respect. The judge [Cooper J] remarked that members of the English bar were admitted to South Australia as general practitioners, and he did not think it was fair to the other lawyers in Adelaide, who could not obtain wigs, to make an invidious distinction, adding 'As long as only one gentleman thought fit to make himself ridiculous by dressing in that which is not the costume of the Court, I did not

---

97. He was a member of Inner Temple, had been called to the Bar in 1827 and practiced on the Oxford circuit until Colonial appointment. He would have been used to wearing the stuff robe and short wig of Counsel.
98. John Emerson, "Why are you wearing a wig: Changes in court etiquette in South Australia," 26/10 *Law Society Bulletin of South Australia* (2004) 31.
99. *Ibid.*
100. McQueen, *supra*, 48.
101. A. J. Hannan, *The Life of Justice Way* (Sydney: Angus and Robertson, 1960) 99.
102. Emerson, *supra.*

say anything about it, when I find others following his example I think it necessary to do so.[103]

The above comments by Cooper J were no doubt also directed to GN Stephen, who initially first wore the wig in court before Cooper J, and who was in fact present in the court wearing the wig when Cooper J made the aforesaid remarks about the 'ridiculous' wigs.[104] Upon hearing those comments, Stephen remarked to Cooper J that:

> having now realised that by wearing a wig in South Australia he might (in contradistinction to the practice in England) offend the bench, he would tear his wig off and throw it to the floor rather than show disrespect to the bench. Mr Justice Cooper, in his most measured tones, tolf Stephen that such an action was unnecessary. Simply removing the wig in the robing room would suffice.[105]

Photograph of Sir Charles Cooper (1795-1887), the first Chief Justice of South Australia, dating circa 1865. He was appointed Chief Justice in 1856 and retired in 1861. This appears to be the first photograph ever taken of a judicial figure from South Australia wearing a wig over court dress. Attributed to the State Library of South Australia

In making the above remarks, Cooper J also alluded to the possibility of wigs being adopted in the future in a new court building and if the legal profession was to be divided between barristers and solicitors as was envisaged at the time:

> If indeed anyone is justified in wearing a wig, it is myself; for in summer I am tormented with the flies settling on my bare head. But I fear that, if I were to adopt it, I should be still more fatigued than I am by the long sittings which I frequently have to endure. At the same time, I do not say that I may not make a change in the costume of the Court and adopt that to which I had long been accustomed to in England, when we have a more convenient Court-house, should the contemplated division be made in the profession and should gentlemen be able to procure wigs.[106]

As a result of this confusion, and in order to clarify the appropriate form of dress to be worn by South Australian practitioners, in 1850 Cooper J made the following rules of court specifying that "the costume of the gentlemen attending the Court should be, as heretofore, a black coat and waistcoat, a white neckcloth and bands."[107] However, this newly stipulated rule of court did not last for long, for later that year on 13 August 1850, Dr George Crawford[108] - the third Judge appointed to the South Australian Supreme Court - presided over his first criminal sessions in a wig:

---

103. Hannan, *supra*, 100.
104. McQueen, *supra*, 48.
105. *Ibid*, 49.
106. Hannan, *supra*, 100.
107. Emerson, *supra*.
108. Crawford J arrived from Ireland and was a member of the Dublin Bar.

Portrait dating circa 1830 of Dr George Crawford (1812-1852), as a young man, prior to his appointment as a judge of the Supreme Court of South Australia. The annotation under the image reads "George John Crawford Esq. appointed 2nd Judge of Supreme Court of SA by Letters Patent, 27th June 1850. Died 24 September 1852". Attributed to the State Library of South Australia

> Mr Justice Crawford opened the sittings this morning, as was expected. His Honour appeared in the wig judicial, which certainly added to his dignity, while in no degree detracted from the comeliness of his appearance.[109]

This appears to be the first time that a Judge has worn a wig in a South Australian court,[110] and it was from this point that the wearing of wigs by both the South Australian Bench and Bar began to be enforced by the courts.[111] It also appears that Cooper CJ must have finally yielded to this custom, for in the full court sittings later that month he also wore a wig, and they have been worn by Judges in South Australia ever since.[112] However, the Judges at this stage continued to wear plain black gowns for both criminal and civil cases.[113] Sir George Cooper's successor, Sir Richard Davies Hanson, seems to have continued the custom of wearing the wig and silk gown over court dress, as can be seen from a photograph of him robed dating from circa 1880, which appears to be the earliest photograph of a Judge of the Supreme Court of South Australia wearing court dress.

Upon his appointment in 1876 as Chief Justice of South Australia, Sir Samuel Way remodeled the Supreme Court on the High Court of Judicature and, as part of his reforms, adopted the scarlet robes worn by English Judges for criminal sittings.[114] Within a year of Way CJ's appointment, the South Australian Register reported the following:

> The forms of the judicial tribunals of the mother-country are being gradually introduced into the Courts of this Colony. The latest innovation on previous practice is the wearing of the time-honoured distinctive costumes by some of the Judges. The Chief Justice, in presiding at the libel action in the Supreme Court, appeared in the scarlet robes trimmed with ermine that has been for centuries the dress worn by judges when presiding in criminal sessions.[115]

Finally, on 13 March 1877, a new rule was brought into operation by the Supreme Court of South Australia requiring all Counsel to appear before the Court in wigs,[116] and this rule still applies to Counsel appearing in criminal sittings of the Supreme and District Courts of South Australia.

---

109. "Law and Police Courts," *South Australian Register*, 13 August 1850, 3.
110. "Barristers' Wig," *South Australian Chronicle and Weekly Mail*, 17 March 1877, 4.
111. McQueen, *supra*, 49.
112. Emerson, *supra*.
113. *Ibid*.
114. Sir Samuel James Way, 1st Baronet of Montefiore (1836-1916) was Attorney-General of South Australia (1875-1876) and Chief Justice of the Supreme Court of South Australia (1876-1916). In 1897, Sir Samuel became the first Australian to be appointed to the Judicial Committee of the Privy Council.
115. "The Judicial Ermine," *South Australian Register*, Thursday 12 July 1877, 5.
116. "Barristers' Wig," *South Australian Chronicle and Weekly Mail*, 17 March 1877, 4.

Painting of Sir Richard Davies Hanson, Chief Justice of South Australia, dated circa 1880, wearing the full-bottomed wig instead of the bench wig. Attributed to the State Library of South Australia

Photograph of William Alfred Wearing QC (1816-1875), who was appointed Crown Solicitor and later the third Justice of the Supreme Court of South Australia. Part of his judicial duties involved holding the Palmerston Circuit Court in the Northern Territory, from where he was returning when the SS Gothenburg he was on was wrecked on the Great Barrier Reef and he drowned there on 24 February 1875. Attributed to the State Library of South Australia

Photograph of Sir Richard Davies Hanson, Chief Justice of South Australia, dated circa 1880, wearing court attire. He is depicted wearing the black silk gown over a court coat and waistcoat, bands and a bench wig, along with a 'chin curtain beard' which was popular at the time. Attributed to the State Library of South Australia

THE HON. RANDOLPH ISHAM STOW, THE NEW JUDGE OF SOUTH AUSTRALIA.

Above left. Portrait of Randolph Isham Stow (1828-1878), who was appointed a Justice of the Supreme Court of South Australia in 1875 following the drowning of Wearing J until his own untimely death in 1878. Attributed to the State Library of Victoria

Above right. Photograph of Sir Samuel Way (1836-1916) dated circa 1900, who was appointed Chief Justice on 18 March 1876 until his death on 8 January 1916, a record of almost 40 years. Attributed to the State Library of South Australia

Photograph of Sir Mellis Napier (1882-1976) wearing the ceremonial robes of scarlet, at the opening of Parliament in Adelaide in 1924. He was later appointed as the fifth Chief Justice of South Australia in 1942 and held that position until his retirement from office in 1967. Attributed to the State Library of South Australia

Left. Photograph of the Judges of the Supreme Court, dated 22 December 1914. Seated left to right: Mr Justice Gordon, Chief Justice Sir Samuel Way, Mr Justice Murray. Standing left to right: E.M. Sabine (Associate), G. C. Ligertwood (Associate), W. L. Stuart (Master of Supreme Court), Fred Balfour Schultz (later known as Fred Balfour McBryde). The Judges are each wearing a black silk gown over a court coat and waistcoat and bands and a bench wig.
Attributed to the State Library of South Australia

Below. Former Chief Justice John Doyle leads his fellow judges at the 2006 Opening of the South Australian Parliament, wearing scarlet robes and hoods faced with miniver, laced jabots and full-bottomed wigs with white gloves in their hands.
© InDaily/Nat Rogers

Newly appointed South Australian Governor, the Hon. Hieu Van Le, reads out his oath of office at his swearing-in ceremony at the Adelaide Convention Centre, Adelaide, on Monday, 1 September, 2014. Chief Justice Kourakis looks on, wearing the scarlet robes faced with silk, scarlet casting-hood, black scarf and black girdle with white bands and a full-bottomed wig.

From 1876 until 2016, the Judges of the Supreme Court of Australia wore different robes for different sittings of the Court. For criminal sittings, the Judges of the Supreme Court of South Australia wore scarlet robes faced with silk or taffeta, with a scarlet casting hood and black cincture, with bands or jabots and a bench wig. For ceremonial occasions however, the practice of the Court has varied. For example, whilst Judges wore black silk gowns and full-bottomed wigs for ceremonial occasions in court, for ceremonial occasions outside of court Judges predominantly wore scarlet robes faced with either miniver or silk. The variation in practice can be seen by the fact that whilst the Judges wore scarlet robes and hoods faced with miniver at the State Opening of Parliament in 2006,[117] Kourakis CJ instead wore scarlet robes faced with silk (without the corresponding hood) and a full-bottomed wig at the swearing-in ceremony of the Governor of South Australia, the Honourable Hieu Van Li on 1 September 2014.[118]

117. On other occasions the Judges of the Supreme Court of South Australia have simply worn their black silk robes with full-bottomed wigs when attending the State Opening of Parliament. At the 2014 Opening of the South Australian Parliament, the Judges wore their scarlet robes faced with silk with a bench wig but without the corresponding hood.

118. The dress of Kourakis CJ at the swearing-in ceremony was arguably more in line with the Judges' Rules of 1635 which stipulated the proper dress when in the presence of the Sovereign (namely, robe and casting hood, rather than the mantle and hood).

In early 2004, the wig was abolished in civil cases in the Supreme Court of South Australia. Recently, the Chief Justice of South Australia advised the Law Society of South Australia that, at a meeting of Judges of the Supreme Court of South Australia on 31 July 2017, the Judges of the Supreme Court had resolved that wigs will no longer be worn by legal practitioners for ceremonial sittings of the Court, including admissions ceremonies.[119] The decision also applies to the Judges of the Supreme Court, as wigs are no longer worn by Justices of the Supreme Court in criminal, civil or appellate proceedings, nor on ceremonial occasions.[120] Wigs continue to be worn by counsel in criminal sittings of the Court. The current practice direction relating to the dress of counsel appearing in the Supreme Court of South Australia is set out in rule 25 of the *Supreme Court Criminal Supplementary Rules 2014* (SA) which provides that:

Ceremonial sitting of the Supreme Court of South Australia, for the welcome to Justice David Lovell held in the Sir Samuel Way Building in Adelaide, South Australia on 25 February 2015. © Greg Higgs/Newspix

119. "Practitioner Alert - Court Attire," *Law Society of South Australia*, <https://www.lawsocietysa.asn.au/LSSA/newsfeeds/Practitioner_Alert_-_Court_Attire.aspx> (assessed 5 April 2018).

120. Correspondence between from the Associate to the Chief Justice, the Hon. Christopher Kourakis, to the writer, 16 April 2018.

> The dress of barristers appearing in Court is to be black court coat or bar jacket, white jabot and gown (silk for Queen's Counsel and Senior Counsel and stuff for junior counsel), dark trousers for men and dark skirt or slacks/trousers for women. As an alternative to the jabot, white bands may be worn with white shirt and wing collar.
>
> Wigs will be worn when the Court is hearing criminal proceedings (not including appeals).
>
> Barristers' attire should be at all times in a clean and neat condition.[121]

As for the dress of the Judges of the District Court of South Australia, the Judges of this Court wore the same robes worn by English circuit Judges and Judges in District Courts throughout Australia, namely the violet robes with casting hood over the left shoulder, black cincture, jabots or bands and a bench wig. Interestingly, unlike other District Court Judges around Australia, the Judges of the District Court of South Australia have worn a lilac casting hood as opposed to a scarlet casting hood over their violet robes. This derived from the lilac casting hood worn by English County Court Judges presiding over civil matters and is also worn by Circuit Court Judges on ceremonial occasions. The symbolic lilac casting hood continues to be worn by South Australian District Court Judges in the form of a lilac sash.

New Robes for the Judges of the Supreme Court and District Court of South Australia

On 18 November 2016, the Court announced that the Judges of the Supreme and District Courts of South Australia had adopted new robes for their respective courts.[122] In designing the new robes, the Judges wanted more practical robes (that is, without any additional items such as casting hoods and scarves or other attachments), and the one robe to be worn for all occasions.[123] In announcing the new robes on 18 November 2016, the Court said that the new robes had been designed by a Committee of Judges of the Supreme and District Courts:

> With effect from January 2017 the Supreme and District Courts have adopted new judicial robes. The new robes were designed by a committee of Supreme and District Court Judges.
>
> The robes are made of Australian merino wool and are designed to be lighter and more practical than the previous three-piece robes worn by the judiciary. The new robe will be worn by the judiciary in both criminal and

121. This paragraph formerly read as "Wigs will be worn only when the Court is hearing criminal proceedings (including appeals) and on ceremonial occasions. Wigs will not be worn in civil proceedings" prior to its amendment by the *Supreme Court Criminal Supplementary Rules 2014* (*Amendment No. 4*) (SA).
122. Supreme Court of South Australia, Media Release, "New Supreme Court and District Court Robes", 18 November 2016.
123. *Ibid.*

> civil jurisdictions. The Courts Administration Authority will meet the cost of the new robes for the current Judges who have paid for their existing robes.
>
> The Supreme Court robe features a scarlet sash while the District Court robe features a lilac sash. The robes have been manufactured in Australia.[124]

The Supreme Court and District Court robes are identical save for the colour of the fixed pleated sash, which is as long as the robe itself, to signify the traditional Supreme Court scarlet casting-hood and District Court lilac casting-hood, although the lilac casting hood is now over the right shoulder when previously was worn over the left shoulder. Whilst the Judges of the Supreme Court no wear wigs on any occasion, the Judges of the District Courts continue to wear the bench wig in the criminal jurisdiction, although some District Court Judges choose not to do so.[125] Wigs are not worn when Judges of the District Court are sitting in civil proceedings or on ceremonial occasions.[126] Previously, on ceremonial occasions and sittings, the Supreme and District Court Judges wore the full-bottomed wig and bench wig respectively.

The new robe of the Justices of the Supreme Court of South Australia © Supreme Court of South Australia

124. *Ibid.*

125. Correspondence between the writer and the Associate to the Chief Justice, the Hon. Christopher Kourakis, 16 April 2018.

126. *Ibid.*

Right. Chief Justice Kourakis seen presiding over the Legislative Assembly as the newly elected South Australian Premier Steven Marshall (standing on the far left) and other members of Parliament taking their oaths or affirmations of allegiance prior to taking their seats in the chamber, on 3 May 2018. He was sworn in alongside Liberal MPs Stephen Patterson and Steve Murray, and Labor MP Stephen Mullighan, in what the clerk of the house (pictured standing on the left wearing a barrister's wig and court dress similar to that worn by clerks of the House of Lords) described as a "quartet of Stephens". The Chief Justice is wearing the new robes with a fixed sash resembling the scarlet casting hood and white bands.

Above. South Australian District Court Judges during a special sitting in their new robes to mark the appointment of the new Chief Judge Michael Evans on 7 February 2017. The Judges are wearing their new black robes with the lilac sash representing the lilac casting hood traditionally worn by South Australian District Court Judges.
© Roger Wyman/ Newspix

Opposite, bottom. Justices of the Supreme Court of Australia seen in the foreground wearing their new robes with the fixed scarlet sash representing the scarlet casting-hood, at the recent Opening of Parliament of South Australia on 3 May 2018 following the state election. The President of the Legislative Council (the Hon. Andrew McLachlan MLC) can be seen on the left wearing the black silk gown over court dress and full-bottomed wig (as is worn by Presidents of the Legislative Council during ceremonial occasions) facing the Governor of South Australia, the Hon. Hieu Van Le.
© AAP Image/David Mariuz

Left. Photograph of the Lord Chief Justice of Northern Ireland (Sir Declan Morgan) with newly appointed Judges Elizabeth McCaffrey and Neil Rafferty QC of the County Court of Northern Ireland. The robes worn by the County Court Judges of Northern Ireland - a violet robe, black girdle, bands, lilac casting hood and bench wig - were the same robes which were, up until recently, worn by the Judges of the District Court of South Australia.
© Lord Chief Justice's Office

TASMANIA

Since the establishment of the Supreme Court of Tasmania, the Judges have worn the robes associated with the Judges sitting in the Court of Chancery, namely a black silk gown over mourning dress and a bench wig. In 1954, the Judges of the Supreme Court of Tasmania began wearing the scarlet robes and hood faced with miniver, along with the scarlet casting hood, black stole and cincture and wig for ceremonial occasions and the same dress but without the hood for criminal matters and appeals.[127] The scarlet robes were adopted in time for Her Majesty the Queen's visit to Tasmania that year.[128]

Photograph of Sir John Stokell Dodds, Chief Justice of Tasmania (1898-1914), dated 1901, wearing the black silk gown over a court coat and waistcoat, bands and a bench wig. This exact dress continues to be worn by Judges of the Supreme Court of Tasmania during criminal sittings and ceremonial occasions. Attributed to the National Library of Australia

Current Chief Justice of Tasmania, the Hon. Alan Blow AO (2013-), sitting in the Supreme Court of Tasmania wearing a black silk gown over a court coat and waistcoat, bands and a bench wig. © Supreme Court of Tasmania

127. Supreme Court of Tasmania, Circular to Practitioners No 9, "Judicial court apparel in criminal trials and appeals", 6 June 2008.

128. Memorandum on Court Dress from Helen Vizer, Supreme Court Legal Research Officer, to the writer, dated 1 June 2018.

Full-bottomed wigs were worn by judges for the church service for the Opening of the Legal Year, when attending the Opening of Parliament, and by the Chief Justice on the swearing-in of a new Governor as well as his own swearing-in ceremony.[129] Historically, however, they were not worn on other ceremonial occasions, although it is also believed that they may have been worn decades ago in the Court of Criminal Appeal.[130] Prior to 1984 every judge had a full-bottomed wig which was worn on all ceremonial occasions.[131] This changed after 1984 when some judges did not acquire full-bottomed wigs, and from 1994 until 2008, those with full-bottomed wigs wore them on ceremonial occasions, but not all judges had them.[132] For civil matters, the Judges wear a black silk gown over mourning dress. Specifically, the Judges wear a waistcoat, a swallow-tailed coat, a black silk gown, and a rosette.[133] Senior Counsel wear a bar jacket, a black silk gown and a rosette.[134]

Judges of the Supreme Court of Tasmania sitting in court wearing a black silk gown over a court coat and waistcoat, and bands, but without a bench wig. © Supreme Court of Tasmania

129. *Ibid.*
130. *Ibid.*
131. *Ibid.*
132. *Ibid.*
133. *Ibid.*
134. *Ibid.*

On 1 February 2005 the then Chief Justice of Tasmania, the late Peter Underwood, issued a practice direction announcing that wigs would no longer be worn by either Judges of Counsel "in all matters within the Civil Jurisdiction of the Court whether at first instance or in Full Court. In such matters, the dress will be gown, bar jacket, jabot or bands",[135] although there was no change to the requirements for court dress in the Criminal Jurisdiction of the Court. On 6 June 2008, the Supreme Court of Tasmania issued a circular to practitioners announcing that the scarlet robes would no longer be worn by Judges of the Supreme Court of Tasmania, and that the Judges would wear their civil robes for all occasions, including criminal sittings, appeals and ceremonial sittings in the Court (however, as of 19 November 2018 the Judges have adopted a black and red gown to be worn over mourning dress when sitting in criminal trials and appeals).[136] It was also announced that the wig would no longer be worn for ceremonial sittings of the Court by both the Bench and Bar, although wigs continue to be worn by Judges when attending the church service for the Opening of the Legal Year, to the Opening of Parliament, and when the Chief Justice swears in a new Governor.[137]

The Judges of the Supreme Court of Tasmaina at the farewell ceremonial sitting in 2008 of the former Chief Justice of Tasmania, the late Hon. Peter Underwood AC (1937-2014), who was appointed a Judge of the Supreme Court in 1984 and was later Chief Justice from 2004 to 2008. The Judges are wearing the scarlet robes and hood faced with miniver which were the ceremonial robes of Tasmanian Judges from 1954 to 2008.
© Supreme Court of Tasmania

135. Supreme Court of Tasmania, Practice Direction No 2 of 2005, "Court of Appeal", 1 February 2005.
136. Supreme Court of Tasmania, Circular to Practitioners No 9, "Judicial court apparel in criminal trials and appeals", 6 June 2008. Recently, it was announced that as from sittings commencing on 19 November 2018 the Judges would adopt a modern black and red gown to be worn in criminal trials and appeals instead of the traditional black robes (wigs will continue to be worn and the black robes will continue to be worn in civil trials); the new gowns are almost identical to the gowns worn by Judges in some of the Provincial Courts in Canada and are worn over a court coat and waistcoat: Supreme Court of Tasmania, Circular to Practitioners No 13 of 2018, "Judicial Robes in Criminal Trials and Appeals", 12 November 2018.
137. Memorandum on Court Dress from Helen Vizer, Supreme Court Legal Research Officer, to the writer, dated 1 June 2018.

The late Chief Justice Peter Underwood with former Premier Paul Lennon during a brief swearing in ceremony at Government House in Hobart on the morning of 2 December 2004. Justice Underwood was sworn in as Chief Justice, succeeding Chief Justice William Cox.
© AAP Image/David Killick

Photograph taken on 18 November 2018 of the Chief Justice of Tasmania, the Hon. Alan Blow AO and the Hon. Justice Michael Brett wearing the new red and black gown which is now worn by the Judges of the Supreme Court of Tasmania in criminal trials and appeals. The red and black gown replaces the traditional black silk gown and is worn over a swallow-tailed coat and waistcoat, along with bands and a bench wig. The new gown is almost identical to the gown worn by Judges in some Provincial Courts in Canada.

The ceremonial dress has reverted to black silk robes with a bench wig instead of a full-bottomed wig, thus relegating the full-bottomed wig to legal history. Justice Shan Tennent and Chief Justice Alan Blow attend the Opening of the Law Year service at St David's Cathedral in Hobart, on 3 February 2017.
© Photo by Nikki Davis Jones / Newspix

WESTERN AUSTRALIA

Supreme Court of Western Australia

It is unclear exactly when court dress was first adopted in Western Australia, although it appears that Richard West Nash, who acted twice as Advocate General in the 1840s while George Fletcher Moore, the first Commissioner of the Civil Court (which was the ancestor of the Supreme Court),[138] was absent on leave, was the first person to wear a wig and gown in the Civil Court in Western Australia in circa 1839.[139]

It is also unclear what robes were adopted by Judges upon the creation of the Supreme Court in 1861. Although there is a painting of Sir Archibald Burt - the first Chief Justice of the Supreme Court of Western Australia - it is not a contemporary one and was only painted during the last decade or so. There in fact do not appear to be any extant photographs of Burt CJ in court dress. The majority of early photographs of Supreme Court Judges depict them wearing the black silk gown over a court coat and trousers or breeches with jabots or bands and wearing either a full-bottomed or bench wig. An article in the West Australian written in 1888 about a judicial conference held in Australia shows that the Judges of the Supreme Court of Western Australia had not yet adopted the scarlet robes worn by their judicial brothers interstate and in England:

> Another question which came up, and one of undoubted importance from a clothes philosophy point of view, was the official costumes of the Judges; and upon this matter, weighty in more senses than one, the collective wisdom of a committee of Chief Justices is to be brought to bear. We trust that this committee will publish a report, for sure we are that the result of their researches and deliberations will be awaited with no little curiosity. With the body gear of Judges there is no great necessity for interference. The crimson robe-which by the way has not made its appearance in the Criminal Court of our own colony-is certainly not suggestive of coolness, when donned in the midst of an Australian summer. But at the same time it is a most imposing habiliament, and seeing to how great an extent the popular mind is impressed with the outward garb, the Judges might wisely remain faithful to a vestment which is both becoming in form, and, respectable in point of antiquity. Even if the heat compels them to abandon their more prosaic outer garments, the sacrifice of these would scarcely be too great if only the official robe were maintained.[140]

---

138. The *Civil Court of Western Australia Act 1832* (WA) (2 Will. IV No. 1) which established the Civil Court vested it with jurisdiction "of all pleas and jurisdiction in all cases as fully and amply in Western Australia, as His Majesty's Courts of King's Bench, Common Pleas and Exchequer lawfully have in England. Similar wording can be found in s 16 of the *Supreme Court Act 1935* (WA) which provides that its successor in the form of the Supreme Court of Western Australia is, *inter alia*, "invested with and shall exercise such and the like jurisdiction, powers, and authority within Western Australia and its dependencies as the Courts of Queen's Bench, Common Pleas, and Exchequer, or either of them, and the judges thereof".

139. Geoffrey Bolton & Geraldine Byrne, *May it Please Your Honour: A History of the Supreme Court of Western Australia 1861-2005* (The Law Society of Western Australia, 2005) 19.

140. "The West Australian," *The West Australian*, 27 August 27 1888, 3.

By 1903, however, Western Australia's Supreme Court Judges had finally adopted the "crimson robe", bringing their attire in sync with the rest of the Australian mainland. There are a number of sources which establish the date of this change to scarlet. One of the earliest photographs of a Judge of the Supreme Court of Western Australia wearing scarlet robes is that of Burnside J (1902-1929), most likely taken at the time of his appointment to the bench in 1902. He is photographed wearing the scarlet hood faced with taffeta with plain bands and a bench wig. There is also an article in the West Australian which states that the Judges of the Supreme Court wore scarlet robes during the opening ceremony of the newly created Supreme Court building in Stirling Gardens on 8 June 1903:

Portrait of Sir Archibald Burt (1810-1879), the first Chief Justice of the Supreme Court of Western Australia (1861-1879). It is important to note that this portrait may not accurately reflect the dress worn by Judges at the time, as it is not a contemporary portrait and was commissioned by the Supreme Court of Western Australia in the early part of the 21st century as part of its project of having portraits of the past Chief Justices of the Supreme Court, as is the custom in many Supreme Courts around Australia.

> With a smiling sun above, ladies were able to attend the ceremony in great numbers, thronging the broad staircase and crowding to the edge of the balustraded gallery surrounding the main hall of the building. Their costumes lent a medley of colour to the brilliant uniforms of the vice-regal party and of the Commandant and military officers, and to the crimson robes of the Chief Justice and puisne Judges, a contrast intensified again by the dazzling whiteness of the walls of the vestibule and the black gowns and white wigs of the members of the Bar who filled the hall. …
>
> On the floor of the hall gathered the members of the Bar, leaving a passage immediately in front of the dais, where the principals were to take their stand. Legislators assembled at the west end of the hall, and the officers of the Court, with the architect (Mr. J. H. Grainger), and the contractors (Mr. W. H. Vincent and his son), were posted at the eastern end. The Chief Justice. Mr. Justice Parker, and Mr. Justice McMillan wore their scarlet robes, Mr. Commissioner Roe his ordinary wig and gown, the Attorney-General his levee costume, with flowing wig and gown of office, and the Sheriff (Mr. Oct. Burt. I.S.O.), his uniform and dangling sword. A small procession went out to the avenue a few minutes before noon to await the Governor's arrival.[141]

---

141. "The New Law Courts," *The West Australian*, 9 June 1903, 5.

Portrait of Sir Henry Wrenfordsley (1825-1908), who succeeded Burt CJ as the second Chief Justice of the Supreme Court of Western Australia (1880-1883). As with all of the portraits of the older Chief Justices, this portrait is not contemporary and is highly unusual in that it rather interestingly portrays Wrenfordsley CJ standing afar, in front of a court building, presumably because the artist could not find any clear or close up photographs of Wrenfordsley CJ.

It is also interesting to note that Western Australia appears to be the only Australian state in which the winter scarlet robes faced with miniver were never adopted by Judges and that Judges only wore the more cooler scarlet silk robes and accompanying hood for ceremonial occasions and removed the hood for criminal sittings. This was most likely due to Western Australia's hot weather, particularly during the summer. The weather has also played a role in the attire worn by the Bench and Bar in Western Australia, for there have been Western Australian Judges who have removed their wigs and permitted counsel to do the same due to heat-waves, one such example taking place during the hot summer in February 1947:

Portrait of Sir Edward Stone (1844-1920), fourth Chief Justice of the Supreme Court of Western Australia (1901-1906).
© Supreme Court of Western Australia

Photograph of Justice Robert Burnside, circa 1912.
© State Library of Western Australia

> What with many spectators within and a glaring sun without, the atmosphere during a murder trial in the Criminal Court yesterday grew more and more oppressive, until at last Mr. Justice Walker - repeating the thoughtful dispensation which he pronounced in similar circumstances a week earlier - informed the jurors that if they felt like removing their coats they had his permission to do so. They did so, instanter, with appreciative smiles. The Judge told advocates at the Bar that they could take off their wigs, if they wanted to. They did want to, and the Judge doffed his own. But, less fortunate than the jury, counsel remained sweltering in their coats and heavy black gowns, their discomfort assuaged some what, perhaps, by the thought that they had a companion in distress--the Judge, who remained swathed in his robes of scarlet.[142]

In any event, by the early twentieth century the custom had become to wear scarlet silk robes and hood, with white bands and full-bottomed wigs for ceremonial occasions, both inside and outside of the Court. This is the dress

142. "News and Notes," *The West Australian* 11 February 1947, 8.

Justices Northmore, McMillan and Draper standing outside of the Stirling Gardens Supreme Court building in circa 1929. They are wearing the ceremonial dress associated with Queen's Counsel, namely a black silk gown over a court coat and waistcoat, with breeches and black stockings, buckled shoes, bands and a full-bottomed wig. This appears to be the most recent photograph showing Judges wearing the breeches, stockings and buckled shoes. © State Library of Western Australia

worn by Sir John Dwyer CJ at the swearing-in ceremonies of Governors Sir James Mitchell and Sir Charles Gairdner in 1948 and 1951 respectively. It is also the dress worn by Sir Samuel Jackson and other Supreme Court Judges at a legal procession to St Mary's Cathedral for the Opening of the Law Term in the early 1970s.[143] However, there are occasional instances where Judges reverted to the black silk gown over court dress for ceremonial occasions, as can be seen in the photograph of welcoming ceremony for Northmore J in 1913, in which the Judges are depicted wearing black gowns over court dress and a bench wig.[144]

143. Bolton & Byrne, *supra*, 222. Western Australian Judges discontinued the practice of having Church ceremonies for the Opening of the Law Term in 1980s during the chief justiceship of Sir Francis Burt.

144. It was also unclear to some in the local media as to what was the most commonly worn attire for Supreme Court Judges, for in one article in 1952 it was presumed that the black silk gown was worn for most court sittings: "the scarlet robes of the judge sitting in criminal sessions date back to a 1635 edict Same grey and scarlet robes are prescribed for other occasions, but are not often used today. In Perth Supreme Court, everyday dress for judges is the black silk of the QC. They wear a different wig" ("The Black Cap is Badge of Mourning," *Mirror* 21 June 1952, 10).

Portrait of Sir John Northmore, Chief Justice of the Supreme Court of Western Australia (1931-1945). © Supreme Court of Western Australia

Above, right. Portrait of Sir John Dwyer (1879-1966), Chief Justice of the Supreme Court of Western Australia (1945-1959), wearing a black silk gown over court dress and jabot and bench wig, which was the customary dress of Judges presiding over civil matters. Judges of the Supreme Court of Western Australia discontinued the wearing of wigs in civil matters in 1999. © Supreme Court of Western Australia

Left. Sir James Mitchell being sworn in by the Administrator Sir John Dwyer CJ as Governor of Western Australia, on 4 November 1948. From left to right: Ralph Doig, Sir John Dwyer, Sir James Mitchell, Premier Ross McLarty MLA. Dwyer CJ is wearing the scarlet summer robes faced with taffeta, a black girdle, bands and a full-bottomed wig. However, he is not wearing black stockings or buckled shoes, which indicates that they were discontinued by Judges sometime between 1929 and 1948. © State Library of Western Australia

Above. Sir Charles Gairdner, (1898-1983) Governor of Western Australia from 1951 to 1963, is being sworn in as Governor of Western Australia by the Administrator Sir John Dwyer CJ, on 6 November 1951. © State Library of Western Australia

Left. Portrait of Sir Albert Wolff (1899-1977), Chief Justice of the Supreme Court of Western Australia (1959-1969). © Supreme Court of Western Australia

Upon the appointment of Sir Francis Burt in 1977 a few changes were introduced to the Judges' robes. The full-bottomed wig was discontinued for ceremonial occasions and was replaced by the bench wig which was now to be worn for all sittings. Another minor change was in the neck-wear of Judges, for in 1982 the Judges decided to wear lace jabots or stocks instead of the more traditional white bands (probably due the High Court's similar change from bands to laced jabots which took place at the same time).[145] Further changes took place when the late Hon. David Malcolm AC, QC succeeded Sir Francis Burt as Chief Justice in 1988. On 17 May 1999, Malcolm CJ announced that Judges in the Supreme and District Courts of Western Australia abandoned the wearing of wigs in civil proceedings and directed counsel to not wear them in civil proceedings either.[146] At the time Malcolm CJ stated that the decision to discontinue the practice of wearing wigs in civil proceedings was strongly supported by both the Western Australian Bar Association and Law Society of Western Australia, although no change was made to the dress worn by Judges and Counsel in criminal proceedings, the then Court of Criminal Appeal and for ceremonial occasions:

> One of my long-term goals has been to ensure that the law of the Courts and its procedures are appropriate for the times in which we live.
>
> There should not be change for change's sake, but we believe that as we approach the 21st century, the time has come to abandon this centuries-old tradition.
>
> I believe this move will be welcomed by the public.[147]

Following the abandoning of wigs civil proceedings in the Supreme and District Courts, the former Chief Justice of the Family Court of Australia, the Hon. Alastair Nicholson AO RFD, issued practice directions stating that "[a]s counsel do not wear wigs in civil proceedings in the Supreme Court of Western Australia or in the the Federal Court of Australia, it is no longer necessary for counsel to wear wigs when appearing before the Full Court

Contemporary portrait of the Hon. David Kingsley Malcolm AC, QC (1938-2014), former Chief Justice of Western Australia (1988-2006) and Lieutenant Governor of Western Australia (1990-2009). Judges replaced the bands with jabots in around 1982 and wore this dress in civil matters until it was replaced by the modern robes in 2003. Supreme Court Judges continued to wear their criminal and ceremonial robes until May 2007 and January 2010 respectively when they were replaced by the simple black robe which is worn without a jabot/bands or wig. © Supreme Court of Western Australia

145. "Robes of District Court Judges," *Brief* (June 1991) 43.

146. Supreme Court of Western Australia, Media Release, "May 17, 1999 - Wigs Abandoned in Civil Proceedings", 17 May 1999.

147. *Ibid.*

of the Family Court of Australia sitting in Western Australia."[148]

In the 2001 *Annual Review of Western Australian Courts*, Malcolm CJ announced that the Supreme Court's Court Dress Committee, which was chaired by Anderson J, was continuing its review of court dress and had produced a report with recommendations which would be considered in early 2002 in consultation with Judges and Magistrates of other Western Australian courts.[149] The Chief Justice noted that the recommendations in the report included simplifying robes and abandoning wigs, although Malcolm CJ acknowledged that there was "still a degree of support for the wearing of wigs by Judges in criminal trials."[150] In the following year's Annual Review, Malcolm CJ announced that on 20 November 2002 the Supreme Court Judges had unanimously agreed to adopt a new simplified black robe, replacing the traditional black silk gown over court dress, which will be worn over normal business attire without any bands or jabots, but that the existing scarlet robes and bench wigs would continue to be worn for criminal trials and ceremonial sittings.[151] The Chief Justice also announced that bar jackets would no longer be worn by Judges in chambers and that Judges will wear normal business attire instead,[152] although to date the Master of the Supreme Court continues to wear the bar jacket when sitting in chambers.

The Hon. David Malcolm AC, QC, former Chief Justice of Western Australia, during his farewell ceremony on 7 February 2006. The black scarf can be clearly seen worn underneath the hood. The robe and hood are faced with shot pink taffeta, which was the traditional facing for summer scarlet robes until the mid-nineteenth century when it was replaced by slate-grey taffeta. ©West Australian Newspapers Limited

The new robes, which were designed by Pullin and Wheeler JJ, are black in colour and have a number of buttons on the edges of the sleeves (which reflects the buttoned sleeves of the Queen's counsels' court coat and bar jacket) as well as a zip which comes up to the bottom of the neck, leaving the neckwear visible, similar in style to the robes worn by Justices of the High Court of Australia. The simplified nature of the robes was humorously alluded to by the then Attorney General, the Hon Michael Mischin MLC, at the farewell ceremony of Wheeler J - one of the designers of the new robes - on 22 February 2010:

> In concluding it would be remiss of me not to mention one other contribution and legacy that she leaves the Court. Some will know that her Honour is

148. Family Court of Australia, Practice Direction No. 6 of 2001, 4 December 2001, issued by the Hon. Chief Justice Alastair Nicholson AO RFD.

149. Supreme Court of Western Australia, *2001 Annual Review of Western Australian Courts* (2002) 5.

150. *Ibid.*

151. Supreme Court of Western Australia, *2002 Annual Review of Western Australian Courts* (2003) 5.

152. *Ibid.*

an enthusiastic and accomplished clothes designer and maker and designed many of the elegant clothes that she has worn. What may not be widely known is that she, together with his Honour Pullin J, designed the practical and functional judicial garb worn by judges today. It is probably illustrative of my ignorance of the subtleties of fashion but I could not help noticing that after no doubt many hours of anguished deliberation and after drawing upon every spark of their combined talent and creativity, and with access to the full range of fabrics and styles and colours available at the disposal of the western world, they came up with what appears to be a zip-up smock in basic black. I blame Pullin J for this and I urge him not to give up his day job.[153]

Photograph of the ceremonial sitting of the Judges of the Supreme Court marking 100 years since the establishment of the Supreme Court building on 9 June 2003. The Judges are wearing their scarlet robes and mantles faced with slate grey taffeta. The Chief Justice is wearing shot pink taffeta facings. The Registrars sitting below are wearing the barrister's wig. © West Australian Newspapers Limited

In May 2006 the Hon. Wayne Martin AC succeeded the Hon. David Malcolm as Chief Justice of Western Australia. At his Honour's welcoming ceremony on 1 May 2006, the Judges appeared in their scarlet robes and hoods of silk, with black cinctures, a scarlet casting hood underneath the hood, with laced jabots and bench wigs. His Honour referred to the scarlet robes which he and his Honour's colleagues were wearing and said that he would be discussing with his judicial colleagues the question of modernising judicial attire although noting that there were differing views held on the subject of judicial dress:

---

153. Transcript of Proceedings at Perth on Thursday, 25 February 2010, Farewell to the Honourable Justice Wheeler, The Supreme Court of Western Australia, 8-9.

The Hon Wayne Martin AC, former Chief Justice of Western Australia, during the ceremonial welcoming of His Honour as Chief Justice on 10 May 2006. On the left is the Hon. Michael Murray QC, the then Senior Puisne Judge of the Supreme Court. © West Australian Newspapers Limited

There are a number of practices of the courts of this state which, in my view, could benefit from contemporary reappraisal. Some might think that observation incompatible with my present attire, given that my head gear derives from a fashion abandoned several hundred years ago by the European nobles who invented it to conceal their loss of hair.

Although, Mr Attorney, it's perhaps not inappropriate that we sit in red on May Day, I would myself have preferred to sit in a plain black robe with my pate exposed to public gaze. I will be asking my colleagues to review the use of wigs and ceremonial gowns in the near future. While there are, of course, differing views, reasonably and often firmly held, on this subject, for my own part I remain to be persuaded that this attire confers any greater respect or authority upon the holders of judicial office. Authority comes from the office itself and respect derives from actions not appearances.

The Federal and High Courts have long since given up the more colourful trappings of office and I hope to persuade my colleagues to follow their example. The adoption of symbols which suggest a preoccupation with European tradition seems to me to at least risk sending the wrong visual message from what should be a vibrant, contemporary Australian institution.[154]

154. Transcript of Proceedings at Perth on Monday, 1 May 2006, Welcome to the Honourable Chief Justice Martin, 24-25.

Photograph of Chief Justice Martin and the Judges of the Supreme Court at a ceremonial sitting of the Court marking the retirement of the Hon Justice McKechnie in 2015. The Judges are wearing the black robes over normal attire. Below the Judges are the Registrars of the Supreme Court.

Prior to his Honour's appointment as Chief Justice, Martin CJ had written on the topic of legal dress and had suggested that, in terms of the robes worn by the Bar, the dress be simplified.[155] In his article entitled "Forensic Fashions", his Honour also outlined the history of wigs and gowns, noting that the English Judges' habit is of European and Roman origin, and argued that the gown should be retained by legal practitioners so as to distinguish them from members of the public, although his Honour acknowledged that any such change may not be applied throughout all the courts:

> I confess to an ambivalent attitude toward the abolition of wigs and gowns. I thought the wastage of time spent robing and disrobing was the strongest argument for abolition, although the recent introduction of the jabot has very significantly reduced the amount of time required. If there is any weight at all in the argument that wigs and gowns assist in depersonalising the Court and its practitioners and in assisting the quest for truth, mere inconvenience should not outweigh those considerations. ...
>
> On balance, I think there are practical advantages in a ready means of identifying members of the Court and its practitioners from the other persons present during a hearing. ... My own view is that those advantages could be achieved by the mere use of a gown, worn over normal clothing. I believe that

155. Martin, *supra*, 7-10.

Photograph of the ceremonial sitting of the Judges of the Supreme Court of Western Australia to mark the opening of the new Supreme Court building in the David Malcolm Justice Centre on July 2016. Below them are the Registrars of the Supreme Court of Western Australia who are wearing the court dress worn by a junior barrister, namely a stuff gown over a bar jacket and bands or jabot.

> such a gown should be the universal badge of office of the legal practitioner when appearing as an advocate and would serve as a useful function in distinguishing practitioners from non-practitioners in such areas as tribunal and arbitration work, and in the rear of a crowded Court of Petty Sessions. However, … one weakness in this proposal is that it could not be universally applied.[156]

On 7 May 2007, just over a year after his Honour's appointment to the Bench, Martin CJ announced at a ceremonial sitting of the Court marking the commencement of Law Week that the Judges of the Supreme Court had resolved in 2006 to discontinue the practice of wearing the traditional scarlet robes, hoods, jabots and bench wigs for ceremonial occasions, but that the use of scarlet robes and wigs for criminal sittings would continue unchanged:

> Some of you may have noticed that we are not as colourfully dressed as on past ceremonial occasions. Last year, the Judges and Masters resolved that we would wear contemporary robes for ceremonial sittings of the Court, and reserve our more traditional regalia for criminal trials in which, it is argued, it confers advantages of anonymity and solemnity.[157]

---

156. *Ibid*, 10.
157. Speech by the Hon Wayne Martin, "The State of Justice Law Week Address - May 2007", Monday, 7 May 2007, 23.

This came to a head in 2009 when a majority of District and Supreme Court Judges agreed to abandon wigs in both courts. In a letter to the then President of the Law Society of Western Australia on 29 October 2009 the Chief Justice first advised the legal profession of the abolition of wigs and scarlet robes with effect from 1 January 2010:

> I write to advise that the Judges of the Supreme Court have resolved to discontinue the practice of wearing wigs and red robes in criminal work, with effect from 1 January 2010. As from that date, the black robe now worn by Judges of the Court in civil proceedings and in the Court of Appeal will be worn in all proceedings in open court (but not, of course, in Chambers work). The Judges have also resolved to direct that counsel appearing in criminal work are to discontinue the wearing of wigs effect from the same date. I will issue an amendment to the relevant Practice Direction in appropriate terms in due course.[158]

The Hon Justice James Edelman, (now a Justice of the High Court of Australia) at his ceremonial welcome as a Justice of the Supreme Court of Western Australia on 25 July 2011. His Honour is wearing the black robe now worn by Supreme Court Judges on all occasions, showing how the sleeves of the robes are derived from the sleeves of the court coat worn by Judges and Queen's/Senior Counsel. © West Australian Newspapers Limited

Finally, on 5 November 2009, Martin CJ publicly announced that the Judges of the Supreme Court and District Court of Western Australia will no longer wear wigs in court as of 1 January 2010, and that the Judges of the Supreme Court will from the beginning of 2010 wear the simplified black robes, rather than the scarlet robes faced with silk, scarlet casting hood, black cincture and laced jabots, for all sittings.[159] In announcing the historic changes, the Chief Justice stated the following:

> I have publicly stated since my appointment that I did not believe the wearing of traditional European court attire was appropriate in Western Australia in the 21st century. ... My judicial colleagues support that view. We believe that a move to more modern court attire better reflects how our Courts go about their work.[160]

It is interesting to note, however, that although 2009 was the last year in which Western Australian practitioners wore wigs in Western Australia's courts, it was not the last year when wigs were worn by Australian practitioners in Western Australia. Wigs were worn by Western Australian lawyers and Judges of the District Court for a commemorative wig photo in March 2010. Furthermore, wigs have continued to be worn by counsel from interstate who appear before the High Court when it is sitting in Perth, due to the fact that the policy of the High Court with regard to dress is that counsel must appear before it in the same dress as is worn in their own jurisdiction's appellate court.[161]

---

158. Correspondence from the Hon Wayne Martin to Mr Dudley Stow, 29 October 2009.
159. Supreme Court of Western Australia, Media Release, Judges change to modern court dress, 5 November 2009.
160. *Ibid.*
161. The writer personally witnessed such an occasion in 2015. Following a special sitting in Perth of the High Court to commemorate the passing of former Justice of the High Court, the Hon. John Toohey AC, QC, the High Court presided over appeals in which one party was from Western Australia (whose counsel appeared without wig) whilst the other party was from interstate, whose counsel appeared wearing a wig.

District Court of Western Australia

Upon the establishment of the District Court of Western Australia in 1970, pursuant to the *District Court Act 1969* (WA), the question arose as to the appropriate form of dress to be worn by the newly appointed Judges of the District Court. Originally, the District Court Judges wore the same robes for both criminal and civil work, namely, a black silk gown, bar jacket, bands and a tie wig.[162] However, prior to the opening of the Central Law Court building in Hay Street in 1982, the Judges of the District Court resolved that they would robe in similar fashion to their judicial colleagues sitting in the equivalent English County Court and interstate County and District Courts in criminal sittings.

The dress of Western Australia's District Court Judges therefore became a navy blue robe with violet facings, cuffs, bands a scarlet casting hood over the left shoulder and a black girdle or cummerband and tie wig, although the District Court Judges did not adopt the corresponding violet hood or the full-bottomed wig for ceremonial occasions, as was adopted by other equivalent Australian courts.[163] In 1982, when the Judges of the Supreme Court of Western Australia replaced the bands with laced jabots, the Judges of the District Court decided to retain the more traditional bands, although counsel were permitted to appear in either jabots or bands when appearing in the District Court. Today, however, Judges of the District Court wear both bands and various types of jabots, some being elaborately laced others being simple plain jabots, while others wear wide laced bands.

The Chief Judge of the District Court of Western Australia, His Honour Judge Kevin Frederick Sleight, speaking at the ceremonial welcome for Her Honour Judge Belinda Jane Lonsdale on 9 October 2017. The Judges are wearing violet robes with lilac facings, bands and a scarlet casting hood over their left shoulders, which are derived from the exact dress worn by Circuit Judges during criminal sittings in England and Wales. © West Australian Newspapers Limited

162. "Robes of the District Court", *supra*, 43.
163. *Ibid.*

Her Honour Judge Julie Wager, a Judge of the District Court of Western Australia and the current President of the Children's Court of Western Australia.

Her Honour Judge Anette Schoombee, a former Judge of the District Court of Western Australia, wearing wide laced bands as her neckwear in the style which was worn by many 19th century Judges.

In November 2009, it was announced that Judges of the District Court will no longer wear wigs as of 1 January 2010.[164] Practitioners were also no longer required to wear wigs for criminal trials with effect from 1 January 2010.[165] Chief Judge Antoinette Kennedy also issued Practice Direction GEN 1 of 2009 setting out the appropriate dress requirements for both the Bench and Bar:[166]

> 3. Civil Trials and appeals from other jurisdictions
> 3.1 In civil trials, and on the hearing by a Judge of appeals from other jurisdictions, court dress will be as follows:
> Judges: Black robe with bar jacket and jabot or bands, without wig
> Counsel: Black robe with bar jacket and jabot or bands, without wig
> Senior/Queens Counsel: The Court dress customarily associated with that office, but without wig.

---

164. Supreme Court of Western Australia, Media Release, Judges change to modern court dress, 5 November 2009.
165. District Court of Western Australia, Notice to Practitioners by Michael Gething, Principal Registrar, 14 December 2009.
166. *Ibid.*

The former Chief Judge of the District Court Antoinette Kennedy and her successor Judge Peter Martino (as his Honour then was) as well as other Judges of the District Court and members of the legal profession of Western Australia stand for a group commemorative wig photograph taken in front of the old Supreme Court building in Stirling Gardens in Perth on 8 March 2010.

4. Criminal and Ceremonial Occasions
4.1 In criminal trials, sentencing and other appearances in the criminal jurisdiction (except for appearances before a Criminal Commissioner or Registrar) and on ceremonial occasions, the court dress will be as follows:

Judges: Navy gown with purple bands, red sash and black cummerbund, jabot or bands, without wig

Counsel: Black robe and bar jacket and jabot or bands, without wig

Senior/Queens Counsel: The court dress customarily associated with that office, without wig.[167]

On 8 March 2010, the Judges of the District Court, along with about 200 members of the legal profession, wore their respective wigs and robes for a commemorative group photograph taken "for posterity".[168] The Judges of the District Court continue to wear their violet robes and scarlet casting hoods, black cummerbands and a variety of jabots or bands for criminal and ceremonial sittings and the black silk robes for civil sittings, although on some occasions the black silk robes have been worn for ceremonial occasions.[169]

Family Court of Western Australia

The Family Court exercises original and appellate jurisdiction throughout Australia except in Western Australia. In Western Australia, original jurisdiction under the *Family Law Act 1975* (Cth) is exercised by the Family Court of Western Australia (which is a state court funded by the Commonwealth Government).[170] Wigs and gowns are not worn by either the Bench or Bar in the Family Court of Western Australia. However, Judges and Counsel wear robes on certain ceremonial occasions as well as in sittings of the Full Court of Family Court of Australia held in Perth.

167. District Court of Western Australia, Practice Direction GEN 1 of 2009 issued by Chief Judge Antionette Kennedy on 27 November 2009 (which was subsequently revised on 27 June 2011 by Chief Judge Peter Martino so as to clarify that robes were not to be worn for appeals from Registrars).

168. Amanda Banks, "Last wearing of the wigs captured for posterity", *West Australian*, 9 March 2010, 12.

169. For example, at Chief Judge Antoinette Kennedy's welcoming ceremony in 1985, the Judges wore the black silk robes, which were the same robes worn for her farewell ceremony in 2010.

170. Since 1987 the Judges of the Family Court of Western Australia have also held commissions of the Federal Court of Australia.

NORTHERN TERRITORY

The Judges of the Supreme Court of the Northern Territory traditionally wore scarlet robes and hoods faced with taffeta, with the scarlet casting hood over the right shoulder underneath the hood, with bands or jabots and a bench wig for ceremonial occasions. The Judges wore the same scarlet robes (without the hood) in criminal sittings and wore a black silk robe over court dress (without a wig) for civil matters. However, on 12 December 2017, the Chief Justice of the Northern Territory, the Hon. Michael Grant, advised the President of the Criminal Lawyers Association that as of that date the Judges of the Supreme Court of the Northern Territory had adopted new robes for both criminal and ceremonial matters similar to the robes recently adopted by the Judges of the Supreme Court of Victoria earlier that year.[171] However, the Judges of the Supreme Court will continue to wear the bench wig with the new Supreme Court robes for both ceremonial and criminal matters.[172] Although court attire is always at the discretion of the presiding Judge, all Judges of the Northern Territory Supreme Court adopted this attire. It has also been confirmed that the new robes also do not replace the black silk gown worn over court dress worn for civil matters, and wigs are not worn in civil matters.[173]

The new robes of the Judges of the Supreme Court of the Northern Territory. © Supreme Court of the Northern Territory

On 12 December 2017, Chief Justice Michael Grant issued Practice Direction No 6 of 2017 outlining the robing requirements for counsel appearing in the Supreme Court of the Northern Territory:

> 4. In ceremonial sittings (including admission ceremonies, installations, farewells and memorial sittings) robes and wigs shall be worn.
> 5. In Full Court sittings court attire shall be as follows:
>   - proceedings concerning the admission or discipline of legal practitioners - robes and wigs
>   - other substantive hearings and decisions - robes and no wigs
>   - directions hearings – no robes or wigs.
> 6. In Court of Appeal and Court of Criminal Appeal sittings court attire shall be as follows:
>   - substantive hearings and decisions – robes and no wigs
>   - directions hearings – no robes or wigs.
> 7. In criminal matters before a single judge, court attire shall be as follows:
>   - trials (including pre-recording of evidence and voir dire hearings), pleas, mentions, arraignments and any other proceedings in which the accused is present – robes and wigs

---

171. Correspondence from the Hon. Michael Grant to Mr Marty Aust, 12 December 2017.
172. Correspondence from Debbie Carr, Chambers Manager and Executive Assistant to the Hon. Chief Justice Michael Grant, to the writer, 12 April 2018.
173. *Ibid.*

- hearings in relation to mental impairment and fitness to plead – robes and wigs
- bail applications and reviews (technically civil proceedings) – robes and no wigs
- all other matters – no robes or wigs.

8. In civil matters before a single judge, court attire shall be as follows:
   - trials and decisions – robes and no wigs Local Court Appeal hearings – robes and no wigs
   - interlocutory/directions hearings – no robes or wigs
   - judge constituting a tribunal (e.g. Motor Accident Compensation Tribunal) – no robes or wigs.[174]

The Practice Direction did not change any existing practices regarding counsel's dress, but simply consolidated and revoked earlier Practice Directions in force which dealt with various aspects of court dress for counsel.[175] However, the Practice Direction did clarify, inter alia, that if counsel are robed and wigged when the presiding Judge is not, they should remove their wigs, and if counsel are unrobed and unwigged when in fact the presiding Judge is robed and wigged, they should formally seek leave to appear unrobed before the Judge.[176]

Ceremonial sitting of the Supreme Court of the Northern Territory for incoming Chief Justice the Hon. Michael Grant. Sitting from left to right: the Hon. Justice Jenny Blokland, the Hon. Justice Stephen Southwood, Chief Justice Grant, the Hon. Justice Judith Kelly, the Hon. Justice Graham Hiley and the Hon. Justice Trevor Riley in Darwin, Northern Territory. © Katrina Bridgeford/Newspix

174. Supreme Court of Northern Territory of Australia, Practice Direction No 6 of 2017, "Court Attire for Counsel", issued by the Hon. Michael Grant, 12 December 2017.

175. Correspondence from the Hon. Michael Grant to Mr Marty Aust, 12 December 2017.

176. *Ibid.*

AUSTRALIAN CAPITAL TERRITORY

The Judges of the Supreme Court of the Australian Capital Territory traditionally wore the black silk gown over court dress which is the dress customarily associated with the office of Queen's Counsel and a bench wig for all matters.

However, in 2002, the Judges of the Supreme Court ceased the practice of wearing wigs in civil proceedings. This was followed in 2003 by discontinuance of wearing wigs by Judges "in any cause before the Court".[177]

Finally, on 30 January 2009, former Chief Justice Terrence Higgins and the other Judges of the Supreme Court appeared for the first time in their new robes at a ceremonial sitting of the Supreme Court marking the seventy fifth anniversary of the establishment of the Supreme Court.[178] At the special ceremonial sitting, Higgins CJ outlined the intricacies of the new robes, noting that they were similar in appearance to the robes worn by their Federal Court counterparts:

Ceremonial sitting of the Supreme Court of the Australian Capital Territory on 15 June 2015 commemorating Magna Carta. © Jamila Toderas/Fairfax

177. Supreme Court of the Australian Capital Territory, Practice Direction No 4/03 "Wigs", 22 August 2003.

178. Speech by the Honourable Terrence Higgins on the occasion of the 75th anniversary of the Supreme Court on Friday 30 January 2009, 16.

> As you may have noticed, the change of attire does not end with horsehair. Today also marks the unveiling of the new Supreme Court judicial robes, the first robes specifically designed for this Court. And they look rather distinctive, if I do say so myself. The new robes are based loosely on the design of the Federal Court robes, reflecting the fact that many Federal Court judges sit as additional judges of this Court. The coloured band running down one side of the front of the robe and continuing down the back of the robe uses the three colours of the ACT flag (white, gold and blue), which in turn combine the livery colours of the City of Canberra (blue and white) and the sporting colours of the ACT (blue and gold). The three horizontal tucks in the robe, of varying size, reflect the variety of work handled by the Court and the several levels of original and appellate jurisdiction exercised by the Court.[179]

In terms of the robing requirements of counsel appearing in the Supreme Court of the Australian Capital Territory, the Court has issued Practice Direction No 2 of 2009 which, inter alia, provides that:

> 3. In general, robes and any related attire are worn for:
>   a. Civil Trials;
>   b. Criminal trials (including pre-trial hearings and pre-trial applications for severance of indictments, admission of tendency evidence, exclusion of other evidence and the like);
>   c. Appeals (including Magistrates Court appeals);
>   d. All other final hearings including the final hearing of a separate issue;
>   e. The delivery of a reserved judgment in any of these matters, including judgments on interlocutory matters raised during any of these matters;
>   f. Any argument in relation to costs or final orders after delivery of judgment in any of these matters, including delivery of any reserved judgment as to costs or final orders.
> 4. Wigs are not worn in civil matters. Wigs are worn for ceremonial sittings, including admission ceremonies and in criminal matters (including Magistrates Court appeals).
> 5. Where practicable, robes should be worn for ceremonial sittings and admission ceremonies.
> 6. Robes are not worn for any other hearing including the hearing of an interlocutory issue or matters before a registrar;[180]

179. *Ibid.*
180. Supreme Court of the Australian Capital Territory, Practice Direction No 2 of 2009.

Federal Court of Australia

The Federal Court of Australia was created by the *Federal Court of Australia Act 1976* (Cth) and began to exercise its jurisdiction on 1 February 1977. It assumed jurisdiction formerly exercised in part by the High Court of Australia and the whole of the jurisdiction of the Australian Industrial Court and of the Federal Court of Bankruptcy. Upon its establishment, Judges of the Federal Court of Australia wore a black silk gown over court dress and a full-bottomed wig for ceremonial occasions and the same dress but with a bench wig for all other occasions, in line with the dress of the Justices of the High Court of Australia at the time.

Judges of the Federal Court in 1986 in their traditional black silk robes and full-bottomed wigs, which were worn on ceremonial occasions until 1997. Federal Court of Australia sits in Melbourne to farewell Sir Reginald Smithers and welcome Justice Ryan. Attributed to National Archives of Australia

In 1997, the Judges of the Federal Court discontinued wearing wigs in court and in 2001, the Judges adopted new robes. The new robes were designed by Bill Haycock, following consultation with a small committee of Federal Court Judges and "were adopted by acclamation after prototypes were exhibited to a meeting of the whole Court"[181] in 2000. Of the design of the new robes, the then Chief Justice of the Federal Court Michael Black stated the following:

181. "New Robes for the Federal Court", *The Queensland Lawyer* 21 (2001) 105.

The robe for trial work is black in colour, symbolising continuity in the law, and is made of wool grown and manufactured in Australia. The robe is base, essentially, upon a square, and is open in character so that it is worn over ordinary street clothes without bands or jabot. It is tailored to fit neatly over the shoulders.

The detail is minimal, but symbolic. There are seven horizontal tucks or 'ombres' spaced widely apart. These symbolise our federation and federal jurisdiction - the seven elements represent the six States and Territories, as in the Federation Star. They also symbolise the geographical and jurisdictional breadth of the Court's work. The detail also includes a vertical band of black silk composed of seven equal segments. This, too, has federal symbolism and it also symbolises equality before the law.

There is a separate appellate robe which differs from the trial robe in one respect only - the vertical silk bank is deep red in colour, rather than black. The red band contrasts with the black woolen fabric, which is the same that [is] used for the trial robe.[182]

Federal Court Judges standing on the left with Queensland Supreme Court judges on the right at a church service to mark the start of the legal year at the City Tabernacle Baptist Church in Brisbane, Monday, February 12, 2018.
© AAP Image/Dan Peled

182. *Ibid.*

Federal Circuit Court of Australia

The Federal Circuit Court of Australia (formerly known as the Federal Magistrates Court of Australia) was established on 23 December 1999 pursuant to the *Federal Circuit Court of Australia Act 1999* (Cth) and is an intermediate court which deals with the increasing workload of the Federal Court of Australia and Family Court of Australia. On 9 August 2010, former Chief Judge John Pascoe AO CVO issued Practice Direction No.1 of 2010 on robing of counsel in the Federal Magistrates Court.[183] The direction became effective from 6 September 2010 and continues to apply to the Federal Circuit Court. The Practice Direction provides the following:

> The following robing requirements apply to the Federal Circuit Court ("the FCC") in all of its jurisdictions:
>
> - Barristers will robe in final hearings before the FCC for all judgments, trials, and contested hearings in which oral evidence is to be adduced. Barristers will robe wherever the Court is sitting (including all circuit locations).
> - Barristers should not robe in duty matters or for interim or interlocutory applications (unless such applications form part of a trial or a contested hearing in which oral evidence is to be adduced).
> - Barristers will robe for ceremonial sittings.
> - Wigs, full-bottomed or otherwise, are not worn in the FCC on any occasion.
>
> These arrangements are subject to contrary directions made by the presiding Judge - to take into account (for example) the nature of the venue in which the FCC is sitting, or the unavailability of air conditioning.[184]

Regarding the dress of Judges of the Federal Circuit Court, in February 2013 former Chief Judge Pascoe met with Margaret Adams to discuss the making of robes for the 65 Judges of the new Federal Circuit Court of Australia. Following the presentation of sketches by Margaret Adams, the Judges decided to adopt the horizontal pleating and seven vertical lines of the Federal Court robes designed by Bill Haycock. Margaret Adams suggested a purple colour for the sash (as it sat well with the maroon of the Federal Court robes and the red of the Family Court robes) which she presented along with the robe to all the Circuit Court Judges at a meeting in Sydney. The robe was subsequently accepted by a small committee of Judges. Margaret Adam's team of machinists worked through the next few months preparing the robes and the robes were delivered to the Judges in December 2013 and January 2014. Similar to the Family Court Judges' robes, the name of each of the Judges are embroidered onto their robe.

In addition to the new gowns, it appears that the Circuit Court Judges have also adopted traditional white bands as part of their official attire. At the recent welcoming ceremony for Judge Kendall on 29 January 2018, the Judges of the Federal Circuit Court also wore traditional white bands over their robes, which

183. Federal Circuit Court of Australia, Practice Direction No.1 of 2010 issued by John H Pascoe.
184. *Ibid.*

indicates that the bands have been adopted as part of the Federal Circuit Court Judge's judicial dress. It also seems that some Circuit Court Judges are wearing bar jackets, instead of a normal suit, underneath the gown.

Family Court of Australia

The Family Court of Australia was established by the *Family Court Act 1975* (Cth). Among the many wide ranging reforms brought about by the its enactment, the Act also dealt with the question of court dress, the first of its kind in Australian legislative history. Section 97(4) of the Act forbade Judges and Counsel to wear robes in matrimonial causes, which was later upheld by a majority of the High Court of Australia in *Russell v Russell*[185] as being a valid exercise of federal jurisdiction and did not interfere with the organisation of the courts.[186]

Notwithstanding the validity of s 97(4), this peculiar legislative interference with respect to court dress in the Family Court was short-lived. Following the shooting of Justice David Opas,[187] the bombing of the homes of Justice Richard Gee[188] and Justice Raymond Watson,[189] and the bombing of the Parramatta Family Court,[190] the Commonwealth Parliament repealed the ban on court dress in 1987. Following the repeal of s 97(4), the Judges of the Family Court - as well as counsel - resumed the wearing of wigs and robes for judgments, trials and contested hearings where oral evidence is adduced.

Following the creation of the Federal Circuit Court which now deals with nearly 80% of all family law matters filed in the federal courts (excluding Western Australian family law matters which are dealt with by the Family Court of Western Australia) the Judges of the Family Court have again abandoned the wig and have adopted a new gown similar to that worn by the Judges of the Federal Court. By August 2011 Margaret Adam's sewing team had completed the making of 35 new robes for the Judges of the Family Court. The design of this new robe employed the symbolism that Bill Haycock had used for the Federal Court robes, namely, the seven vertical rows of ribbon and horizontal pleats of different widths. The wool was also the same wool used in the making of the Federal Court robes. The judges required only one robe each.

The colour of the sash and ribbon was selected by the then Chief Justice Bryant. The colour of the sash is a vivid red. The sash is 100% red silk fabric with the seven rows of matching red polyester ribbon. At first, the red sash was made separately, and could be worn or not worn with the robe. However, shortly after the adoption of the new robes, the decision was made to permanently attach the sash to the robe. Another difference between the Family Court and

185. (1976) 134 CLR 495.
186. See more above at 184, 186.
187. 23 June 1980.
188. 6 March 1984 in which Mrs Pearl Watson was also killed.
189. 4 July 1984.
190. 15 April 1984.

Federal Court robes is that, rather than fall straight at the front opening as does the Federal Court robe, the Family Court robe has more 'wrap' and has snap fasteners at the front so as to allow the Judge to close the front of the robe should they so choose. Each Judge also has their name embroidered on the back neck facing of the robe. The court has also recently released a new robing policy for counsel. Unless a Judge otherwise orders, having regard to the nature or circumstances of a particular matter. Wigs are not worn by Counsel on any occasion. Counsel are to be robed for:

- trials
- appeals
- all other final hearings, including the final hearing of a separate issue
- and for the delivery of judgment after all such hearings
- ceremonial sittings.

However, robes are not worn for any other hearing, including the hearing of an interlocutory issue and matters before a Registrar of the Family Court.[191]

High Court of Australia

The dress of the Justices of the High Court of Australia has also been subject to changes over the last few decades. When the High Court was first established in 1903, the decision was made to adopt the working dress customarily worn by English Judges at circuit and in the Old Bailey, namely the black silk gown over a morning coat and waistcoat with white bands and a full-bottomed wig.[192] This has been attributed to the fact that the High Court was a creature of statute with a defined jurisdiction, having been created by s 71 of the *Commonwealth Constitution*, in contrast to the inherent jurisdictions of the various state Supreme Courts throughout Australia, who were able to adopt the traditional Judges' habit of scarlet.[193]

In early photographs of the first sittings of the Court, the Justices of the High Court can clearly be seen wearing the traditional white bands. In other contemporary photos, they can sometimes be seen wearing a white bow tie as well. There are also formal portraits of both Isaacs and Gavan Duffy JJ showing each wearing lace jabots instead of the white linen bands. Nonetheless, bands seem to have been the ordinary dress for the Justices up to around 1980, when a laced jabot (said to have been designed by Lady Aickin) replaced the more traditional white bands.[194] Up until the 1970s, the Justices of the High Court

191. "Court Attire," *New South Wales Bar Association*, <https://www.nswbar.asn.au/coming-to-the-bar/court-attire>(accessed 1 March 2018).

192. T. Blackshield, M. Coper & G. Williams, *The Oxford Companion to the High Court of Australia* (Oxford University Press, 2001), 168.

193. *Ibid.* However, the Judges of the Supreme Court of Canada, which was also created by statute, wear scarlet robes faced with miniver for ceremonial occasions, although without out a wig.

194. It is thought that Gibbs CJ brought the idea of the jabot back from a visit to South Africa: *ibid.*

Photograph of the first three Justices of the High Court of Australia in 1903. Attributed to State Library of Queensland

The Justices of the first High Court of Australia. Justice Edmund Barton, Chief Justice Samuel Griffith, Justice Richard Edward O'Connor with two associates. Probably taken at the inauguration of the High Court in Melbourne on 6th October 1903. Attributed to National Archives of Australia

Official photograph of the first session of the High Court of Australia in the Banco Court of the Supreme Court of Victoria building on 6 October 1903. The mounting is autographed by the three foundation justices, from left to right Justice Edmund Barton, Chief Justice Samuel Griffith, Justice Richard Edward O'Connor. Attributed to National Library of Australia

wore traditional court dress for ceremonial occasions, namely a morning coat and waistcoat, with breeches, silk stockings and buckled shoes, as part of their ceremonial costume, but the breeches were replaced by morning striped trousers, although earlier photographs of Justices of the High Court show them wearing striped or dark trousers instead of the more elaborate breeches and stockings. It therefore seems that there was no particular policy as to the dress of High Court Justices, with variations taking place over the years.

Regarding the wearing of the wig, the Justices of the High Court wore full-bottomed wigs for ceremonial occasions, and the bench wig in ordinary sittings of the court, although some Judges (such as Starke and Murphy JJ) on some occasions did not wear the bench wig during sittings of the court. However, both the full-bottomed and bench wig were discontinued at the same time as the new robes were adopted by the Justices of the High Court in 1988.

Justices of the High Court also used to carry the tricorne hat during ceremonial occasions.[195]

On 2 August 1988 the Justices of the High Court appeared in Court wearing large black gowns made of Australian wool, replacing the black silk gowns and jabots. The change in court dress was introduced without any new rule of

195. The Justices of the Supreme Court of Canada continue to carry the tricorne hat.

Lawyers watching the opening of the first session of the High Court on 6 October 1903. Attributed to the State Library of Queensland

The High Court bench of 1964, featuring (ordered from left to right) Justice Windeyer, Justice Taylor, Justice McTiernan, Chief Justice Dixon, Justice Kitto, Justice Douglas Menzies and Justice Owen. Attributed to National Archives of Australia

Lawyers sitting in the same banco court in exactly the same dress, exactly 100 years later. John Howard, former Prime Minister of Australia (1996-2007), is addressing the Justices of the High Court on the centenary of the establishment of the High Court on 6 October 2003. The courtroom included the Chief Justice and Justices and the Prime Minister John Howard and the Governor General Michael Jeffery. © AAP Image/POOL/Stuart McEvoy

Sir Isaac Isaacs wearing ceremonial lace and laced cufflinks as part of his dress. New South Wales, ca. 1930. Attributed to National Library of Australia

court or practice direction, and was simply explained in a Press Statement issued by the then Clerk of the Court Mr R. G. Rose:

Portrait by Sir William Dargie (1912-2003) of Sir Harry Gibbs (1917-2005), Chief Justice of the High Court of Australia (1981-1987) wearing the black silk robes over court dress and a laced jabot and full-bottomed wig, which was the ceremonial dress of High Court Judges until their adoption of simple black robes in 1988. Reproduced with the permission of the Department of Justice and Attorney-General, Queensland © Department of Justice and Attorney-General

> As of today, Tuesday, 2 August, the Chief Justice and Justices of the High Court of Australia will wear black gowns when sitting in court instead of the traditional attire of a robe, jabot and wig.
>
> The decision is not intended to establish a model for other courts. The fact that the High Court is a constitutional and appellate court and not a trial court has been significant in the decision to alter the dress. Different considerations may well apply to other courts. The nature of their work, particularly that of trial courts, differs from that of the High Court.
>
> This decision does not affect counsel. They will continue to wear their customary dress when appearing before the High Court.[196]

The editor of the Australian Law Journal at the time made the following analysis of the new robes and the reason for why they were adopted specifically by the Justices of the High Court:

> The last paragraph of this Press Statement shows that the High Court will, in effect, be assimilated to the International Court of Justice, where counsel are expected to be attired in the same way as before the superior courts of their own country; thus counsel for the United Kingdom appear bewigged and robed before the International Court.
>
> The second paragraph of the Statement serves to explain one basic reason for the change. Significantly, it is declared that the High Court is "not a trial court". Due to the amendments of recent years to the Judiciary Act 1903 (Cth), with powers inter alia to remit cases to State and Federal Supreme Courts and the Federal Court of Australia ... which powers are in fact exercised, the High Court has become exclusively an appellate court and constitutional review tribunal; it does not try matters of fact or hear actions or suits, other than those of a constitutional nature.[197]

196. "Change of traditional Court garb by Justices of the High Court," *The Australian Law Journal* 62 (1988) 749.
197. *Ibid.*

The Justices of the High Court in their silk robes and full-bottomed wig sitting in their newly created High Court building in 1987 in Canberra. Attributed to the National Archives of Australia

Chief Justice Anthony Mason, Justice Dawson, Justice Toohey, Justice Wilson, Justice Brennan, Justice Mary Gaudron and Justice William Deane, in 1987 wearing their working robes.
Attributed to the National Archives of Australia

These robes continued to be worn by the Justices until the High Court's October sittings in 2016, when it was announced that the justices of the High Court had adopted new judicial robes, designed by Mr Bill Haycock (who has previously designed judicial robes for the Federal Court of Australia and the Federal Circuit Court of Australia). The High Court has described the new design of their robes as follows:

> The design of the new robes juxtaposes Australian merino wool with silk. They are made to be lighter and more practical than the previous robes, with a design reflecting the function of the High Court in the Australian Federation.
>
> The robes embody three symbolic features. There are seven equal tucks reflecting the seven components of the Federation — the States and the Commonwealth. There is a hand-woven element in the sleeve ends based on sand ripple patterns and a triangular motif suggestive of the High Court's function as the final court of appeal for Australia.
>
> The robes were developed as a collaboration with Mr Haycock's creative colleagues Margaret Adam as cutter, Saffron Firkins as maker and Kay Faulkner as weaver.[198]

---

198. High Court of Australia, Press Release, "New High Court Robes", 6 October 2016.

The Hon. Susan Kiefel being sworn in as a Justice of the High Court of Australia in Canberra on 3 September 2007. Her Honour was only the third woman appointed to the High Court.

Former senator and Commonwealth Attorney-General, the Hon. George Brandis QC, makes a speech as Chief Justice Susan Kiefel (C) looks on after being sworn in as Chief Justice of the High Court in Canberra on 30 January 2017.

The current High Court robes have a hand-woven fabric incorporated into the design. The sleeves are made from hand-woven silk and wool, and the silk and wool create a pattern in the weave. The female Justices of the High Court have a silk and wool neckpiece, which was designed by Margaret Adam.

As for the dress worn by the Bar when appearing before the High Court, counsel are expected to robe in accordance with the rules governing their appearance before the Court of Appeal or Full Court of the state in which they primarily practise.[199] If in that state it is normal for the legal practitioner to wear a wig when addressing the Court of Appeal or Full Court, that is how counsel should be attired when addressing the High Court. As a result of this rule, it is not unusual for to see counsel on one side of the bar table wearing wigs and counsel on the other side appearing without wigs.[200]

The Chief Justice of the High Court, the Hon. Susan Kiefel AC, and Attorney-General George Brandis QC following her Honour's swearing-in as Chief Justice of the High Court on 30 January 2017. © AAP Image/Mick Tsikas

199. Blackshield, Coper Williams, *supra*.

200. The writer witnessed an example of this in action during a High Court sitting in Perth in 2015, where counsel from the eastern states appeared before the Court in wigs whereas counsel from Western Australia appeared wigless. The same can also be seen in ceremonial occasions in the High Court, with one example being that upon the appointment of Chief Justice Kiefel the head of the Queensland Bar Association appeared before the Court with a full-bottomed wig whereas later that day at the swearing-in ceremony of Western Australia's Justice James Edelman, the head of the WA Bar Association appeared before the Court without a wig.

BIBLIOGRAPHY

BOOKS/PUBLICATIONS

A. Amos, *Fortescue De Laudibus Legum Angliae: The Translation into English* (London: J. Smith, 1825)

C. J. Baker, *Sydney and Melbourne* (London, 1845)

Sir John Hamilton Baker, *An Introduction to English Legal History* 4th ed. (London: Oxford University Press, 2002)

Sir John Hamilton Baker, *Collected Papers on English Legal History: Volume I* (Cambridge University Press, 2013)

Sir John Hamilton Baker, *Collected Papers on English Legal History: Volume II* (Cambridge University Press, 2013)

Sir John Hamilton Baker, *Serjeants-at-Law* (London: Seldon Society, 1984)

Sir John Hamilton Baker, ed., *The Reports of Sir John Spelman* (London: Seldon Society, 1977)

W. P. Baildon, ed., *The Records of the Honourable Society of Lincoln's Inn: The Black Books, Vol. II from AD 1586 to AD 1660* (London: Lincoln's Inn, 1898)

D. Beanland, *A Court Apart: The District Court of Queensland* (Supreme Court of Queensland Library, 2009)

Edward T. Beaumont, *Ancient Memorial Brasses* (London: Oxford University Press, 1913)

J. M. Bennett, *A History of Supreme Court of New South Wales* (Sydney: Law Book Company, 1974)

J. M. Bennett, *Portraits of the Chief Justices of NSW 1821-1977* (St Ives: John Ferguson, 1977)

J. M. Bennett, *Sir Alfred Stephen: Third Chief Justice of New South Wales 1844-1873* (The Federation Press, 2009)

J. M. Bennett, ed., Some papers of Sir Francis Forbes : First Chief Justice in Australia (Sydney: New South Wales Parliament, 1998)

T. Blackshield, M. Coper & G. Williams, *The Oxford Companion to the High Court of Australia* (Oxford University Press, 2001)

Geoffrey Bolton & Geraldine Byrne, *May it Please Your Honour: A History of the Supreme Court of Western Australia 1861-2005* (The Law Society of Western Australia, 2005)

Edmund Bolton, *The Elements of Armories* (London: George Eld, 1610)

John Bruce, ed., *Diary of John Manningham of the Middle Temple and of Bradbourne, Kent, Barrister-at-law, 1602-1603* (Westminster: J. B. Nichols & Sons, 1868)

Una Campbell, *Robes of the Realm: 300 Realms of Ceremonial Dress* (London: Michael O'Mara Books Limited, 1989)

E. Chamberlayne, *Angliae Notitia or the Present State of England* (1671 ed.)

Sir Henry Chauncy, *The Historical Antiquities of Hertfordshire, Vol 1*, (London: JM Mullinger)

Court Dress: a consultation paper issued on behalf of the Lord Chancellor and The Lord Chief Justice (Lord Chancellor's Department, 1992)

C. H. Currey, *Sir Francis Forbes, The first Chief Justice of New South Wales* (Sydney: Angus & Robertson, 1968)

Malcolm Henry Ellis, *Lachlan Macquarie* (Sydney: Dymocks, 1947)

Phillis Emily Cunnington & Catherine Lucas, *Costume for Births, Marriages and Deaths* (New York: Barnes & Noble, 1972)

James Derriman, *Pageantry of the Law*, (London: London, Eyre & Spottiswoode, 1955)

C. R. Dodwell, *Anglo Saxon Art, A New Perspective* (Manchester: University Press, 1982)

Herbert Druitt, *A Manual of Costume as illustrated by Monumental Brasses* (Philadelphia: George W. Jacobs & Co, 1907)

Sir William Dugdale, *Origines Juridiciales* 3rd ed. (London, 1680)

Sir William Dugdale, *The Antiquities of Warwickshire illustrated* (London, 1656)

Sir William Dugdale, *The History of St Pauls Cathedral in London from its Foundation untill these Times* (London: Tho Warren, 1658)

Charles du Fresne Du Cange, *Glossarium mediæ et infimæ latinitatis*, (La Favre, 1883)

Reginald James Fletcher, ed., *The Pension Book of Gray's Inn (Records of the Honourable Society) 1569-1669*, (London: Chiswick Press, 1901)

Halsbury's Laws of England, Volume 66 (2015) para 909

A. J. Hannan, The *Life of Justice Way* (Sydney: Angus and Robertson, 1960)

W. N. Hargreaves-Mawdsley, *A History of Legal Dress in Europe until the end of the eighteenth century* (Oxford: Clarendon Press, 1963)

William Herbert, *Antiquities of the Inns of Court and Chancery* (Vernor & Hood, 1804)

Richard Hooker, *Of the Laws of Ecclesiastical Polity in Two Volumes - Volume II (Book V)* (London: Dent, 1907)

Charles Henry Hopwood, *Middle Temple Records Volume I* (London: Butterworth & Co, 1904)

Mary G. Houston, *Medieval Costume in England and France: The 13th, 14th and 15th Centuries* (Dover Publications, 1996)

F. A. Inderwick, *A calendar of the Inner Temple Records Vol. I.* (London: Stevens & Sons, 1896)

F. A. Inderwick, *The King's Peace: A Historical Sketch of the English Law Courts* (London: Swan Sonnenschein & Co, 1895)

Arthur Robert Ingpen ed., *Master Worsley's Book on the History and Constitution of the Honourable Society of the Middle Temple* (London: Chiswick Press, 1910)

Croake James, *Curiosities of Law and Lawyers* (London: Sampson Low, Rasten & Co, 1896)

John Cordy Jeaffreson, *A Book About Lawyers* (New York: G. W. Carleton & Co, 1867)

David Jenkins ed., *The Cambridge History of Western Textiles* (Cambridge University Press, 2003)

G. Kane ed., *Piers Plowman: The A Version* (Talbot Donaldson, 1960)

William Lack, H. Martin Stuchfield & Philip Whittemore eds., *The Monumental Brasses of Huntingdonshire* (Stratford St. Mary, 2012)

Bora Laskin, *The British Tradition in Canadian Law* (London, 1969)

David Lemmings, *Professors of the law: barristers and English legal culture in the eighteenth century* (Oxford: Oxford University Press, 2000)

Narcissus Luttrell, *A Brief Historical Relation of State Affairs from September 1678 to April 1714* (1857)

William Lyndwood, *Provinciale* (Oxford, 1679)

Wharton B. Marriott, *Vestiarium Christianum: the origin and gradual development of the dress of holy ministry in the church* (London: Rivingtons, 1868)

John McKenna, *Supreme Court of Queensland: A Concise History* (St Lucia: University of Queensland Press, 2012)

B. H. McPherson, *The Supreme Court of Queensland 1859-1960 History Jurisdiction Procedure* (Butterworths, 1989)

Rohan McWilliam, *The Tichborne Claimant: A Victorian Sensation* (London: Hambledon Continuum, 2007)

Stephen E. Moore, *Church Words: Origins and Meanings* (Forward Movement Publications, 1996)

Edward Nares, *Heraldic Anomalies or Rank Confusion in our Orders of Precedence with Disquisitions moral, philosophical, and historical, on all the existing Orders of Society - Volume 2* (1823)

James Oldham, *English Common Law in the Age of Mansfield* (University of North Carolina Press, 2004)

David Pannick, *Judges* (Oxford, 1988)

H. Phillips, *Mid-Georgian London: A Topographical and Social Survey of Central and Western London about 1750* (London: Collins, 1964)

Portraits of the Worthies of Westminster Hall, with their Autographs (London, 1823)

Wilfrid Prest, ed., *The Diary of Sir Richard Hutton 1614-1639*, (London: Selden Society, 1991)

Sir Alexander Pulling, *The Order of the Coif* (1887)

James Robinson Planche, *Cyclopedia of Costume* (London Chatto and Windus, 1876-1879)

George Ruggle, *Ignoramus*, ed. E. Hawkins (London, 1787)

John Schofield, *St Paul's Cathedral before Wren*, (Historic England Publishing, 2011)

Walter W. Skeat, *The Book of Husbandry by Master Fitzherbert* (London: Trubner & Co, 1882)

John Thomas Smith, *Antiquities of Westminster* (London: T. Bensley, Bolt Court, 1807)

John Stow, *Annales, Or a Generall Chronicle of England* (London, 1631)

John Stow, *Survay of London* (London, 1598)

H. Stanford, *The Queen's Beasts* (London: Newman Neame Ltd, 1953)

J. Strype, ed., Stow's Survey of London (London, 1720)

Supreme Court of Victoria, *Annual Report 2015-2016* (Melbourne: Supreme Court of Victoria, 2017)

Supreme Court of Western Australia, *2001 Annual Review of Western Australian Courts* (2002)

Supreme Court of Western Australia, *2002 Annual Review of Western Australian Courts* (2003)

The Annual Register: World Events 1790 (ProQuestrel, 1793)

The History of the King's Works: Volume V 1660-1782, ed., H. Colvin; J.M. Crook, K. Downes & J. Newman (1976)

Tom Tierney, *Byzantine Fashions* (Mineola: Dover Publications, 2002)

J. Trenchard, *A Collection of all the Humorous Letters in the London Journal* (London: J. Roberts, 1721)

James William Norton-Kyshe, *Law and Customs relating to Gloves* (London: Stevens & Hayens, 1901)

Thomas Woodcock, *Legal Habits: A Brief Sartorial History of Wig, Robe and Gown* (London: Ede & Ravenscroft, 2014)

Edward Wynne ed., *Observations touching the Antiquity and Dignity of the Degree of Serjeant at Law* (1765).

D. Yarwood, *English Costume: From the Second Century B.C. to the Present Day, with Introductory Chapters on the Ancient Civilisations* (B.T. Batsford, 1967)

JOURNAL ARTICLES

Murray B. Blok, "A Brief History of Court Attire," *The Advocate (Vancouver)* 64 (2006) 65

E.W. Brabrook, *Trans. London & Middlesex Archaelogical Society* 7 (1877) 249

E. Cave, "Ancient form prescribed for robing the Judges &c," *The Gentleman's Magazine, and Historical Chronicle* 38 (1768) 457

"Change of traditional Court garb by Justices of the High Court," *The Australian Law Journal* 62 (1988) 749

G. R. Corner, "Observations on Four Illuminations," *Archaeologia* 39 (1863) 357

County Courts Chronicle 5 (1852) 59

"Judicial Costume," *Leisure Hour* 26 (1877) 707

"Judicial Costume," *The Law Times* 103 (1897) 577

L. Edwards, "The Professional Costume of Lawyers illustrated principally by Monumental Brasses," *Transactions of the Monumental Brass Society* 8 (1936-1938) 155

John Emerson, "Why are you wearing a wig: Changes in court etiquette in South Australia," 26/10 *Law Society Bulletin of South Australia* (2004) 31

G. J. French, *Notes & Queries - 1st series* 10 (1854) 38

Paul James Healy, "Of Wigs, Wig Bags and Rosettes," *Brief* (April 2000) 20

Paul James Healy, "The Dress of Queen's Counsel and Senior Counsel," *Brief* (November 2001) 22

Robert Kinsey, "Each according to their Degree: the Lost Brasses of the Thorpes of Northamptonshire," *Transactions of the Monumental Brass Society* 18 (2012) 311

C. Langford, "The prerogative writs and the origins of English administrative law," *Australian Law Journal* 88 (2014) 567

Law Journal, County Court Reporter 5 (1916)

"Legal Retrospections," *The Law Magazine or Quarterly Review of Jurisprudence* 31 (1844) 54

E. MacCulloch, *Notes & Queries - 1st series* 10 (1854) 213

F. D. MacKinnon, "Judges' Robes - The Gun-Case," *The Law Quarterly Review* 61 (1945) 30

Wayne Stewart Martin, "Forensic Fashions," *Brief* (June, 1986) 7

Rob McQueen, "Of Wigs and Gowns: A Short History of Legal and Judicial Dress in Australia," *Law Context: A Socio-Legal Journal* 16 (1999) 31

J. G. McLaren, "A brief history of wigs in the legal profession," *International Journal of the Legal Profession* 6/2 (1999) 241

"New robes for the Federal Court", *The Queensland Lawyer* 21 (2001) 105

F. N. Newark, "Judicial Robes," *Northern Ireland Legal Quarterly* 6 (1944-1946) 206

F. H. Newark, "Notes - The Gun Case," *The Law Quarterly Review* 62 (1946) 181

"Robes of District Court Judges," *Brief* (June, 1991) 43

F. E. Sawyer, *Notes & Queries - 6th series* 9 (1884) 465

J. C. Sikes, *Notes & Queries - 7th series* 1 (1886) 468

F. W. Steer "A Medieval Household: The Urswick inventory," *Essex Review* 63 (1956) 4

Sir Bernard Sugerman, "The Wearing of the Wig," *The Australian Law Journal* 47 (1973) 39

E. K. Williams, "Judicial Robes," *Advocate* 10 (1952) 109

Sir Viktor Windeyer, "Of Robes and Gowns and Other Things," *The Australian Law Journal* 48 (1974) 394.

"To Wig or be Damned," *Brief*, Volume 15, Number 7 (August, 1988).

CASES

Lord Coleridge v Sotheby's [2012] EWHC 370 (Ch)

McPherson v McPherson [1936] AC 177

R v Whittaker (1844) 8 JPJO 390

Re Douglas (unreported) NSWSC, 1 September 1998 (BC9804579)

Russell v Russell (1976) 134 CLR 495

St Edmundsbury Diocesan Board v Clark [1973] 1 Ch 323

The Queen v Matthews (1887) 8 LR (NSW) 45

LEGISLATION

3 Edward IV, c. 5

Act of Apparel 1532 (24 Hen. VIII, c. 13)

Civil Court of Western Australia Act 1832 (WA) (2 Will. IV No. 1)

Civil Procedure Act 2005 (NSW)

County Courts Act 1846 (9 & 10 Vic c 95)

District Courts Act 1858 (NSW) (22 Vic No 18)

District Court Act 1973 (NSW)

Family Law Act 1975 (Cth)

Legal Practice Act 1996 (Vic)

Legal Profession Amendment (National Practising Certificates) Act 1996 (NSW)

Supreme Court Act 1935 (WA)

Supreme Court Act 1970 (NSW)

Supreme Court Act 1986 (Vic)

Supreme Court of Judicature Act 1873 (36 & 37 Vic. c. 66)

Supreme Court of Judicature Act 1875 (38 & 39 Vic. c. 77)

Supreme Court Criminal Supplementary Rules 2014 (Amendment No. 4) (SA)

Supreme Court Criminal Supplementary Rules 2014 (SA)

MANUSCRIPTS

Bodleian Library MS Ashmole 854

British Library, MS. Add. 35329

British Library, MS Add. 71474, f. 121

British Library MS Add. 28330, folio 29

British Library MS Harley 361 ff. 75-80, 85v

British Library MS Harley 1498, folio 76

Cambridge University Library, MS. Add. 6862, 6863 II.

Rijksuniversiteit-Gent MS 2466, folio 67

Royal MS 6 Edward VII, folio 52

Royal MS 6 Edward VII, folio 356v

Royal MS. 6 Edward VII, folio 345

Royal MS. 6 Edward VII, folio 150v

GOVERNMENT RECORDS

House of Commons, *Debates*, 4 March 1830, vol 22 cc. 1293-1294

Public Record Office, Exchequer: King's Remembrancer and Treasury of the Receipt: Inventories of Goods and Chattels, Inventory of the goods of Thomas Ursewyk paper, E 154/2/2

Public Record Office, Lord Chancellor's Office, LCO 12/43

Public Record Office, Lord Chancellor's Office, LCO 66/42

Public Record Office, Lord Chancellor's Office, LCO 2/6697

Will of Sir Edmund Mervyn, 16 November 1553, Probate Records of the Prerogative Court of Canterbury, PROB 11/36/285

Will of Peter Arderne of Latton, Essex, 10 July 1466, Probate Records of the Prerogative Court of Canterbury, PROB 11/5/245

Will of Thomas Lytilton or Lyttleton, 8 November 1481, Probate Records of the Prerogative Court of Canterbury, PROB 11/7/74

Will of Thomas Tremayll, of East Meon, Hampshire, 19 September 1508, Probate Records of the Prerogative Court of Canterbury, PROB 11/16/104

PRACTICE DIRECTIONS/ GUIDANCE

Criminal Practice Directions 2015 [2015] EWCA Crim 1567

"Court Attire Policy" issued by J J Spigelman AC Chief Justice of New South Wales, 20 September 2007

Court Dress: Revised Guidance from the Chairman of the Bar Council of England and Wales, Desmond Browne QC, 2 June 2009

District Court of Western Australia, Notice to Practitioners by Michael Gething, Principal Registrar, 14 December 2009

District Court of Western Australia, Practice Direction GEN 1 of 2009 issued by Chief Judge Antionette Kennedy on 27 November 2009

Family Court of Australia, Practice Direction No. 6 of 2001, 4 December 2001, issued by the Hon. Chief Justice Alastair Nicholson AO RFD

Federal Circuit Court of Australia, Practice Direction No.1 of 2010 issued by John H Pascoe.

High Court of Australia, Press Release, "New High Court Robes", 6 October 2016.

Judicial Communications Office, Lord Chief Justice announces reforms to court working dress, Press Release, 12 July 2007

Judicial Communications Office, Practice Direction handed Down for Court Working Dress, Press Release, 31 July 2008

Rani Kulkarni, Associate to the Honourable Justice J Forrest, Notice to the Profession "Wearing of wigs in Common Law Division proceedings", 26 May 2016

Practice Direction (Court Dress) (No 5) and Amendment No 20 to the Consolidated Criminal Practice Directions (Court Dress), issued by Lord Phillips of Worth Matravers on 31 July 2008

Supreme Court of Queensland, "Supreme Court adopts a New Robe", Media Release, 14 August 2017

Supreme Court of South Australia, Media Release, "New Supreme Court and District Court Robes", 18 November 2016

Supreme Court of Tasmania, Circular to Practitioners No 9, "Judicial court apparel in criminal trials and appeals", 6 June 2008

Supreme Court of Tasmania, Practice Direction No 2 of 2005, "Court of Appeal", 1 February 2005

Supreme Court of the Australian Capital Territory, Practice Direction 2002/1, 27 May 2002

Supreme Court of the Australian Capital Territory, Practice Direction No 4/03 "Wigs", 22 August 2003

Supreme Court of the Australian Capital Territory, Practice Direction No 2 of 2009

Supreme Court of the Northern Territory of Australia, Practice Direction No 6 of 2017, "Court Attire for Counsel", issued by the Hon. Michael Grant, 12 December 2017

Supreme Court of Tasmania, Circular to Practitioners No 13 of 2018, "Judicial Robes in Criminal Trials and Appeals", 12 November 2018

Supreme Court of Victoria, Practice Note SC Gen 4 - Custom and Protocol, 30 January 2017

Supreme Court of Victoria, Transcript, 24 May 2016 (the Hon. Justice Bell)

Supreme Court of the United Kingdom, Revised guidance on court dress at the UK Supreme Court, Press Notice No 12/2011, 12 November 2011

Supreme Court of Western Australia, Media Release, "May 17, 1999 - Wigs Abandoned in Civil Proceedings", 17 May 1999

Supreme Court of Western Australia, Media Release, Judges change to modern court dress, 5 November 2009

SPEECHES

Speech by Judge JM Robertson, "Children as Witnesses," Paper delivered at Child Witness Support Conference, Brisbane 7 June 2007

Speech by the Honourable Terrence Higgins on the occasion of the 75th anniversary of the Supreme Court on Friday 30 January 2009

Speech by the Honourable Paul de Jersey AC at the University of Queensland - TC Bierne School of Law, "Welcome to Students", 9 February 2000

Speech by the Honourable Justice Margaret Wilson, "The Banco Court - Talk given to QUT 1st year architecture students", 23 September 2008

Speech of Lord Hailsham of St Marylebone at a dinner in Lincoln's Inn on 30 October 1971, reported in 121 *New Law Journal* at 985

Speech by the Hon Wayne Martin, "The State of Justice Law Week Address - May 2007", Monday, 7 May 2007

Transcript of Proceedings at Perth on Thursday, 25 February 2010, Farewell to the Honourable Justice Wheeler, The Supreme Court of Western Australia

Transcript of Proceedings at Perth on Monday, 1 May 2006, Welcome to the Honourable Chief Justice Martin

LETTERS/CORRESPONDENCE

Correspondence from Bridie Kelly, Senior Associate to the Chief Judge of the County Court of Victoria, to the writer, 4 December 2017

Correspondence from Debbie Carr, Chambers Manager and Executive Assistant to the Hon. Chief Justice Michael Grant, to the writer, 12 April 2018

Correspondence from the Rt. Hon. The Lord Thomas of Cwmgiedd to the writer, 11 September 2017

Correspondence from the Associate to the Chief Justice, the Hon. Christopher Kourakis, to the writer, 16 April 2018

Correspondence from the Hon. Michael Grant to Mr Marty Aust, 12 December 2017

Correspondence from the Hon. Wayne Martin to Mr Dudley Stow, 29 October 2009

Memorandum on Court Dress from Helen Vizer, Supreme Court Legal Research Officer, to the writer, 1 June 2018

NEWSPAPER ARTICLES

Australian, Sydney, Friday, 16 March 1832, 3

Australian, Sydney, 22 October 1844, 807

Amanda Banks, "Last wearing of the rings captured for posterity", *West Australian*, 9 March 2010, 12.

"Barristers' Wig," *South Australian Chronicle and Weekly Mail*, 17 March 1877, 4

Brisbane Courier, 10 May 1910

Brisbane Courier, 25 February 1881

"Civil Side," *Australian*, Thursday 21 April 1842, 2

Courier Mail, Brisbane, Friday, 3 November 1939, 1

"Court of Probate and Divorce," *The Exeter and Plymouth Gazette*, Thursday, 31 July 1868, 3

Evening News, 17 February 1896, 6

John Gay, "Sciences of *Poetry* and *Dress*," *The Guardian*, no. 149, 1 September 1713

Herald, 8 December 1886, 6

"Judicial Intelligence," *Port Phillip Patriot and Morning Advertiser*, Tuesday, 21 July 1846, 3

"Law and Police Courts," *South Australian Register*, 13 August 1850, 3

"Law Intelligence," *Daily News*, Thursday, 23 July 1868

"Law Intelligence," *Sydney Herald*, Monday 3 June 1839, 2

"Law Intelligence," *Sydney Herald*, Tuesday 11 January 1842, 2

"Law Intelligence," *Sydney Herald*, Tuesday 18 July 1843, 2

Letter to the The Times, 21 August 1995, 15

"Miscellaneous," *The Leeds Mercury*, Saturday, 1 August 1868

"Monthly Full Court", *Telegraph*, Brisbane, Tuesday, 8 March 1887, 5

"News," *The Chelmsford Chronicle*, Friday, 24 July 1868, 4

"News and Notes," *The West Australian*, 11 February 1947, 8

"Notes by the Way," *Nottinghamshire Guardian*, Friday, 31 July 1868

"Robes Day", *Brisbane Courier,* Wednesday, 10 March 1926, 6

"Supreme Court", *Brisbane Courier,* Wednesday, 6 December 1893

"Supreme Court," *Sydney Gazette and New South Wales Advertiser*, Saturday, 17 September 1836, 3

"Supreme Court," *Sydney Monitor and Commercial Advertiser*, Wednesday, 20 October 1841, 2

Sydney Morning Herald, 20 November 1873, 7

"Sydney News," *Maitland Mercury and Hunter River General Advertiser,* Saturday 22 April 1843, 3

"Sydney News," *Maitland Mercury and Hunter River General Advertiser*, Wednesday, 30 December 1846, 2

Telegraph, Brisbane, Friday, 22 March 1929, 2

"The Black Cap is Badge of Mourning," *Mirror* 21 June 1952, 10

"The Full Court", *Brisbane Courier*, Wednesday, 16 March 1904, 4

"The Judicial Ermine," *South Australian Register*, Thursday 12 July 1877, 5

"The New Law Courts," *The West Australian*, 9 June 1903, 5

The Times, 24 July 1868, 5d, lla and 12a

The Times, 23 July 1868, 5f

"The West Australian," *The West Australian*, 27 August 27 1888, 3

WEBSITES/DIGITAL ARTICLES

"£140,000 bill for Supreme Court robes judges will hardly wear," *Daily Mail*, 13 December 2009, <http://www.dailymail.co.uk/news/article-1235344/140-000-Supreme-Court-robes-judges-hardly-wear.html> (accessed 14 June 2018)

"Court Attire," *New South Wales Bar Association*, <https://www.nswbar.asn.au/coming-to-the-bar/court-attire> (accessed 1 March 2018)

Examples, Courts and Tribunals Judiciary, <https://www.judiciary.uk/about-the-judiciary/who-are-the-judiciary/court-dress/examples/> (accessed on 5 June 2018)

Caroline Ford, "Court couture on show," *Law Institute Victoria*, <https://www.liv.asn.au/Staying-Informed/LIJ/LIJ/March-2018/Court-couture-on-show> (accessed 1 April 2018)

"Judges ditch wigs," *Lawyers Weekly*, 10 August 2007 <https://www.lawyersweekly.com.au/news/861-judges-ditch-wigs> (accessed 29 March 2018)

National Portrait Gallery, London: https://www.npg.org.uk/collections/search/person/mp127114/sir-william-seymour [11 March 2018])

"Practitioner Alert - Court Attire," *Law Society of South Australia*, <https://www.lawsocietysa.asn.au/LSSA/newsfeeds/Practitioner_Alert_-_Court_Attire.aspx> (assessed 5 April 2018)

The Hon. Catherine Holmes, "Presentation of Queen's Counsel; recognition of newly -admitted barristers; and traditional exchange of Christmas Greetings Banco Court Wednesday 13 December 2017, 9.15am" <https://archive.sclqld.org.au/judgepub/2017/holmes131217.pdf> (accessed 19 March 2018)

The Hon. M. Gleeson, 17 May 1999 at the 175th Anniversary Dinner of the Supreme Court of New South Wales <http://www.supremecourt.justice.nsw.gov.au/Documents/Publications/Speeches/175th%20Anniversary%20Speeches/175_06_anniv_scnsw_1999.05.17_gleeson.pdf> (accessed 1 March 2018)

The Hon. Michael Kirby, Australian Bar Review Book Review, J.M. Bennett, Sir Alfred Stephen: Third Chief Justice of New South Wales 1844-1873 (Lives of the Australian Chief Justices series), 2010, 6. *See*: <http://pandora.nla.gov.au/pan/96901/20160929-0803/www.michaelkirby.com.au/images/stories/speeches/2000s/2010_Speeches/2447.BookReview-Sir-AlfredStephen.pdf> (accessed 26 November 2017)

"Wearing of Wigs," *Queensland Bar Association* <https://www.qldbar.asn.au/#/president-message?messageId=43> (assessed 23 November 2017)

INDEX

CPSIA information can be obtained
at www.ICGtesting.com
Printed in the USA
BVHW020253081221
623495BV00005B/524

9 781616 195854